# THE GUYANA COURT OF APPEAL

# THE GUYANA COURT OF APPEAL

## THE CHALLENGES OF THE RULE OF LAW IN A DEVELOPING COUNTRY

**Dr Bertrand Ramcharan, LLM, PhD**
Barrister-at-Law (Lincoln's Inn),
Commissioner of the International Commission of Jurists,
Member of the Permanent Court of Arbitration,
Fellow of the London School of Economics
and Political Science (LSE)

Routledge
Taylor & Francis Group
LONDON AND NEW YORK

Ramcharan, BG

The Guyana Court of Appeal: the challenges of the rule of law in a developing country

1 Guyana Court of Appeal 2 Criminal law – Guyana

I Title

345.8'81'01

First published in 2002 by Cavendish Publishing Limited

Published 2022 by Routledge
4 Park Square, Milton Park, Abingdon, Oxon OX14 4RN
605 Third Avenue, New York, NY 10017

*Routledge is an imprint of the Taylor & Francis Group, an informa business*



British Library Cataloguing in Publication Data

ISBN 13: 978-1-85941-686-0 (hbk)

# CONTENTS

# PREFACE

Developing countries the world over are struggling for decent life-chances for their peoples in difficult global conditions. The international economic order presents many difficulties to them in their quest for development. For the peoples of many developing countries the right to development is still only a mirage. Economic, social and cultural rights, as well as civil and political rights, remain illusory for millions throughout the world.

In these circumstances, governance takes on a particularly crucial significance for the peoples of the developing countries. It is through good governance that a people can efficiently utilize its national resources with a view to giving the best chances possible to every member of the polity. It is by demonstrating good governance that a people can stake a claim to international equity and to international co-operation.

The rule of law is at the base of good governance, of democracy and of respect for human rights. It is also the starting point for development efforts in any country. The rule of law is thus a topic of strategic significance for every country, and particularly for every developing country. The breakdown of the rule of law has led to the impoverishment of too many developing countries.

With this in mind, it is essential to draw lessons on how the rule of law has fared in the countries that achieved their independence as part of the process of self-determination launched by the United Nations Charter. When the United Nations was established in 1945, it had just over 50 member countries. Today, it has nearly 200. The majority of these are developing countries whose peoples still aspire to decent life-chances.

In order to be able to provide better life-chances to the peoples of the developing countries, studies of how the rule of law has fared in those countries take on particular urgency. In this work, we look at the fate of the rule of law in one such country, Guyana, which achieved its independence in 1966 and which took on republican status within the Commonwealth a decade later.

For four decades the courts of Guyana have had to chart a course for the rule of law in a newly independent country, maintaining the core protections of the common law and modernizing the common law where necessary to meet the conditions of an evolving developing society. They have had to wrestle with the challenges of governance and power sharing in a multi-ethnic country with six races which aspire to a future 'one nation, one people'.

The travails of the rule of law in a developing country are examined in this work through the lens of its highest court, the Court of Appeal. The peaks and valleys of the rule of law are revealed when it comes to democracy and human rights. The brilliance of local lawyers is demonstrated in non-political areas of the law, such as the criminal law, the law of contracts, the law of torts and property law. The protection of human rights is shown to have been victim of the vagaries of political benches.

It is hoped that this study will help lead to the strengthening of the rule of law in this country as well as in other developing countries.

This is the first study of the Guyana Court of Appeal. Parts of its jurisprudence presented here are necessarily introductory, as one has had to work on the basis of unpublished decisions. The *Law Reports of Guyana* were last published in 1975. It is hoped that legal practitioners in Guyana will offer suggestions of cases to be added to subsequent editions of this work.

*BG Ramcharan*
*31 December 2001*

# INTRODUCTION

The struggle for justice and human rights has been a part of Guyana's history from early times. Guyana partakes of the Caribbean experience that has seen efforts to uphold the rights of indigenous people, to abolish the scourge of slavery, to uphold the dignity of indentured people and to advance the cause of equality and justice for all. One of our leading Caribbean historians, the late Eric Williams of Trinidad and Tobago, has recorded the history of the Caribbean as one of the great historical theatres in the struggle for freedom of the oppressed peoples of the world:[1] 'In Guyana, our ancestors had to face the tyranny of the law as colonial subjects. A Guyanese constitutional historian found evidence of the prostitution of the law as an instrument of managerial oppression and of oppression through the instrumentality of the law.'

He also found that:

> The use of the legal machinery as an adjunct to the managerial powers of the employers was perhaps most visible in the practice which they developed of bringing numerous prosecutions for labour offences without either hope or intention or proving their cases, but with the object, which almost always succeeded, of cowing the defendant ... into submission, when the prosecution would be withdrawn and his detention pending trial terminated on condition that the costs were paid by him and that he did whatever was required of him.

We were, sadly, to repeat this experience in our subsequent history, even as he was writing.

## The Demerara slave rebellion of 1823

One hundred and seventy-seven years ago, during the night of 17 August 1823, the then British colony of Demerara saw the start of one of the most massive slave rebellions in the history of the Western hemisphere, in which nearly 12,000 slaves took up arms against their masters. Emilia Viotti da Costa, Professor of History at Yale University, reconstructs this compelling story of the struggle for universal human rights through the eyes of the Demerara slaves. It is an important work in the historiography of Guyana.[2]

The rebellion started on plantation Success, which belonged to John Gladstone (father of the future British Prime Minister), and spread to about 60 plantations along the east coast. At the time, Demerara society was experiencing growing confrontation between masters and slaves. Torn from their societies of origin in Africa with their rules, norms and decorums, slaves had sought to redefine their identities, to recreate their past, to control their

---

1 Williams, E, *A History of the West Indies*, 1970, London: Andre Deutsch.

2 Viotta da Costa, E, *Crowns of Glory, Tears of Blood – The Demerara Slave Rebellion of 1823*, 1994, New York, Oxford: OUP. See also Shahabuddeen, M, *The Legal System of Guyana*, 1973, Georgetown: Guyana Printers, p 365.

present and to shape their future. They framed their demands in terms of rights.

The slave rebellion of 1823 and the Reverend John Smith's role in it have universal value. Professor da Costa places the rebellion in the historical stream of the fight for human rights that had seen the American Declaration of Independence, the French Revolution and its Declaration on the Rights of Man and the Haitian Revolution which, by challenging the power masters had over slaves, had brought the question of slavery to the forefront. The Demerara slave rebellion of 1823 would see the articulation by slaves themselves of universal human rights.

What the Demerara slaves of 1823 had to cope with was made clear in a book published by Alexander McDonnell in 1824, *Considerations on Negro Slavery with Authentic Report Illustrative of the Actual Conditions of the Negroes in Demerara*. McDonnell argued that slavery was a legitimate institution, sanctioned by law and history and that slave property should be treated like any other property. Hence, the British Parliament had no right to take away from the planters 'without indemnification, the privilege of obtaining from their slaves six days labour in the week'.

Against such views the Demerara slaves defended their 'customary rights'. They were quick to learn about their 'legal' rights. They learned that they could bring their complaints to the Fiscal, and they did do so – although in the early period their complaints often fell on deaf ears. Women often complained that their rights had been violated.

When norms for labour performance, food and clothing allowances and medical assistance were violated, the slaves protested. From law and custom they derived notions of 'rights'. And it was in the name of these rights that, individually or in groups, slaves went to the Fiscal to complain, rejected their allowances when these were insufficient or spoiled, did not perform their tasks when they thought the assignment was unreasonable, and from time to time even resorted to strikes, collectively refusing to do any work until their demands were met.

While the masters considered that they held total power over the slaves and were entitled to blind obedience, the Demerara slaves perceived slavery as a system of reciprocal obligations. They assumed that between masters and slaves there was an unspoken contract, an invisible text that defined rules and obligations, a text they used to assess any violation of their rights.

The slaves' notion of rights had taken on a new dimension in the late eighteenth century when revolutionary discourse gave universality and thus new legitimacy to the notion of rights. The language of the universal rights of man conferred a new meaning on the slaves' struggles, since it acknowledged the slaves' 'humanity' and their right to be free. The slaves henceforth had the language of human rights on their side.

With this intellectual ferment the idea of rebellion was always latent in Demerara. The downward trend in commodity prices and the transition to sugar on some plantations of the east coast had caused masters to intensify labour exploitation and to encroach on the slaves' customary rights. This came precisely at a time when the slaves' notion of rights and commitment to freedom had been enhanced and expanded by the efforts of abolitionists and the preaching of missionaries. The spark in Demerara came in May 1823 when Governor Murray reissued an earlier proclamation forbidding the slaves from attending chapel without passes. The second occurred a few weeks later when rumours of emancipation began to spread in the colony.

Tension rose from May to August until the famous night of 17 August. The rebellion started at Success and quickly spread to neighbouring plantations. Beginning around six in the evening, to the sound of shell-horns and drums, and continuing through the night, 9,000 to 12,000 slaves from about 60 east coast plantations surrounded main houses, put overseers and managers in the stocks and seized their arms and ammunitions. When they met resistance, they used force. The slaves spoke of laws and of rights. They put their masters in the stocks and used their whips. They broke doors and windows, destroyed furniture, set buildings afire. They whipped managers and masters, took their clothes and money and drank their wine. And when whites fired at them, they shot back. Unfortunately, by the middle of the night the old African shells and drums were silent and only the sound of European guns could be heard.

That the rebellion was put down is a matter of history. What is not well known is that the Demerara slave rebellion of 1823 had been the culmination of one of the great historical struggles for universal human rights. This marks the Demerara slave rebellion as one of the great historical moments in the development of universal human rights.

## Resistance on the plantation

In his work *A History of East Indian Resistance on the Guyana Sugar Estates, 1870–1950* (1996, Lewiston, Lampeter: Edwin Mellen), Basdeo Mangru recalled that during the century and a half of the Indian presence in the Caribbean most of their history had been embedded in the plantation:

> It was a history, like that of their African counterparts, which was rooted in bondage, brutality, exploitation and human degradation. This exploitation began when the wily recruiter first established a psychological hold over them through euphoric promises and money advances. It continued in the emigration depot and in transit to the Caribbean, reaching its zenith in the 'logies', the old slave barracks with a history of oppression. As low paid, largely unskilled 'bound' workers they were exploited and despised as well and their rich culture denigrated. The epithet 'coolie', a term of opprobrium still in use, attested to their degraded status.

He identified two broad categories of resistance on the plantations – passive and active:

> Passive or covert resistance refers to such actions as malingering, feigning ignorance of authority instructions, deliberately doing shoddy work and such inward directed aggression as suicide, maiming or creating ulcers to avoid field labor. In active or overt resistance workers resorted mainly to industrial action, such as strikes and riots, physical assaults on the upper echelons of estate management and wanton destruction of estate property including sabotage. These everyday forms of resistance, often called the 'weapons of the weak', have been largely spontaneous and localized requiring little organization.

The harsh conditions on estates, he found, provoked considerable resistance and retaliation:

> Although their spirit of resistance which stemmed from their strong family, religion and community life would fail to prevent them from being 'knocked down' on the estates, it would preserve them from being 'knocked out'.

## The independence struggle

The struggle for human rights ran throughout the independence struggle. At the 1950 Caribbean Conference in Curacao, Dr Cheddi Jagan moved a motion calling for the implementation of the proclamation of the Universal Declaration of Human Rights that 'the will of the people shall be the basis of the authority of government'.

The 1953 manifesto of the original People's Progressive Party, the predecessor of the current PPP and PNC, called for universal suffrage, free health services, workmen's compensation to cover industrial diseases, more secondary school scholarships, more nursery schools, land reform, security of tenure for farmers and low rental housing – all core human rights issues. This was the vision of a nationalist PPP, embraced by our first three presidents, Presidents Cheddi Jagan and Burnham, President Janet Jagan, and other Guyanese patriots such as Senior Counsel Ashton Chase.

The mood of the times was captured by our national poet Martin Carter in his poem *Let Freedom Wake Him*:

> Comrade the world is loud with songs of freedom
> Mankind is breeding heroes every day
> On high the scarlet banner flies aloft
> Below the earth re-echoes liberty!

This spirit has inspired a consistent commitment among Guyanese to international human rights as defined in the Universal Declaration of Human

Rights, in the International Covenants on Human Rights and in similar United Nations documents.

Nearly half a century later, addressing the European Union in 1994, Dr Jagan called for '[T]he fullest exercise of human rights – civil and political, as well as economic, social and cultural, in keeping with the UN Covenants on Human Rights'. No less than the highest, the fullest exercise, was sufficient for him.

As a petitioner to the Committee of 24, the Decolonisation Committee of the United Nations, Dr Jagan had championed the cause of human rights in Guyana. Throughout Dr Jagan's 28 years in opposition he campaigned relentlessly for Guyana to ratify the UN Covenants and the Optional Protocol to the Covenant on Civil and Political Rights.

Dr Jagan wrote consistently to the United Nations Division of Human Rights after the disputed general elections of 1968. He sent successive memoranda to the United Nations complaining about violations of human rights in Guyana. On 15 April 1981 Dr Jagan petitioned the United Nations Commission on Human Rights in the following terms:

> The People's Progressive Party requests that the Guyana situation should be discussed by the forthcoming meeting of the United Nations Commission on Human Rights.

Attached to his letter was a 'Memorandum on the Violation of Human Rights in Guyana'.

Dr Jagan's championship of human rights issues was echoed by other voices in Guyana. In an editorial in *The Mirror* on 26 August 1977 a trenchant plea was made for human rights and fundamental freedoms in Guyana. Two days earlier, on 24 August 1977, an editorial in *The Mirror* had complained:

> There is marked concern, both locally and regionally, about the question of human rights in Guyana. This was manifested in the report of a meeting held in Trinidad over the last weekend which pointed an accusing finger at four Caribbean territories where human rights are in jeopardy. Guyana headed the list, with attention being drawn to five areas of violations.

A story in *The Mirror* on 9 January 1979 reports the PPP welcoming the setting up of a Committee for the Defence of Human Rights in Latin America. An Editorial in *The Mirror* dated 21 November 1988 entitled 'CARICOM and Human Rights' argued that there was 'need for CARICOM to discuss human rights'. The 21st Congress of the PPP, held from 31 July – 2 August 1982, adopted a resolution on 'Human Rights and Civil Liberties in Guyana' complaining that 'since our last Congress the human rights and civil liberties situation in Guyana has further deteriorated'. The Congress called for respect of the judicial process and a halt to interference therein.

In a similar vein, in an editorial on 14 December 1988, *The Stabroek News* counselled:

> ... the International Covenant on Civil and Political Rights adopted in 1966 ... and the Optional Protocol thereto were widely acclaimed by human rights activists everywhere. The latter gives jurisdiction to a human rights committee appointed by members who have subscribed to the covenant to receive complaints of human rights abuses from individuals in a State. The State can reply and the committee then forwards its views to both parties and makes an annual report of its activities.
>
> The publicity involved in such a procedure gives some muscle to human rights though there are no further enforcement provisions. We strongly commend them to the attention of the government [of President Hoyte].

Dr Jagan's address to the 24th PPP General Congress, in 1991, contained the following article of faith by the late President:

> As regards political and economic rights, we will honour and guarantee them. We will go one step further than the PNC. They have paid lip service to the two United Nations covenants on civil and political and economic, social and cultural rights. They have implemented neither and they refused to sign the protocols attached to them. We propose to sign the Optional Protocol to those covenants and to give everybody the right to invite the United Nations Commission of Human Rights to come at anytime to Guyana. (Address by Dr Cheddi Jagan to the 24th PPP General Congress, 1991, Georgetown: Freedom House.)

One of President Jagan's early acts upon his election to the presidency in 1992 was to ratify the Optional Protocol. This would be eviscerated shortly after his death.

## A continuing struggle for human rights

The struggle for human rights in Guyana is far from over. In the foreword to a recent Guyanese book on human rights, a leading Guyanese senior counsel, Mr Rex McKay, lamented:

> The history of the people of the Commonwealth Caribbean is a history of struggle for human rights and freedoms over many years. [Unfortunately], the excesses of government action ... sadly is all too apparent in many States of the Caribbean.[3]

We need to recall that the Universal Declaration of Human Rights was proclaimed to the end that every individual, and all organs of society, shall strive to realize its precepts. This means that the governments of all countries should have their legitimacy in respect for human rights and should be organized so as to uphold those rights.

The international covenants on human rights ratified by Guyana place upon governments solemn legal obligations to pursue human rights policies

3 Address by Dr Cheddi Jagan to the 24th PPP General Congress. Published by Freedom House, Georgetown (1991).

and strategies of governance. One of the fundamental human rights strategies of governance contained in the Universal Declaration of Human Rights and in the international covenants is the principle of equality and non-discrimination in the enjoyment of human rights. The principle of equality and non-discrimination is especially pertinent to multi-racial societies such as Guyana. Such societies have a special duty to develop constitutional principles, institutional arrangements and the necessary processes for constantly guarding over, and promoting, the practical application of the principle of equality and non-discrimination. A wise multi-racial society is one that keeps under constant scrutiny the adequacy of its fundamental guarantees and its related institutions and processes.

The guiding principle of equality and non-discrimination is a fundamental norm for the development process, understood as the pursuit of all human rights. The measure of poverty elimination when viewed in the prism of human rights is not how high is the standard of living, but how equal is the access of all vulnerable sectors to whatever benefits the society has to offer. International conventions on the rights of the child and omen, the guiding principles on equalizing opportunities for people with disabilities, and the ILO conventions on the treatment of indigenous peoples offer a guiding framework for national policies for specific sectors whose rights need special protection in the rough and tumble of daily governance and priority setting.

On the development of a culture of human rights in Guyana, it would be fitting to recall the declaration of an eminent group of Commonwealth human rights judges and lawyers meeting in Georgetown in September 1996. They authoritatively affirmed that:

- Fundamental human rights and freedoms are universal and are inherent in all human kind. They find expression in constitutions and legal systems throughout the world; they are anchored in the international human rights instruments by which all genuinely democratic States are bound; their meaning is illuminated by a rich body of case law of international and national courts.

- The universality of human rights and freedoms derives from the moral principle of each individual's personal and equal autonomy and human dignity. That principle transcends national political systems and is in the keeping of the independent judiciary.

- The international human rights instruments and their developing jurisprudence enshrine values and principles of equality, freedom, rationality and fairness, now recognised by the common law. They should be seen as complementary to domestic law in national courts. These instruments have inspired many of the constitutional guarantees of fundamental human rights and freedoms within and beyond the Commonwealth; they should be given constitutional status in all dependent territories.

- Both civil and political rights and economic, social and cultural rights are integral, indivisible and complementary parts of one coherent system of global human rights. The implementation of economic, social and cultural rights is a primary duty for the legislative and executive branches of government. However, even those economic, social and cultural rights which are not justiciable can serve as vital points of reference for judges as they interpret their constitutions and develop the common law, making choices which it is their responsibility to make in a free, equal and democratic society. Respect for human rights under the rule of law provides the best environment for the economic, social and cultural development of everyone in all parts of the world.

- Fundamental human rights and freedoms are more than mere pious aspirations. They form part of the public law of every nation, protecting individuals and minorities against the misuse of power by public authorities of all kinds. It is the special province of judges to see to it that the law's undertakings are realised in the daily life of the people. In a society ruled by law, all public institutions and authorities – legislative, executive and judicial – must act in accordance with the constitution and the law.

- The legislative and executive branches of government have a duty to provide the necessary means to secure the equal protection of the law, speedy and effective access to justice, and effective legal remedies. To achieve this, there is a need for adequate funds for the proper functioning of the courts, and adequate legal aid, advice and assistance for people who cannot otherwise obtain legal services. It is also essential for each branch of government to introduce and maintain appropriate rules and procedures to promote compliance, in discharging their functions, with the international human rights instruments by which they are bound.

- The provision of equal justice requires a competent and independent judiciary and legal profession trained in the discipline of the law and sensitive to the needs and aspirations of all the people. It is fundamental for a country's judiciary and legal profession to enjoy the broad confidence of the people they serve.

- Judicial review and effective access to the courts are indispensable, not only in normal times, but also during periods of public emergency. It is at such times that basic human rights are most at risk and when courts must be especially vigilant in their protection.

- Freedom of expression must be jealously protected as essential to the safeguarding of democracy and human rights. The courts must be zealous to protect free speech and expression in their widest sense and at all times.

The Chancellor of the Judiciary and other eminent Guyanese judges participated in the drafting and adoption of the Georgetown Conclusions. At the pinnacle of the Guyanese judicial system stands the Guyana Court of Appeal whose task is to watch over the protection of the human rights of Guyanese. It is to this court that we shall now turn.

# THE CHALLENGES

*1*

The Guyana Bar Association is now affiliated to the International Bar Association. Its application for membership was approved at the 19th Biennial Conference of the International Bar Association held in New Delhi, India, in October 1982.

Following the refusal of the Bank of Guyana to give the Guyana Bar Association permission to remit £15.00 to pay for its affiliation, Guyanese attorney Dr BG Ramcharan, now residing in Segny, France, offered the Guyana Bar Association President to pay the dues. The offer was accepted.

The Association has expressed its gratitude to Dr Ramcharan, who works in Geneva, for his kind gesture.

*The Guyana Bar Association Review, NS Vol 3, December 1982, p 73.*

2

In much of our legislation since 1967 there is discernible the fine hand of one or more craftsmen who had a hidden agenda. ... Words are used to obfuscate not to elucidate. There are traps, exclusions, exceptions, deliberately grey areas, in fact one comes to realize the law is being used as a technique to destroy legality. For at the end of the day the concept of legality is not infinitely flexible but is based on certain inarticulate major premises which inform western democracies and free societies everywhere.

*The Stabroek News, 29 June 1991, p 4.*

3

A duty devolves upon the courts to pronounce on the validity of executive action when it is challenged, to determine whether such action goes beyond constitutional power. The first allegiance of the courts is to the Constitution.

*RH Luckhoo JA, Seeram Teemal case, Civil Appeal No 43 (1982), p 24.*

4

Many legal analysts and other specialists have long referred to the 'gap' which has developed between the present Constitution as a document and its practical implementation, eg the gap between the theory and practice of constitutionalism.

The feeling has been expressed that the judiciary has been somewhat less than diligent in dealing with abuses and infringements of the Constitution by the Executive. It has been claimed that more often than not it has avoided confrontation with the Executive, through a combination of sophistry, exploiting the absence of common law remedies, and resorting to antiquated legal principles which are not in keeping with the present age of citizens' rights.

The invocation of the legality of 'dismissal at pleasure', the failure of the judiciary to order exemplary damages against the Executive where the abuse of its authority is grave, and its failure also to address abuses of the electoral machinery, illustrate that since independence the judiciary has not been prepared to use its weight against abuses by the Executive authorities of the State.

Given the situation, it is important, therefore, that the Select Committee find every means possible to assert the independence of the judiciary in its constitutional review. The new Constitution must assure the public that a real balance of power between the separate arms of the State exists. As experience elsewhere has shown, in the long run the judiciary is expected to be one of the most important bulwarks in protecting the rights of citizens under the Constitution.

*Professor Clive Thomas, submission to the Select Committee on Constitutional Review, 1996.*

*5*

'Chancellor should withdraw his offensive statement.'

During a recent television interview Chancellor of the Judiciary Mr Cecil Kennard made offensive remarks about women in the legal profession. When asked how he reacted to the growing number of women in the profession, he replied to the effect that '[t]he legal profession is for men'. He went on to describe the legal profession as difficult, but stated that if women work in the DDP's office and AG's chambers, they will do well.

Such patronizing comments, while offensive in themselves, are completely unacceptable coming from one charged with ensuring such prejudice becomes a thing of the past.

Art 29(1) of the current Constitution states that 'men and women have equal rights and the same legal status in all spheres of political, economic and social life'. Article 29(2) continues, 'the exercise of women's rights is ensured by according women equal access with men to academic, vocational and professional training, equal opportunities in employment, remuneration and promotion' ... The Constitutional Reform Commission recommended these rights be elevated to the status of fundamental rights in the new Constitution.

The Chancellor's comment has repercussions not only for women lawyers but for all women, should cases involving women's rights come before him. The GHRA believes the Chancellor should completely withdraw the remarks and apologize for any offence they may have caused.

Whatever course of action he chooses to take, however, the chilling effect of the Head of the Judiciary harbouring views so out of step with the Constitution and international human rights norms cannot be removed.

*Executive Committee, Guyana Human Rights Association (GHRA), 20 October 2000.*

# THE GUYANA COURT OF APPEAL

## CHANCELLORS OF THE JUDICIARY, 1966–2000

| | | |
|---|---|---|
| 1 | Sir KS Stoby | 1966–68 |
| 2 | Sir EV Luckhoo | 1968–75 |
| 3 | Mr JOF Haynes | 1976–80 |
| 4 | Mr VE Crane | 1980–84 |
| 5 | Mr KS Massiah | 1984–88 |
| 6 | Mr KM George | 1988–95 |
| 7 | Mr AFR Bishop | 1995–96 |
| 8 | Mr CC Kennard | 1996– |

## JUSTICES OF APPEAL, 1966–2000

| | | | | |
|---|---|---|---|---|
| 1 | Mr | Justice | EV Luckhoo | 1966–68 |
| 2 | Mr | „ | GLB Persaud | 1966–76 |
| 3 | Mr | „ | PA Cummings | 1966–77 |
| 4 | Mr | „ | VE Crane | 1967–79 |
| 5 | Mr | „ | JOF Haynes | 1974–75 |
| 6 | Mr | „ | RH Luckhoo | 1975–86 |
| 7 | Mr | „ | D Jhappan | 1976–79 |
| 8 | Mr | „ | KS Massiah | 1976–84 |
| 9 | Mr | „ | KM George | 1976–81 |
| 10 | Mr | „ | CJE Fung-a-Fatt | 1980–87 |
| 11 | Mr | „ | JC Gonsalves-Sabola | 1981–85 |
| 12 | Mr | „ | F Vieira | 1982–84 |
| 13 | Mr | „ | R Harper | 1985–88 |
| 14 | Mr | „ | CC Kennard | 1985–95 |
| 15 | Mr | „ | AFR Bishop | 1987–92 |
| 16 | Mr | „ | C Churaman | 1988–2000 |
| 17 | Ms | „ | DP Bernard | 1992–96 |
| 18 | Mr | „ | LL Perry | 1992–2000 |
| 19 | Mr | „ | P Persaud | 1995–2000 |
| 20 | Ms | „ | C Singh | 2000– |
| 21 | Mr | „ | I Chang | 2000– |
| 22 | Mr | „ | N Kissoon | 2000– |
| 23 | Mr | „ | C Singh | 2000– |

# SELECTED DECISIONS OF THE COURT OF APPEAL*

## *NOTE*

The *Law Reports of Guyana* were last published in 1975. The library of the Court of Appeal has a set of bound decisions for use by judges and lawyers. The list is meant to provide an indication of what is available at the library of the Court. The citations are reproduced as received.

### *1966*

Appana v Berbice Estates Ltd .......... 21/66
Abrams v Dookhoo Narayan .......... 10/66
BWIA v Bart .......... 12/66
Bijil v Salik Ram .......... 14/66
Berbice Estates Ltd v Appana .......... 21/66
Bart v BWIA .......... 12/66
Chitra v Takenarine .......... 15/66
Commissioner of Inland Revenue v Gomes .......... 17/66
Deokenanan v R .......... 19/66
Darsan v Enmore Estates Ltd .......... 16/66
Enmore Estates Ltd v Ramkellawan Darsan .......... 16/66
Forde v R .......... 6/66
Fraser v James Lewis .......... 18/66
Gomes v Commissioner of Inland Revenue .......... 17/66
Harris v Toolsie Persaud Ltd .......... 8/66
Lowe v R .......... 4/66
Lewis v Fraser .......... 18/66
Mayers v R .......... 5/66
Mohabeer et al v Sooknarain Singh and Sookram Bhagaloo .......... 11/66
Marshall v Texeira .......... 2/66
Mortimer v AP Singh .......... 13/66
Narayan v DA Abrams .......... 10/66
Persaud v R .......... 3/66
Persaud v Harris .......... 8/66
Pooran v R .......... 20/66
Ram v Bijil .......... 14/66
Rambeharry v Ressouvenir Estates Ltd .......... 9/66
Ressouvenir Estates Ltd v Rambeharry .......... 9/66
R v Courtney Low .......... 4/66

* 1966–2000. The decisions listed here were selected by the staff of the Court of Appeal for binding.

## *1967*

*1968*

*1969*

Sankar, Ahmad v Chintamanie Ajit .......... 36/69
Sarran, Gerriah v In Re .......... 27/69
Shipping Association of Georgetown et al v Ivan Bentinck .......... 13/69
Siebs v Siebs .......... 7/69
Singh, Khemraj et anor v Habi Bulah Khan et al .......... 17/69
Weber, Walter R et anor v Chintamanie Ajit .......... 28/69
West Bank Estates v Alexander Phillips .......... 9/69

*1970*

JW Evelyn v William Chichester .......... 1/70
Benjamin Semple v R .......... 2/70
Chintamanie Ajit v Town Clerk .......... 3/70
Shalim Ghanie v Bookers Shipping .......... 4/70
Kalion Motelall v State .......... 5/70
Jaichand Persaud v Vincent Lewis .......... 6/70
FHW Ramsahoye v Ramjit Singh et anor .......... 7/70
F White et al v Marics and Co Ltd .......... 8/70
George Sutherland v R .......... 9/70
Omar Khan v R .......... 10/70
Footoo Parasram v Kirpalanie Bros .......... 11/70
J Gafoor v Bookers Dem Sugar Estates Ltd .......... 12/70
Ogle Co v Mangre Ragnarine .......... 13/70
Alladat Khan v K Bhairo and John DeCastro .......... 14/70
Solomon Mohan v Guyana National .......... 15/70
Peter Persaud et al v Versailles and Schoon Ord .......... 16/70
Dhanwantie Rambharose v Bookers Dem Sugar Estates Ltd .......... 17/70
Edgar Ince v State .......... 18/70
Lindon Harper v State .......... 19/70
Lennox Da Costa v State .......... 20/70
Enmore Estates v Majid Noor .......... 21/70
State v Sankar Sudama .......... 22/70
State v Terrence Fowler .......... 23/70
Motilall Sudeen v Salamanie Naiken .......... 24/70
Vibert De Santos v Francis Approo .......... 25/70
Aubrey D Hunte v JW Evelyn and T and HD .......... 26/70
Kadar Lall Gobin v HS Cameron et al .......... 27/70

*1971*

Rolf Brandt v Attorney General of Guyana and Commissioner of Police . . . . . . . . . .1/71
Rolf Brandt v Attorney General and Carl Austin . . . . . . . . . . . . . . . . . . . . . . . . . . . . .3/71
State v Rakla Persaud . . . . . . . . . . . . . . . . . . . . . . . . . . . . . . . . . . . . . . . . . . . . . . . . . .6/70
Rambeharry v Ressouvenir Estates Ltd . . . . . . . . . . . . . . . . . . . . . . . . . . . . . . . . . . . .31/69
State v Jabez Carlton McRae . . . . . . . . . . . . . . . . . . . . . . . . . . . . . . . . . . . . . . . . . . . .64/70
John Leonard v Stanley Erskine . . . . . . . . . . . . . . . . . . . . . . . . . . . . . . . . . . . . . . . . .46/70
Maud Inez Lambert v Mary Caldeira . . . . . . . . . . . . . . . . . . . . . . . . . . . . . . . . . . . . . .40/69
McBool Shah v Public Trustee of Guyana . . . . . . . . . . . . . . . . . . . . . . . . . . . . . . . . . .17/70
Sowatilall v Kalika Persaud et al . . . . . . . . . . . . . . . . . . . . . . . . . . . . . . . . . . . . . . . .47/69
Hubert Dash et al v Bhagwan Jairam Persaud . . . . . . . . . . . . . . . . . . . . . . . . . . . . . .50/70
Prince Barnwell v Enmore Estates Ltd . . . . . . . . . . . . . . . . . . . . . . . . . . . . . . . . . . . .21/70
Abdulla et al v State . . . . . . . . . . . . . . . . . . . . . . . . . . . . . . . . . . . . . . . . . . . . . . . .37–39/71
Frank Sookram v State . . . . . . . . . . . . . . . . . . . . . . . . . . . . . . . . . . . . . . . . . . . . . . . . .45/71
Nazreen R Hanoman v Kathleen Hanoman . . . . . . . . . . . . . . . . . . . . . . . . . . . . . . . . .28/70
Ogle Co Ltd v Mangri Rajnarine . . . . . . . . . . . . . . . . . . . . . . . . . . . . . . . . . . . . . . . . .31/71

*1972*

Thomas Bijadder v State . . . . . . . . . . . . . . . . . . . . . . . . . . . . . . . . . . . . . . . . . . . . . .28/71
Lillowtie v Sumintra . . . . . . . . . . . . . . . . . . . . . . . . . . . . . . . . . . . . . . . . . . . . . . . . . .53/71
Ronald Gibson v Lucianne Gibson . . . . . . . . . . . . . . . . . . . . . . . . . . . . . . . . . . . . . . . .27/71
State v Lalta Persaud et al . . . . . . . . . . . . . . . . . . . . . . . . . . . . . . . . . . . . . . . . . . . . .3–7/71
Etwaroo v Jagdeo, Persaud Jagsarran . . . . . . . . . . . . . . . . . . . . . . . . . . . . . . . . . . . .65/71
Olga Appiah et al v Winnifred Hookumchand . . . . . . . . . . . . . . . . . . . . . . . . . . . . . . .47/71
Mazahar Bacchus v Suraj Booklall . . . . . . . . . . . . . . . . . . . . . . . . . . . . . . . . . . . . . . .40/70
Mustapha Ally v State . . . . . . . . . . . . . . . . . . . . . . . . . . . . . . . . . . . . . . . . . . . . . . . . .45/72
Chitaria Outram v Saffie Mohamed . . . . . . . . . . . . . . . . . . . . . . . . . . . . . . . . . . . . . . .25/72
Una Welch et al v Shafi Janali . . . . . . . . . . . . . . . . . . . . . . . . . . . . . . . . . . . . . . . . .27–33/72
Bephia v Sahijaram Thani . . . . . . . . . . . . . . . . . . . . . . . . . . . . . . . . . . . . . . . . . . . . . .30/70
Claude Vieira v State . . . . . . . . . . . . . . . . . . . . . . . . . . . . . . . . . . . . . . . . . . . . . . . . .140/71
In Re Lennox Arthur and Calvin Hermanstyne . . . . . . . . . . . . . . . . . . . . . . . . . . . . . . .34/70
Samuel Glen v Raphal Sampson . . . . . . . . . . . . . . . . . . . . . . . . . . . . . . . . . . . . . . . . . . .9/71
Maisie Harris et al v The Guyana and Trinidad Mutual
Fire Insurance Co Ltd . . . . . . . . . . . . . . . . . . . . . . . . . . . . . . . . . . . . . . . . . . . . . . .41/71
Ogle Co Ltd v Moses Douglas . . . . . . . . . . . . . . . . . . . . . . . . . . . . . . . . . . . . . . . . . . .13/71
Kirpaul Sookdeo et al v State . . . . . . . . . . . . . . . . . . . . . . . . . . . . . . . . . . . . . . . . . . .3–5/72
Frederick Mahaica v Derek Phang et anor . . . . . . . . . . . . . . . . . . . . . . . . . . . . . . . . . .39/71

## *1973*

Gladys Tappin v Francis Lucas .............................................................1/73
Janet Jagan and New Guyana Co Ltd v Linden Forbes
Sampson Burnham ....................................................................46/72
Jagroo v George Wimpey and Co Ltd ................................................35/72
Dhannie Ramsingh v State ..........................................................48/72
Jagrani Das v Surujpaul ...........................................................8/72
Cyril Durbeej v Bhagwan Persaud ...................................................132/72
Peter Taylor and Co Ltd v Commissioner of Inland Revenue ..........................5/71
Wycliffe Sookra v Kumar Singh, Officer of Customs and Excise .......................30/72
Mohamed Zaman v State .............................................................9/73
Vishnu Narine Sarju v Felix Walker ................................................49/73

## *1974*

Asad Khan v Zaitoon Khan ..........................................................8/73
Petition by Shafi Janali ..........................................................47/73
The Demerara Bauxite Co Ltd v Joseph R Hunte ......................................49/70
Walter Seepersaud v Port Mourant Ltd ..............................................21/71
Vishnu Narine Sarju v Felix Walker ................................................49/72
Sarabjeet Ramlakhan v Boodnie Farouk ..............................................50/73
Enmore, Hope Village v District Council v
Mohamood Shaw et al ...............................................................23/74
Ramlakhan v The Commissioner of Inland Revenue .....................................49/73
Philip Nurse, Senior Public Health Inspector v Khalil Rahaman ......................41/74
Paul Burnett v Smulex Frankel .....................................................3/74
Winston Hamilton Romalho v
(1) Lalta Persaud and Sons Ltd
(2) Omadatt Samaroo v
Leonard Wharton ...................................................................10/74
State v Lloyd Harris ..............................................................42/74
Hubert Dash, Fransic Gregory, Louisa Green et al v Bhagwan Jairam Persaud ...37/72
John Nagreadie v Noor Abjal .......................................................35/71
(1) Clement Vigilance
(2) H Barry Massay v Chase Manhattan Bank ..................................52 and 53/72
Gordon Yaw v VJ Correia ...........................................................12/73
State v Reuben Khan ...............................................................80/73
Harold Roberts Polycarp Dennison v Roydon GB
Field-Ridley et al .................................................................26/73
Mervyn Linton v Donald Haynes v Samuel Facey ......................................15/73

State v George Mootoosammy, Henry Budhoo .......................32 and 33/74
The Village Council of Stewartville v David Powdar and Others ..............61/73
Rosaline v Babu Imrit Singh ..........................................18/73
Berbard Singh v Alice Nixon and Rupert Castello .....................22 and 23/73
Kaimraj Powaroo et al v Philip Busgith ...............................6/72

## *1975*

State v Ivor Moonilall ..............................................18/73
Lynden Reece DC v Hakim Abdulia ......................................79/74
Ramdat Sookraj v Edward Ceres ........................................68/74
The Shipping Association of Georgetown and Bookers
Shipping (Demerara) Ltd v Arthur Hayden ..............................15/74
Omar Persaud v Jaitoon ...............................................70/74
State v Balram Gobin et al ...............................26, 27, 28 and 29/75
State v Carl Van Rossum and Carrol Halley ...........................47 and 48/75
John Fernandes (Ins) Ltd v Commissioner of Inland
Revenue and Attorney General .........................................19/74
State v Henry Roberts and Michael Roberts ...........................43 and 44/75
Toolsie Persaud Ltd v Durga Persaud ..................................9/74
Rosita Pearl Smith v Samad Yassin ....................................32/74
Eileen Sumintra Bankay et al v Sukdai Sukhdeo ........................27/74
State v Sydney Purdassy ..............................................103/74
State v Sookraj Evans ................................................82/74
Herman Jaipergas v Veelmattie Jaipergas ..............................38/73
State v Alfred Kellman ...............................................94/74
State v Kowshall Persaud .............................................84/74
State v Rudolph Doris ................................................90/74
State v Hansraj Ori and Tulsie Persaud ..............................83 and 85/75
State v Basdeo .......................................................101/74
Commissioner of Inland Revenue v Isahack .............................54/71
State v Mohamed Khalil ...............................................69/74

## *1976*

Tula Ram Det Const 7325 v Vishnu Ramdass ..............................1/76
The Enmore Estates Ltd v DR Singh ....................................2/76
State v Cleveland Clarke .............................................3/76
State v Robert Lewis .................................................4/76
State v Prince Adams and Eon Poole ...................................5/76
State v Neil Daniels .................................................6/76

In the Matter of Trade Marks Act and In the Matter of an Application by General Foods Corp ........ 7/76
Henry Chester Det Const 7294 v Hardatt Called Ghanie ........ 8/76
State v Ken Barrow ........ 9/76
State v Jaigobin Bissessar ........ 10/76
John Perira and Lily Rohan v Winston Jeune Supernumerary Const ........ 11/76
Aleem Ali and Yacoob Ali v Basil Williams DC 7845 ........ 12/76
State v Dennis Pryce ........ 13/76
Elvira Small v Winifred Melville ........ 14/76
State v Vibert Hodge ........ 15/76
Deonarine Singh v Transport and Harbour Department ........ 16/76
State v Oswald Gobin, PB Griffith ........ 17/76
State v Gowkarran Persaud et al ........ 18/76
State v Abdool Azim Sattaur et anor ........ 19/76
Panchu a/k Namkoo v Rampersaud a/k Poonoo ........ 20/76
State v Guy Simmons ........ 21/76
Bata Shoe Com, Guy Ltd et al and Guyana Unit Trust Management Co Ltd et al v CIR and Attorney General ........ 22/76
Ramroop Tiwari and Jagessar v Harry Narine Singh et anor ........ 23/76
State v Fitzpatrick Darrell ........ 24/76
State v Phillip Plowell ........ 25/76
State v Lynette Scantlebury ........ 26/76

## *1977*

Mohammed Yasseen v Janki Persaud ........ 1/77
Moneram Hazari v Paul Burnett, Officer of Customs and Excise ........ 2/77
State v Neville Corbin ........ 3/77
The East Demerara Water Conservancy Board v Saliman et al and Ivan Samaroo et al ........ 4/77
John Patin v J D'Oliveira, Officer of Customs and Excise ........ 5/77
State v Albert Stanislaus Browne ........ 6/77
Continental Biscuit Co Ltd v Albert Joseph Shanks ........ 7/77
Johannes Waaldyk v Rupert Trim George Eastman ........ 8/77
Patrick Bowen PC 7094 v Varnie Johnson ........ 9/77
Doolarie c/d Fatty v Police Constable English ........ 10/77
State v Mohamed Gaznabbee ........ 11/77
Abdool Hack v Rahieman ........ 12/77
Peter Mangroo v Dhanmatie Singh c/d Bissessar ........ 13/77

Stanley Erskine Det Supt v Jaiprakash Goel ..............................14/77
Hugh Desmond Hoyte v Liberation Press Ltd and
Cast Papers Ltd ..............................15/77
Deolall Triloti, Ramratti Triloti v Clefrin Broomes and
Cyril Sookhai ..............................16/77

*1978*

Nellie Rajbahadur Singh v Winston Benjamin ..............................1/78
Adjodhia Persaud Singh v Chuni Lall ..............................2/78
State v Jaipaul Naipaul ..............................3/78
State v Parbu Sharma and Williams ..............................4/78
State v Mohamed Nazir ..............................5/78
Bharose v Patricia Pulcoomarie Courtherm ..............................6/78
Doodnauth Heeralall v Hack Bros and Joseph Benn ..............................7/78
State v Brahmanand Again ..............................8/78
The Editor, The Evening Post v Satrohan Singh ..............................9/78
Sheik Mohamed Hyder Ali v The Public Service Commission ..............................10/78
John Charles v Llewellyn Skeete ..............................11/78

*1979*

Major Harry B Hinds v Chang Woon Lee ..............................73/78
Gung Rin Kim ..............................74/78
Frank Hope v New Guyana Co Ltd ..............................33/76
Attorney General v Vincent Teekah ..............................33/76
State v Michael Greene ..............................24/78
State v Cyril Denham ..............................63/77
Elsie Persaud v Charles Ogle ..............................3/76
State v Derick Robinson ..............................34/78
James Britton v Charles Paul ..............................16/79
Muhisar v Bookers Demerara Sugar Estate Ltd ..............................85/75
State v Lennox Thomas ..............................61/78
Carlton Weithers v Rene Walters ..............................12/78

*1980*

Kwame Apata v Morris Roberts Constable 7763 ..............................2–3/80
State v Owen Alleyne ..............................19/80
Hardyal and Sarah Sawh v Soukhia, Administratrix of
Ramgobin Estate ..............................12/80

*1981*

State v Ashraf Haniff .......... 23/80
Seeta Ramoutar v Rampersaud .......... 40/78
Gladys Brandis v Neville Craig .......... 70/79
State v Douglas James .......... 17/80
State v Chandica P Sanichar .......... 30/79
Mahindra Persaud c/d Vishnu v Kennard Barran .......... 36/80
Bhupal Persaud v Daneshwar Ramsumeer .......... 37/80
Thakur Persaud
Sookmanth c/d Cuttie
State v John France .......... 69/78
State v Moses Dey .......... 10/81
State v Wilbert Beckles .......... 9/81
Ivan Charran and Grace Kacobs v Savitri Singh .......... 27/78
Victor Johnson v Sterling Products Ltd .......... 17/80
State v Keith Mayers .......... 6/79
Badr Prasaud v Dem Mutual Life Insurance .......... 68/79

*1982*

Kwame Apata v Morris Roberts DC .......... 40–41/80
Badri Prasad v The Demerara Mutual Life .......... 68/78
RH Nielsen v Loyd Barker, DPP .......... 57/82
The Guyana Labour Union v McLukk McKenzie .......... 22/78
Bhanmat Santokie v Guyana Transport Services .......... 60/80
The New India Ass Co Ltd v Gangaram .......... 8–9/78
Ricardo Solomon v State .......... 60/78
Edward Burke v Phyllis Gill .......... 1/78
National Milling Co v Allen .......... 34/80
Vidyadat Mohabir v Dhanpaul Kissoon .......... 37/80
Inshan Bacchus v Ali Khan .......... 24, 27, 28 and 29/79
Srinivasan MEI v Pretam Lall .......... 14/79
Charles Ramson v Lloyd Barker .......... 16/80
State v Ronald Gajraj v Brigadier Clarence Price .......... 13/79
Sedley Phoenia v State .......... 42/79
Latchman Outer v State .......... 27/80
George Alves v State .......... 35/80
Kunti v Dem Mutual Life Assurance .......... 47/77
Sheik Mohamed Houssain v Sheik Mohamed Yaccob .......... 61/79
Bertie Ramjohn v Jagdeo Ramdin .......... 31/79

## *1983*

Deryck Price v State ........ 31/80
American Life Insurance Co v Sumintra ........ 20/82
Bruce Baptiste v The General Manager of Transport ........ 12/82
Mohamed Farouk v
(1) S Persaud
(2) K Persaud ........ 47/80
Jennie Waldron v E Ewards, DC 9936 ........ 19/83
Basil Williams, DC 7845 v
(1) J Halloran
(2) SNG Quian ........ 26/74
State v Colin Armstrong and Leslie Johnson ........ 77–78/75
The Guyana Sugar Corp Ltd v Seeram Teemal ........ 45/82

## *1984*

The Guyana Trinidad Mutual Life Insurance Ltd v Rentokil ........ 4/84
Ramdehol Samaroo v Jagdeo ........ 5/84
Caledonian Insurance Co Ltd v S Ramkisoon ........ 9/81
Alan Outridge v State ........ 9/84
Balkarran and Others v State ........ 10/84
Josephine Burnett v The Comptroller of Customs and Excise ........ 11/84
Sheik Mahuzadin v Guyana Sugar Co ........ 23/82
Wahid Alli v Mohamed Yasseen ........ 5/82

## *1985*

Sainchand v Deonarine ........ 61/83
Oscar Haynes v Ivan Walters ........ 24/85
Lochan Arjune v State ........ 28/78
Mayheu Heyliger v Lakeram Deokarran ........ 20–21/80

## *1986*

Patrick Grant v Haimwant Ramdehol ........ 29/85
Dora Westmoreland v Clifton Chan-a-Yun and Others ........ 49/84
Sulficar Hussain and Errington Herbert v Godfrey De Freitas ........ 28/85
Amar Bholananth v State ........ 4/85
Lloyd Barker v Eric Douglas ........ 59/84
Whitfield Rhyma v Transport and Harbour Department ........ 56/82
Pelham Gray et al v State ........ 30–34/85

## *1987*

Roland Hetsberger v State ....................................... 1/87
American Life Insurance Co v Dolly Ann ....................................... 2/87
Frank David v State ....................................... 3/87

## *1988*

Attorney General of Guyana v Mohamed Ali et al ....................................... 1/88
State v Cevil Levine ....................................... 2/88
Mohamed Omar v State ....................................... 3/88
Patrick Zephyr v Bank of Nova Scotia ....................................... 4/88

## *1989*

Patrick Perreiro v Dick Manning et anor ....................................... 1/89
Frank Martin v State ....................................... 2/89
Rampersaud Sewkaran v State ....................................... 3/89
Bebi S Yassin v David Joseph ....................................... 4/89
Shomsheer Khan c/d Sherry et al v State ....................................... 5/89
Albert Dorsett, Malcolm Somersett v State ....................................... 6/89
Godfrey Caesar v Attorney General of Guyana ....................................... 7/89

## *1990*

Stanley Collynse v Anthony Hilary Gomes ....................................... 36/85
Eric Gilbert and Gloria Henry v James Britton ....................................... 20/84
Gwendline Singh v Cecil Ram Doobay ....................................... 7/86
Cpl Williams and the Attorney General
Osman Khan et al v State ....................................... 47, 48, 49 and 50/88
Ramdat BR v Mahadeo Doobay ....................................... 57/88
Sheik Mohamed Adam v Mohamed Mursalin ....................................... 72/87
Ramdas Persaud et al v Bephia Persaud and Deodas ....................................... 87/84

## *1991*

Abool Salim Yasseen v State ....................................... 38 and 39/88
Noel Thomas and K Zaman Alli v DPP ....................................... 8/90
Ursula De Freitas v Alphonso Modern Record Store ....................................... 27/89
R Sattaur v Sarojni Das ....................................... 68/88
Kent Garment Factory v Attorney General and Minister of Trade and Tourism ....... 58/89

## *1992*

Ramdas Persaud v Deodas, Ramdas Persaud .............................. 81/84
Sumair Singh v Chase Manhattan N/A et al .............................. 36/86
Rajpaul Singh v Balgobin and Bephia .............................. 46/86
Mohamed Alli v Teaching Service Commission .............................. 65/88
Ramesh Ramdat v State .............................. 40/88
Jennifer Swamy v State .............................. 28/88
J Goel v Attorney General .............................. 33/89
Steven Edward King v DPP .............................. 85/91
Nandalall-Sukhram v DAT .............................. 44/87
Charles Bazil and Others v May Wharton .............................. 21/88
Winston Humphrey v Dr Mohamed Hallim Rahat .............................. 71/88
Ramsamaugh et anor v Hand-in-Hand Mutual Insurance Co Ltd .............................. 71/88
Siri Hari Ram and Com v Umanath Ketwaroo .............................. 88/89
Fazal Osman v Vernon Annamanthadoo .............................. 22/86
GTM v Chandroutie and Others .............................. 42/89

## *1993*

Ramdat Soukraj Trading v Paul Burnette Customs and Excise .............................. 55/91
David Mangroo v Ramrattan, Jagmohan, Bhanmattie Singh .............................. 80/90
GP and TWU v Winston James et al .............................. 64/91
Noel Fraser v GTM et al .............................. 40/92

## *1994*

Bibi Shamina v Sompat Dyal .............................. 51–56/83
Rameall v Tulsie Narine and Das .............................. 69 and 73–77/89
Juliet Vicilorie v Food World Int'l Ltd .............................. 36/90
Neil Lafferty v Attorney General of Guyana .............................. 50/92
GTM v Chandroutie and Others .............................. 42/89
Kenneth W Barnwell v Attorney General of Guyana, the Judicial Service Commission and Others .............................. 84/91
Dropratte Singh v Raymond Bayse .............................. 61/91
Anand Mohankissoon v State .............................. 2/93
Lennox Thomas v State .............................. 21/90
G T and T LTD v PUC .............................. 90/91
Clement Johnson v Attorney General of Guyana .............................. 21/91
Kemp Roberts v Attorney General of Guyana .............................. 35/91
Sasenarine and Inez Seepaul v Attorney General of Guyana .............................. 50/91
Kandasammy v Lall .............................. 14/94

## *1995*

Ambrosine Thomas v Abdool Hamid ........................................4/86
Adams and Archer v State ........................................5 and 6/91
Ambrose v Boston ........................................74/90
Sharma v Sharma ........................................49/91
Omadai Sattaur v State ........................................10/93
Clement Singh v State ........................................29/90

## *1996*

Yasseen and Thomas v Attorney General et al ........................19 and 20/96
Hiemelia Ram Gobin v Premnauth Persaud ........................26/96
Oswald Lewis v R Joseph Eleezer ........................26/96
Donald Gunputh v State ........................17/91
Yasseen and Thomas v Attorney General et al ........................40/96
Leon Vansluytman v New Building Society, CJ Thrift Shop Ltd ................68/92
Hari Persaud v Ganesh Persaud et al Kumar et al ........................59/92
Ramasingh v Janakdai Bacchus ........................4/95
Spencer and Fraser v State ........................10–11/96

## *1997*

Godwin Patterson v Cpl Byrne ........................30/96
David Persaud v Bohir Rampersaud ........................103/85
K Juman Yassin v Ganga Deolall ........................31/95
MCC v Hughes, Stoby and Field ........................56/98
Zaman Ali v Oswald A Gouveia ........................8/97
Errol Leung v Romanie Gouveia ........................79/96
Lawrence Chang v State ........................2/96
Michel Adams v Minister of Finance and Comm of Police ....................16/97
Meer T Tiwari v Gautama Kamal Maraj ........................11/93
State v Rabindra Deo ........................3/96

## *1998*

Michael Gordon v State ........................13/97
Simon Fairbain v Attorney General ........................5/97
Eric Williams v State ) ........................3 and 4/94
Dinidal Khublall )
Bharatraj Mulai v State ) ........................9/96
Lallman Mulai )

Raymond Persaud v Attorney General, DPP .....55/97
Edgar Aaron v Writ of Certiorari .....41/97
Jai Naraine Prashad v State .....26/96
Attorney General of Guyana v Caterpillar Americas Co .....43/94
Asthon Chase v Audrey Chase .....66/96
Matthews v State .....15/96

*1999*

John Lawrence v State .....1/99
Guyana Consumer Advisory Bureau Public Utilities Comm v GT and T .....2/99
Shazam Ibrahim, Surendranauth Chattergoon v State .....3/99
Keith Thomas v State .....4/99
Vivekanand Singh, Hazath Hussein et al v State .....5/99
Donovan Caesar v State .....6/99
Stanley Singh, Janet Jagan v Esther Perreira .....7/99
Avis Whaul v Joy Reid, Clarence Hughes .....8/99
State v Hardat Ketwaru .....9/99
Dereck Jagan v Karran Ganpat .....10/99
Jeffery Edwards, David Baptise v State .....11/99
Peter Rodney v State .....12/99

*2000*

Garfield Sobers v Director of Prisons .....1/2000
VCT v National Frequency Mang Unit .....2/2000
Attorney General of Guyana v Caterpillar Americas .....3/2000
Irfan Ally v State .....4/2000
Joseph D'Agrella v Attorney General .....5/2000
Attorney General, Mala Drepaul and Andrew Wade v Errol Alphonso .....6/2000
MH Wong v ED Ellis .....7/2000
Raldolph Rodrigues v State .....8/2000

# TABLE OF CASES

# THE ROLE OF THE GUYANA COURT OF APPEAL

## INTRODUCTION

Guyana has been independent since 1966 and by the turn of the century the Guyana Court of Appeal had three and a half decades of experience. As the highest court in the land, the Guyana Court of Appeal outranks in importance any other constitutional institution. In the final analysis the liberties and rights of Guyanese are in its hands. If necessary, the court must be willing to uphold the Constitution even against Parliament itself. For the future of Guyana, therefore, the Court of Appeal warrants the closest study. This chapter will offer an initial assessment of the court. Such an assessment is important not only for the legal history of the country, but might also help pave the way for the eventual entry onto the scene of a Caribbean Court of Appeal.

### The role of the courts

The role of the highest court of *any* country is especially important. The role of the highest court of a developing country takes on added significance. The court must help steer the country towards a path of development grounded in democracy, the rule of law and respect for human rights. The role of the highest court in a multi-ethnic country is even more crucial still; for it is the court that must help stitch together the national fabric with the threads of the rule of law and respect for human rights.

In today's world the first responsibility of a judge is to seek to uphold constitutionally and legally guaranteed human rights, guided by the internationally proclaimed human rights norms. A judge should *know*, *apply* and *promote* international human rights norms. A judge, in the words of the famous Indian Chief Justice, Mr Justice Bhagwati, should seek to 'fashion new tools', to 'invent new strategies' and to 'develop a human rights jurisprudence' bringing human rights within the reach of the citizen.[1] A judge should always be independent and impartial, and refuse to submit to any form of political pressure.

Law in a free and moral society, according to Lord Justice Sedley, is concerned centrally with the abuse of power wherever it resides. Justice is a process of principled negotiation of interests through law on the basis of constitutionally and legally guaranteed human rights grounded in

1 Interview with Mr J Bhagwati, Geneva, 30 March 1999.

international norms.[2] International laws and, in particular, human rights jurisprudence can greatly assist domestic courts in interpreting a Bill of Rights or human rights provisions in a constitution. It can also help expand the scope of a Bill of Rights, making it more meaningful and effective. Judges should adopt a generous and purposive approach in interpreting a Bill of Rights. This is particularly important in countries which are in the process of building democratic traditions.[3] Judges have a vital part to play in developing and maintaining a vibrant human rights environment.

## Post-independence justice in Guyana

At a welcoming ceremony for the Chancellor of the Guyana Court of Appeal on 2 May 1984, the then President of the Guyana Bar Association, Mr Miles Fitzpatrick, told the court: 'The task of the courts in Guyana is to establish a jurisprudence that responds to the needs of our people and our times and in so doing to recognize the ascendancy of none but the law.' 'The courts', he added, 'have a long way to go in carrying out this task'. He warned the assembled judges, lawyers, diplomats and guests of the need for continuity of the law:

> However revolutionary and progressive the changes may be, if we lose sight of the basic verities of the common law, we would cast ourselves adrift on the rocks of dictatorship and intolerance ... We can either go forward to a new flowering of the law, where the courts cast their protective cloak over the ordinary citizen, upholding his fundamental rights against ever-increasing encroachment by an ever more powerful authority, or we can go backwards, to an authoritarian system, in which the power and interests of the establishment take precedence over the freedom, integrity and welfare of the underprivileged citizen.[4]

The President of the Bar Association was addressing a chancellor of the judiciary who would later resign his position to move across to the political arm of government and become its principal legal adviser as Attorney General. The incoming chancellor was succeeding one who, as Chancellor, had addressed the Bar on 28 October 1981 in the following terms:

> In Guyana the rule of law is very necessary so as to provide the right environment for socialist orientation and nation building, which are the dominant preoccupations of Parliament and the Government of the Co-operative Republic of Guyana. The judiciary is now a necessary and integral

---

2 Sedley LJ, 'Freedom, Law and Justice', *The Fiftieth Hamlyn Lectures*, 1999, London: Sweet & Maxwell, p 56.

3 See Hatchard, J and Linn, S, *Parliamentary Supremacy and Judicial Independence. A Commonwealth Approach*, 1999, London: Cavendish Publishing. See also Dickson, B and Carmichael, P, *The House of Lords; Its Parliamentary and Judicial Roles*, 1999, London: Hart.

4 Report in the *Guyana Chronicle*, 2 May 1984.

> part of the political, economic and social system, and the judiciary must look upon itself as having a crucial role to play in this task by ensuring that in the all-important field of socialist development, basic values like the rule of the law and, consequently, justice, are to be maintained. This is, without any doubt, one of the most important of the judiciary's functions in contemporary Guyana.

He added:

> The high point of the present day arrangement is that while he maintains his judicial independent conscience, the Guyanese judge works in cooperation with the administration for the advancement of socialism.[5]

The peaks and valleys of the Guyanese courts led an eminent Guyanese scholar, Professor Clive Thomas, to submit to the Constitutional Reform Commission of the Parliament of Guyana in 1996:

> The past three decades have been littered with breaches in, and the erosion of, the rights of the citizens of Guyana, as they are traditionally recognized in democracies. The courts have played no small role in this unfortunate situation, despite the catalogue of entrenched fundamental rights in the 1980 Constitution, which were carried over from the original Independence Constitution. The provision of 'exceptions' to these rights under the 1980 Constitution have also helped to pave the way for this outcome. Emergency legislation has been invoked without the prior declaration of a State of Emergency and has been used as a weapon clearly aimed at regime survival as distinct from protection of the State against serious security threats. The National Assembly has also failed to make any noticeable progress in the provision of court practice and procedures, for the enforcement of fundamental rights. These matters, essential to the fundamental rights of all citizens, should receive a clear delineation in the new Constitution.[6]

This harsh but fair judgment would need to be kept in mind in any assessment of the Guyana Court of Appeal. There is surely much that can be said that would be critical of the court and of the judiciary in Guyana. The purpose of critical assessment of the court should, however, in our view, be to draw lessons with a view to strengthening judicial independence in the future and to build upon the positive aspects of the work of the court in helping to set in place a jurisprudence inspired by the highest standards of national and international human rights law. The rest of this chapter will seek to distill some of the key doctrines of the Guyana Court of Appeal that might represent the juristic philosophy of the country and provide the basis for a strengthened judiciary of the future.

---

5 *The Guyana Bar Association Review*, NS, December 1981, Vol 1, pp 43–52.

6 Submission obtained from the Constitutional Reform Commission. During this period, the Attorneys General of Guyana included Mr SS Ramphal, who later became Secretary General of the Commonwealth Secretariat and Mr M Shahabuddeen, who became a judge on the International Court of Justice.

## The position of the Court of Appeal under the 1980 Constitution

As a preliminary comment, it should be noted that the 1980 Constitution is widely acknowledged to have been brought in by a government that took power in massively fraudulent elections. The Constitution itself was approved in a referendum also widely acknowledged to have been a massive fraud. The architect of the Constitution during this process was Dr M Shahabuddeen, who was later elected to the International Court of Justice.

Chapter IX of the 1980 Constitution of Guyana provides for a Supreme Court of Judicature consisting of a Court of Appeal and a High Court, with such jurisdiction and powers as are conferred on them by the Constitution or any other law.[7] Each of these courts is a superior court of record. The Judges of the Court of Appeal are the Chancellor, who is President, the Chief Justice and such number of Justices of Appeal as may be prescribed by Parliament. The Chancellor and the Chief Justice are appointed by the President acting after consultation with the 'Minority Leader'. Judges other than the Chancellor and the Chief Justice are appointed by the President acting in accordance with the advice of the Judicial Service Commission.

In the closing months of 2000 a controversy arose over the role of the President in appointing judges to the Court of Appeal and whether it was mandatory for the President to follow the letter of the advice of the Judicial Service Commission. The facts are that at a meeting held on 1 September 2000, the Judicial Service Commission decided to recommend three persons to act as Justices of Appeal. The Commission further recommended that a fourth judge be appointed a Justice of Appeal after she had given decision in an election petition, the hearing of which had been completed. Following her appointment, the first three judges should be confirmed. The aim of the Commission was to preserve the seniority of the judge whose decision in the election petition was pending. Instead of proceeding as the Commission recommended, the President proceeded to appoint all four persons as Justices of Appeal. Members of the legal profession and the Guyana Bar Association contended that the President was bound to accept all of the recommendations of the Commission. If he had reasons to do so he should have referred their advice back to the Commission for reconsideration. Thereafter the President would be bound by the advice tendered by the Judicial Service Commission. On this view the four judges were improperly appointed.

The issue gave rise to protests by the Guyana Bar Association. Reportedly the Guyana Bar Association wrote to the Judicial Service Commission asking for clarification of the advice tendered to the President. The subject was much debated in the local media and was the focus of a public conference by the

7 Constitution of Guyana 1980, Art 123(1).

Guyana Bar Association. At that conference Senior Counsel strongly advocated more stringent rules to ensure judicial independence.[8]

Article 130 of the Constitution provides that Parliament may make provisions for the exercise of the jurisdiction and powers of a Justice of Appeal by such puisne judge as may be requested by the Chancellor to sit as an additional Justice of Appeal at sittings of the Court of Appeal.[9] Parliament may also make provision for the exercise of the jurisdiction and powers of a puisne judge by such Justices of Appeal as may be requested by the Chancellor to sit as an additional puisne judge.

Under Art 133 of the Constitution, an appeal to the Court of Appeal lies as of right from decisions of the High Court in the following cases:

(a) final decisions in any civil or criminal proceedings on questions as to the interpretation of the Constitution; and

---

8 See *The Stabroek News*, 13 November 2000: 'Judicial Service Commission Considers Bar Association's Request'; 16 November 2000, editorial: 'Appointing Judges'; 26 November 2000 and 29 November 2000, 'Letters to the Editor' (www.stabroeknews.com).

9 See on this the following letter of Senior Counsel in *The Stabroek News* of 6 October 2000, p 2:

> *'Two judges of High Court cannot sit as additional judges of Court of Appeal'*
>
> Dear Editor,
>
> I observe from reports in the print and electronic media that the Chancellor sat and heard appeals with two judges of the High Court, Justices Carl Singh and Nandram Kissoon.
>
> The Constitution of the Court of Appeal is set out in Art 124 of the Constitution as:
>
> The Judges of the Court of Appeal shall be the Chancellor, who shall be the President of the Court of Appeal, the Chief Justice and such number of Justices of Appeal as may be prescribed by Parliament.
>
> In keeping with the provisions of Art 124 of the Constitution – s 34(1) of the Court of Appeal Act, states: 'The Judges of the Court of Appeal shall include not less than two and not more than five Justices of Appeal.' In 1978, s 34 of the Court of Appeal Act was amended and made provision for 'any' judge of the High Court to sit as an additional judge of the Court of Appeal. Section 12(3) of the Administration of Justice Act, No 21 of 1978 reads:
>
> Notwithstanding anything to the contrary in sub-s (1) the Chancellor may request the attendance at any time of any judge of the High Court to sit as an additional judge of the Court of Appeal at any sittings of the Court, and any judge whose attendance is so requested shall attend accordingly.
>
> The clear and unambiguous language of the enabling legislation does not authorise two judges of the High Court to sit as additional judges of the Court of Appeal.
>
> In my view therefore where two judges of the High Court sit as additional judges of the Court of Appeal it is not properly constituted and decisions given by it are constitutionally invalid.
>
> It is hoped that the Honourable Attorney General will see fit to address the issue raised herein.
>
> Yours faithfully,
>
> Rex H McKay, SC

(b) final decisions given in exercise of the jurisdiction conferred on the High Court by Art 153 of the Constitution, which relates to the enforcement of fundamental rights and freedoms.[10]

Article 153 of the Constitution provides that if any person alleges that any of the provisions of Arts 138 to 151 has been, is being, or is likely to be contravened in relation to him (or, in the case of a person who is detained, if any other person alleges such a contravention in relation to the detained person), then, without prejudice to any other action with respect to the same matter which is lawfully available, that person (or that other person) may apply to the High Court for redress. The High Court has original jurisdiction to hear and determine any application made by any person in pursuance of this competence. It may make such orders, issue such writs and give such directions as it may consider appropriate for the purpose of enforcing or securing the enforcement of any provisions of Arts 138 to 151. However, the High Court may not exercise its powers under this paragraph if it is satisfied that adequate means of redress are or have been available to the person concerned under any other law.

If in any proceedings in any court subordinate to the High Court any question arises as to the contravention of any of the provisions of Arts 138–51 (inclusive), the person presiding in that court is required to refer the question to the High Court unless, in his or her opinion, the raising of the question is merely frivolous or vexatious. Where any question is referred to the High Court in pursuance of this provision, the High Court is called upon to give its decision upon the question and the court in which the question arose is required to dispose of the case in accordance with that decision or, if that decision is the subject of an appeal under the Constitution to the Court of Appeal, in accordance with the decision of the Court of Appeal.

Parliament may confer upon the High Court such additional powers as may appear to Parliament to be necessary or desirable for the purpose of enabling the High Court more effectively to exercise the jurisdiction conferred upon it. Parliament may make provision with respect to the practice and procedure of the High Court in relation to the abovementioned jurisdiction and powers; of the High Court and the Court of Appeal in relation to appeals to the Court of Appeal from decisions of the High Court in the manner prescribed above; and of subordinate courts in relation to references to the High Court.

The Court of Appeal is given competence under Art 163 of the Constitution to hear appeals from decisions of the High Court regarding:

(a) the qualification of any person to be elected as member of the National Assembly;

10 Constitution of Guyana 1980, Art 133(1).

(b) whether:
   (i) either generally or in any particular place, an election has been lawfully conducted or the result thereof has been, or may have been, affected by any unlawful act or omission;
   (ii) the seats in the Assembly have become vacant; or
   (iii) a seat in the Assembly has become vacant; or
   (iv) any member of the Assembly is required under the provisions of Art 156(2) to cease to exercise any of his functions as a member thereof;

(c) the filling of a vacant seat in the Assembly; or

(d) whether any person has been validly elected as Speaker of the Assembly from among persons who are not members thereof or, having been so elected, has vacated the office of Speaker.

An appeal can be brought to the Court of Appeal:

(a) from the decision of a judge of the High Court granting or refusing leave to institute proceedings for the determination of any question referred to above;

(b) from the determination by the High Court of any such question, or against any order of the High Court made in consequence of such determination.

Parliament may make provision with respect to the circumstances and manner in which, and the conditions upon which proceedings for the determination of any question under Art 163 may be instituted in the High Court and an appeal may be brought to the Court of Appeal in respect thereof; the consequences of the determination of any question under Art 163 and the powers of the High Court in relation to the determination of any such question, including provision empowering the High Court to order the holding of a fresh election throughout Guyana or a fresh ballot in any part thereof, the re-allocation of seats in whole or in part; and the practice and procedure of the High Court in relation to the jurisdiction and powers conferred upon it by or under Art 163 and of that Court and the Court of Appeal in relation to appeals to the Court of Appeal under this Article.

In the ensuing sections we shall seek to identify parts of the jurisprudence of the Court of Appeal showing pillars of its jurisprudence which can be said to characterize its legal philosophy.

## The protection of rights

Even if the Guyanese courts have had a chequered record when it comes to the protection of human rights, there are important pronouncements in the jurisprudence of the court when it comes to the protection of the rights of the individual. In the *Seeram Teemal* case,[11] RH Luckhoo JA had the following to say about the protection of legal rights:

> I think it is not in doubt that a vested legal right carries with it a right of recourse to the courts for its enforcement. Rights are legally protected interests. Salmond, Jurisprudence, 12th edn, 221, sets out the characteristics of a legal right. It is vested in a party and it avails against another party upon whom lies a correlative duty. As Salmond has put it, the legal right obliges the person bound to an act or omission in favour of the person entitled. If a legal right cannot be enforced it ceases to be a right. A person has a constitutional right of recourse to the courts for a determination of the existence or extent of any civil right and for relief for an infringement of that right. I would accept that a tribunal other than a court can be established by law for the determination of the existence or extent of any civil right or obligation. Parliament can confer on such a tribunal power to decide not only questions of fact but also questions of law, but in my view, clear words will be required to confer such a power. An essential characteristic of the right of a citizen is that it carries with it a right of recourse to the courts unless some statute decreed otherwise.

Chapter II of the Constitution of Guyana contains a number of social and economic rights, including the rights to work, education and public participation. Unlike the Constitutions of India and Ireland, the Constitution of Guyana does not state that Chapter II rights are non-justiciable. In the 1980s, Guyana's Court of Appeal had to decide whether or not one of the Chapter II provisions – Art 11 – was justiciable. Article 11 concerns the right of trade unions to participate in certain matters of national significance. The court held that Chapter II provisions are not 'mere political rhetoric' and that Art 11 was justiciable:

> There are some provisions in Chapter II that are so widely and generally formulated as to be incapable of enforcement at present, requiring legislation to define their proper juristic boundaries ... But Art 11 is not one of those incognizable provisions; its efficacy and utility do not depend on the future enactment of any auxiliary legislation. And it is drawn with consummate preciseness and declarative lucidity in absolute and unambiguous terms.[12]

In the case of *Yasseen and Thomas*,[13] the Court of Appeal had to address the situation of an Attorney General who had been Defence Counsel for a convicted murderer and then participated in the Advisory Council that advised the President of the Republic on the exercise of the prerogative of mercy. The court held that the Attorney General, as the former legal adviser of the appellants in the self same charge for the offence of murder which engaged the attention of the Advisory Council on the prerogative of mercy, ought not to have presided as its chairman. His presence as the chairman of

11 Civil Appeal No 43 (1982).

12 *Attorney General v Alli and Others* (1989) LRC (Const) 474, p 502.

13 Constitutional Appeal No 40 (1996).

the council at which the sentences of the appellants were considered vitiated those deliberations. The opinion expressed by him to the President in that capacity was null and void. Hence, the decision of the President that he would not intervene must be vacated.

## The right of appeal

In *Bata Shoe Co Guyana Ltd* and the *Commissioner of Inland Revenue*, Civil Appeals Nos 10 and 12 (1975), the Court of Appeal addressed squarely the question, 'did the Constitution of Guyana itself confer a right of appeal to the High Court in tax assessment matters?'. RH Luckhoo JA declared that a right of appeal is a matter of jurisdiction. It has to be expressly conferred by the Constitution. Save where the Constitution has itself given jurisdiction, it is Parliament which normally makes provision for jurisdictional rights. The position at common law had been that a right of appeal had not existed. He held that there was no express provision in any of the articles of the then Constitution conferring a right of appeal to a court of law in tax assessment matters. His function was to uphold the law, even though he might not approve of it, if that law had not overstepped the constitutional limitations.

## The final Court of Appeal

In *Samuel Glen v Raphael Sampson*, Civil Appeal No 9 (1971), Crane JA asked the question, 'Does our present situation justify us in not merely *declining to follow*, but in *overruling* the decisions of former courts of co-ordinate jurisdiction, such as the former West Indian Court of Appeal, Federal Supreme Court, or the British Caribbean Court of Appeal?'. He answered this question as follows:

> Speaking for myself, I believe our present position justifies our so doing. Admittedly, overruling is the act of a superior authority but with the Privy Council no longer at the summit in the hierarchy of authority, are we not now possessed, for that very reason, of an authority that is ultimate and superior to that formerly held by our immediate predecessor, the British Caribbean Court of Appeal and of jurisdiction to overrule its former judgments?
>
> Authority is lacking on this point in the West Indies, no doubt because we have been the first of former colonial territories in these parts to abolish the appellate jurisdiction of the Privy Council from our legal system. Nevertheless, the true position would seem to be that the Guyana Court of Appeal cannot now be regarded merely as of co-ordinate jurisdiction with the British Caribbean Court of Appeal if there is not to be an impasse ...
>
> It seems to be there is no alternative in our present situation but for us to *overrule* former judgments of the British Caribbean Court of Appeal, and refuse to follow even those of the Privy Council if they conflict with later decisions of our Court of Appeal. There being no higher authority to look up to, we cannot

permit matters to remain at large and conflicting and competing precedents to militate against certainty and development in the law. This question, however, as will be seen presently, is by no means academic in view of the fact that we are of unanimous opinion that *Dhanrajie v Baijnauth* was wrongly decided (by the British Caribbean Court of Appeal).

## The inherent jurisdiction of the court

In the case of *Mustapha Ally v Hand-in-Hand Fire Insurance Co Ltd,*[14] the Court of Appeal made an important pronouncement on its inherent jurisdiction. The appellant had filed a notice and grounds of appeal challenging the decision of a High Court judge made in favour of the respondents. On 6 September 1966, a justice of appeal in Chambers ordered that the appellants should provide security for costs in the sum of $1,300 within eight weeks, failing which, the appeal should stand dismissed. The appellant did not comply with the order as the result of a genuine and unfortunate mistake and the appeal stood dismissed. On 9 November 1966, the appellant filed a notice of motion which was amended with leave at the hearing to request a discharge or variation of the order in accordance with Order II, Rule 16(2) of the 1959 Rules.

The Court of Appeal held: (i) it has an inherent jurisdiction to control its own procedure and, in a proper case, where no rules have been made, the court will itself make rules necessary for dealing with matters within its jurisdiction; (ii) Order I, Rule 8 of the 1959 Rules, authorizing as it does a departure from the rules where the rules of practice so require, was intended to confer on the Court of Appeal jurisdiction to grant or refuse relief upon an application such as the present one.

## Sources of law

In the *Yasseen and Thomas* case referred to earlier, Fitzpatrick JA made the following important pronouncement touching on the sources of law and possible recourse to the principles of natural justice:

> The principles of natural justice do not have to be recognized in writing by the legislature for them to be effective. They hover over all written laws, their collective eye constantly fixed on the citizen sparrows of this world.
>
> In this case justiciability concerning the exercise of the prerogative of mercy applies not to the decision itself but to the manner in which it is reached. It does not involve telling the Head of State whether or not to commute. And where the principles of natural justice are not observed in the course of the processes leading to its exercise, which process are laid down by the

14 Law Reports of Guyana (1967), p 310.

> Constitution, surely the court has a duty to intervene, as the manner in which it is exercised may pollute the decision itself.[15]

## The role of the court in reviewing findings of fact

Mr Justice RH Luckhoo JA in *Abdool Hack v Rahieman*, cast the role of the Court of Appeal in the following terms:

> Though [the Court of Appeal] is a court of re-hearing it should be borne in mind that we, sitting here, see only the recorded testimony in cold print, coming, as it were, at second hand, and deprived of the advantages of the recorder who obtained it at first hand. We are robbed of that appeal which only a live version can have on the senses, robbed of the ring of truth in the spoken word which only the trained sensitive ear can detect, robbed of the manner in which the testimony was given which only the keen judicial eye can perceive, robbed of the whole atmosphere in which the examiner and cross-examiner elicited that testimony. We are called upon to assess and analyze that evidence which in print might look formidable but which when given must, indeed, have been devoid of the qualities of conviction.[16]

This was cited with approval by Churaman JA in *Bibi Sahieman Yassin v David Joseph*.[17] In the case of *Dereck Jagan v Karran Ganpat et al* (1999), the Court of Appeal again upheld this approach.

In *Wilfred Methews v State*, Criminal Appeal No 15 (1996), Kennard C, confirmed the position of the Court of Appeal with regard to criminal cases as follows:

> In passing I must mention that this court cannot set aside a conviction on the ground that it is unsafe or unsatisfactory as can be done in England ...
>
> In Guyana we can set aside a conviction on the ground that the verdict of the jury was unreasonable or cannot be supported having regard to the evidence, that is, where the verdict of the jury was obviously and palpably wrong. This was decided in *State v Kissoon and Singh* ... where the court considered both the English and the Guyanese provisions which are not similar ... Section 13(1) of the Court of Appeal Act, Cap 3:01 provides:
>
> The Court of Appeal on any such appeal against conviction shall allow the appeal if they think that the verdict of the jury should be set aside on the ground that it is unreasonable or cannot be supported having regard to the evidence or that the judgment of the court before whom the appellant was convicted should be set aside on the ground of a wrong decision on any question of law or that on any ground there was a miscarriage of justice, and in any other case shall dismiss the appeal.

15 *New Guyana Bar Review*, December 1996, p 51.

16 Civil Appeal No 12 (1977), Court of Appeal.

17 Civil Appeal No 63 (1984), Court of Appeal.

## The right to a fair trial

In the case of *Fitzpatrick Darrell,*[18] the appellants argued that the trial judge erred when he rejected the application of counsel at the trial for the recall of an injured man and two other eye-witnesses for further cross-examination. The court held:

> A trial must be fair to an accused in every respect, the refusal of the judge to allow the recall of the witnesses was, in the circumstances of the present case, a miscarriage of justice.
>
> The importance of the fair trial of persons charged with criminal offences is recognized as one of the fundamental rights of the individual by the Constitution of Guyana. *Inter alia,* Art 10(2) guarantees to anyone who is charged with a criminal offence the right to adequate time and facilities in order to prepare his defence and the right to be defended either in person or by a legal representative of his own choice. It also guarantees that the person charged 'shall be afforded facilities to examine in person or by his legal representative the witnesses called by the prosecution before the court'. This guarantee which is provided in Art 10(2)(e) of the Constitution is but a re-statement of the common law right referred to by Lord Maugham in *Galos Hired v R.*
>
> In arriving at the conclusion that there was a miscarriage of justice in the present case, we must not be thought to be saying that a court must always exercise its discretion in favour of a recall of a witness when so requested by the accused person or his counsel. The court's function must at all times be to examine the justice of the request in the particular case as it affects all the parties concerned and exercise its discretion only after taking into account all the circumstances thereof.
>
> We therefore allow this appeal and remit the case to the High Court for trial *de novo.*

## *Stare decisis*

In a Civil Appeal of 1971, *Walter Seepersaud v Port Mourant Ltd,* Luckhoo Ch declared:

> As I have said earlier, I am conscious that there was error in the *Abhiraj* case. It is my view that this court must not allow itself to perpetuate an error of which it has become aware and convinced, and is in a position to rectify subsequently.
>
> Lord Gardiner, LC, before judgments were given in the House of Lords on 26 July 1966, made the following statement on behalf of himself and the Lords of Appeal in Ordinary:
>
> Their Lordships regard the use of precedent as an indispensable foundation upon which to decide what is the law and its application to individual cases. It

18 Criminal Appeal No 12 (1975).

> provides at least some degree of certainty upon which individuals can rely in the conduct of their affairs, as well as a base for orderly development of legal rules.
>
> This is an admirable statement of the desirability to stand by precedent of proven value. But as their Lordships realized and recognized, 'too rigid adherence to precedent may lead to injustice in a particular case and also unduly restrict the proper development of the law'. Their Lordships consequently proposed 'to modify their present practice' and, while treating former decisions of their house 'as normally binding, to depart from a previous decision when it appears right to do so'. (See (1966) 3 All ER 77.)

He continued:

> However ... I hasten to accept the proposition that if this court is satisfied that a previous decision of the court was wrong, then if the point arises again, the court is at liberty to reverse its previous stand. To hold otherwise would be to stultify the growth and development of the law, particularly where it is incumbent on the court, as I believe it is on this court, to develop the jurisprudence of an independent country, even though it might do so along principles that have long been accepted and applied.

The cases of *Oswald Gobin and Boniface Griffith v State*[19] represented one of the great decisions of the Court of Appeal which would subsequently be endorsed by the Privy Council on important points of law. Among other things, the cases raised issues of whether there is jurisdiction in the Guyana Court of Appeal to overrule its previous decisions and whether there should be unanimity in doing so. Haynes, C, Crane, VE, Luckhoo, RH and Jhappan, D JJA, held that the principle underlying *stare decisis* in the Guyana Court of Appeal is not the same for criminal as for civil cases. In criminal cases it is less rigid. Jurisdiction of the court to overrule previously decided cases is a continuing one. The court will exercise judicial review whenever there is to be determined 'some broad issue of justice, public policy or question of legal principle'; and in a criminal cause or matter which is plainly wrong and manifestly unjust, the court will overrule it without hesitation.

## Judicial standards

On 15 March 1996, the Guyana Bar Association issued a statement reiterating its opposition to retired judges returning to practice in the courts. 'It is undignified, indecent, inappropriate and totally unacceptable,' the statement complained. It continued: 'What started as an exception or isolated trickle over our objections has now turned into a deluge and appears set on becoming a norm ... It is a most unfortunate development and strikes a crucial blow against our legal system and the independence of the judiciary, which is one of the main pillars of justice in the Republic ... It signals a further decline

19 Law Reports of Guyana (1975), p 113.

in the standards of the judiciary in this country and is going to bring the law into ridicule and disrespect,' said the GBA.

The statement continued: 'It is undignified and indecent for a retired chancellor, chief justice or a judge of first instance or an appellate judge to return to practice in the courts before persons they may have helped to appoint as judges or who were subordinate to them and to be citing their own judgments as authority for any proposition they may put forward ... The Guyana Bar Association remains firmly opposed to a breach of the convention and its own Code of Conduct in retired judges returning to practice in the courts of this country.'[20]

A few days later, three of the four retired judges who had returned to practice at the Bar reacted to the stinging criticism by the lawyers' professional grouping. They stated: 'The Bar Association should feel strange on the moral high ground that it has now sought to occupy, for it has not been making public pronouncements on the great moral and social issues of the day.' They continued: 'We totally disagree with the Bar Association's febrile and insubstantial reasoning.' They concluded: 'And of course we do not and will never accept that the Bar Association has the authority to erode our cherished human right to work, without even affording us an opportunity to be heard on the matter. We are not yielding our rights.'[21]

Later in the month the fourth judge involved, a former Chief Justice, wrote:

> May I remind the Bar Association of Art 22(1) of our Constitution:
>
> > Every citizen has the right to work and its free selection in accordance with social requirements and personal qualification. He has the right to be rewarded according to the nature, quality and quantity of his work. Women and men have the right to equal pay for equal work.
>
> Is the Bar Association endeavouring by its stated code of discipline – the less said of that code the better – to deprive us of that right to work which is enshrined in the constitution?
>
> It is better that the Bar Association try to discipline those many in its fold who with daring impunity rob their clients, whose recourse to the Legal Practitioners' Committee is almost a waste of time.
>
> We shall always reserve the right to appear before any forum where our services are legitimately needed.[22]

When a former Chancellor of the Court of Appeal resigned and became Attorney General, the Organization of Caribbean Bar Associations expressed disappointment and dismay. It noted that under the constitutional system which the English-speaking Caribbean proudly shared, the judiciary had the

20 *Guyana Chronicle*, 16 March 1996, pp 4–5.

21 *Guyana Chronicle*, 23 March 1996, p 3.

22 *The Stabroek News*, 29 March 1996, p 7.

sacred responsibility of protecting the citizen against legislative and executive infringements of his or her legal rights and of dispensing justice between the State and the individual. It continued:

> Accordingly, the separateness and independence of the judiciary are vital elements in our democratic system.
>
> It is in recognition of the essential characteristics and lofty purposes of the judiciary that there are well-established ethical rules and a long-standing tradition that judges do not after retirement join the ranks of the political executive and in most cases are not permitted to practise in the courts over which they hitherto presided. It would appear that (his) acceptance of this office will conflict with both aspects of the rule and traditions of the legal profession.
>
> Even more seriously, this unfortunate precedent can only serve to undermine public confidence in the judiciary and administrative justice. The lawyer will find it difficult to accept that the loss of his case against the government had no connection with the fact that the person who headed the judiciary is now a member of that government.

In Barbados, *The Advocate* criticized the development in the following editorial comment:

> The Chancellor of the Judiciary stepped down from his exalted position which is the office in which is epitomized the independence and impartiality of the entire judiciary. For this reason the confident expectation of small people, who know no one, for a just resolution of their problems, that there is a forum before which the high and the mighty and meek and the lowly are all reduced to a status of equality.
>
> It is not only how judges behave during their term of office on which reputations and expectations are founded. When they demit office their conduct continues to be an important consideration. The question must never arise whether by accepting gifts or appointments from any source the judge may be receiving compensation for deeds of associations performed or formed during his term of office. Judges are not even to be seen practising law among lawyers before whom they presided and there are few offices to which they ought to welcome appointment. Certainly an appointment to a political office is out of the question.

## Concluding observations

The foregoing is a sample taken from the records of the court and the related public record. The cases chosen touch on core aspects of the functioning of a body such as the Court of Appeal. From the discussion above and taking the records of the court as a whole, the following concluding observations may be offered:

- The Guyana Court of Appeal has had and has in its midst some of the finest legal talent in the country.

- The jurisprudence of the court, on occasions, matches for excellence that of prestigious institutions such as the Privy Council which has, on occasion, followed the pronouncements of the court as stating the correct position in law.
- In cases outside the realm of politics, the jurisprudence of the court and the quality of its judgments often soar in quality and eloquence.
- The foundations of a Guyanese jurisprudence anchored in the common law and in Commonwealth doctrines can be detected.
- The court has been more reticent when it comes to the invocation and application of international human rights norms in its jurisprudence – even though individual judges of the High Court have been more forthcoming on this subject.
- The court has unfortunately not escaped the taint of yielding to executive pressure, especially during the decades of the sixties, the seventies and the eighties.
- It is a sad fact that whereas the *Law Reports of British Guiana* had been published for a century before independence, of the three and a half decades since independence the *Law Reports of Guyana* have only been published in respect of 1967–75 – and the last two volumes had to be issued by charitable institutions. Nearly a quarter of a century of the law reports unfortunately remains unpublished.
- The call by a serving chancellor for the courts to be in partnership with the political and the executive branches within the framework of socialist legality raised many eyebrows, to say the least.
- The resignation of a chancellor of the judiciary to become the legal adviser of the government caused consternation and despair.
- The return of judges to practice, including a former chancellor turned Attorney General and a former chief justice, raises troubling legal, economic and social issues.
- The quest to strengthen the independence of the judiciary by further insulating it from political influence has been much emphasized in the recent efforts at constitutional reform. The leadership of senior members of the Bar has been encouraging on this issue.
- The courage of individual members of the Court of Appeal during the three and a half decades of peaks and valleys needs to be recognized. It would be fair to say that following the restoration of democracy in 1992 the judges of the Court of Appeal are striking out on a course towards more judicial independence, even if the quality of some appointments to the court has been the subject of comment.

Against this background, we may now turn to the place of the legal profession in the legal order of Guyana, drawing upon some cases of the Guyana Court of Appeal.

# CHAPTER 2

# THE LEGAL PROFESSION

## INTRODUCTION

Article 40 of the Constitution of Guyana endows every person in the country with 'the protection of the law', which carries the entitlement, as laid down in the United Nations Basic Principles on the Role of Lawyers, to call upon the assistance of a lawyer of one's choice to protect and establish one's rights. Legal representatives in Guyana are defined in Art 154 of the Constitution as persons entitled to practise as an attorney-at-law before a court or tribunal. Upon admission to practice at the bar of Guyana, an attorney swears:

> I, AB, do swear (or solemnly, sincerely and truly declare and affirm) that I will well and truly serve the people of Guyana according to the best of my learning and knowledge in the law, and I will truly counsel and advise them that retain me according to the best of my skill, and I will not defer, protract, or delay their causes willingly for lucre or hope of reward – so help me God. (Laws of Guyana, Cap 4:01, s 6.)

The United Nations Basic Principles on the Role of Lawyers provides a good indication of what is expected of governments and the legal profession: It is the duty of governments to ensure that efficient procedures and responsive mechanisms for effective and equal access to lawyers are provided for all persons. Governments, professional associations of lawyers and educational institutions must ensure that attorneys-at-law are aware of the ideals and ethical duties of the lawyer and of human rights and fundamental freedoms recognized by national and international law. 'Lawyers shall at all times maintain the honour and dignity of their profession as essential agents of the administration of justice.' The duties of lawyers towards their clients include advising clients as to their legal rights and obligations, and as to the working of the legal system insofar as it is relevant to the legal rights and obligations of the clients. Professional associations of lawyers are expected to contribute 'to ensure that everyone has effective and equal access to legal services. Codes of professional conduct for lawyers must be established by the legal profession through its appropriate organs, or by legislation, in accordance with national law and custom and recognized international standards and norms'.

### Right to counsel

In *State v Fitzpatrick Darrell*, Criminal Appeal No 12 (1975), decided on 17 November 1976, the appellant who, at the time of his conviction was 28 years old, was found guilty by a Demerara Assize jury of causing grievous bodily harm to Archibald Batson with intent to maim, disable or disfigure him. He appealed against this conviction on several grounds, but the Court of Appeal considered only one of them, viz, the refusal by the trial judge to allow the recall of three of the prosecution's witnesses for cross-examination by counsel who represented him.

The matter came up for trial on Tuesday, 9 December 1975, when the accused intimated to the trial judge that he was represented by counsel who was absent. He was nonetheless arraigned and he pleaded not guilty. Two counsel entered appearance on behalf of the State and a panel was struck. The trial judge then adjourned the case to the following day at 9am to enable the accused to consult with counsel who, it was stated, was at Linden.

On the resumption at 9.45 am on 10 December, counsel did not appear nor was any reason given for his non-appearance. The accused was put in the charge of the jury, and then it was that another barrister appeared and informed the trial judge that counsel whose services the accused said he had engaged, had asked him to state that proper arrangements had not been made for his appearance. The trial judge then proceeded with the trial. Three witnesses, including the victim, Archibald Batson, all as eye-witnesses, were called during the morning session, which ended at 11.30 am. They were cross-examined by the accused, but the brevity of the cross-examination as well as the nature of the questions asked of them indicated, in the opinion of the Court of Appeal, how inadequate he was to the task.

On the resumption at 1.40 pm, the medical doctor, who had examined the victim on the night of the incident, gave evidence, and he too was cross-examined by the accused. After the doctor had completed his evidence, the accused requested an adjournment to 2.30 pm to enable another legal practitioner, whom he named, to be present and appear on his behalf. This request was granted and the adjournment was taken at 1.48 pm. On the resumption at 2.45 pm, still another barrister, Mr R Hanoman, entered appearance on behalf of the accused and he requested and was granted leave to further cross-examine the doctor. Then the prosecution called its final witness, a detective sergeant, who gave evidence of having gone to the scene on the night of the accident, of an oral statement made to him by the accused, and also of a subsequent written statement, both of which were under caution. After this witness had been cross-examined, Mr Hanoman made a request to have the three eye-witnesses recalled for further cross-examination, but the trial judge refused the request. The note he made reads as follows:

> Mr Hanoman requests that three witnesses be recalled – Archibald Batson, Pearl Cooper and Theodore Williams on the grounds that in the interest of justice (*sic*) that because of the fact that the accused was unrepresented until now that an opportunity be given to counsel to cross-examine. Application refused.

Counsel for the State then closed his case and the accused made a statement from the dock which could be construed either as a plea of self-defence or accident. He called no witnesses and was eventually found guilty and sentenced to a term of five years' imprisonment and ordered to receive a whipping of 10 strokes.

On the basis of the above facts counsel for the appellant argued before the Court of Appeal that the trial judge erred when he rejected the application of counsel at the trial for the recall of the injured man and the two other eye-witnesses for further cross-examination. See s 74(4) of the Evidence Act, Cap 5:03, empowering a judge 'if he thinks fit, [to] permit a witness to be recalled, either for further examination-in-chief or for further cross-examination'. The question to be determined was whether the trial judge in the circumstances of the case exercised the discretion given him by the sub-section, judicially. No reasons were given by him for his refusal to allow the witnesses to be recalled, although it was clear from a reading of the notes of evidence, the Court of Appeal noted, that if either the plea of self-defence or accident was to succeed a much more careful and searching cross-examination of those witnesses would have been required than that done by the accused or, possibly, of which he was capable.

The Court of Appeal observed that this was not a case of an attempt to obtain the services of counsel at the last moment. The accused had intimated from the very inception that he not only desired to be represented but that he had actually retained the services of a barrister. The learned trial judge, no doubt conscious of the desirability of an accused being so represented, had granted him an adjournment to the following day. And, though one could not be certain of this, it was possible that he was also moved to grant the adjournment in the full knowledge that, because of the procedure used in calling up cases for trial at the criminal sessions, an accused person might well receive less than 24 hours' notice as to the time when his case would come on for trial. Such a short period of notification, the Court of Appeal remarked, could be a source of acute embarrassment, not only to the accused, but possibly even more so to his legal adviser who might well find himself faced with a clash of fixtures. Indeed, in such circumstances it quite frequently happened that the accused person's case was adjourned in an attempt to accommodate the practitioner. Be that as it may, the pre-trial efforts of the accused to retain the services of a practitioner having proved abortive, he must have found himself faced with what, to him, must have been the daunting prospect of conducting his case on his own – a prospect which he did not seem to have anticipated – and with two lawyers arrayed against him on behalf of the State.

The Court of Appeal cited Lord Denning, MR, as having very aptly portrayed the dilemma of the man undefended by counsel in *Pett v Greyhound Racing Association Ltd* [1968] 2 WLR 1471, pp 1475–76:

> It is not every man who has the ability to defend himself on his own. He cannot bring out the points in his own favour or the weaknesses in the other side. He may be tongue-tied or nervous, confused or wanting in intelligence. He cannot examine or cross-examine witnesses. We see it every day. A magistrate may say to a man, 'You can ask any questions you like', whereupon the man immediately starts to make a speech. If justice is to be done, he ought to have the help of someone to speak for him.

Those rather graphic observations of the Master of the Rolls, the Court of Appeal commented, portrayed an all too familiar occurrence in all courts of trial in Guyana.

Another example of the anxiety of the courts that there should be adequate legal representation of a person charged with a criminal offence, the Court of Appeal continued, was to be found in the case of *R v Din* (1971) CLR 601. The facts were as follows:

> Din was convicted of being in charge of a motor vehicle when unfit to drive through drink, and with a blood alcohol concentration above the prescribed limit ... His defence was that he was not in charge of the car ... When he arrived at the trial court his solicitor was not present. He telephoned his solicitor who said that his case had been overlooked but he would try to instruct counsel at once. Counsel was instructed and he took the view that the defence would be handicapped by the absence of witnesses (one was out of the country) but there was no application for an adjournment. The summing up contained a number of misdirections.

It was held, allowing the appeal, that even if there had been no defect in the summing up the court would probably have quashed the conviction, as it was considered one of the essential features of justice that those entitled to be defended should be defended adequately, and that Din was entitled to feel strongly that justice did not appear to have been done. In *Galos Hired v R* [1944] AC 149, an advocate was assigned to the appellant 'for the preparation and conduct of his appeal against his conviction of murder, and the advocate, through no default on his part, was unable to reach the court in time to conduct the appeal which was conducted by the appellants in person and dismissed'. It was held that the appeal had not been effectively heard and must be restored for hearing in circumstances which would enable an advocate to conduct it. Although the judgment of the Judicial Committee was concerned primarily with the construction of a provision in the Poor Persons Defence Ordinance of the Somaliland Protectorate, the observations of Viscount Maugham (p 155) were of much wider significance and import. He said:

> The importance of persons accused of a serious crime having the advantage of counsel to assist them before the courts cannot be doubted by anybody who remembers the long struggle which took place in this country and which ultimately resulted in such persons having the right to be represented by counsel.

Representation included cross-examination, which was of primary importance.

In the *Darrell* case, the Court of Appeal found, the trial judge had recognized the desirability of the accused being represented by counsel and rightly allowed such representation. Counsel had appeared at a time when all the main witnesses who could testify as to the alleged attack, as well as the doctor who examined the victim, had all completed their evidence. He had allowed the doctor to be recalled but not the vital witnesses, concerning the cross-examination of whom so much depended if any credence was to be given to the accused's defence or any reasonable doubt cast on the case for the prosecution. The case was a short one and there was no evidence that any inconvenience would have resulted if the application of counsel had been granted.

The permitting of counsel to appear at the trial, on the one hand, and the refusal of his request to recall for further cross-examination the vital witnesses on whom the prosecution relied for a conviction, on the other, could not but be considered in the circumstances a denial of proper representation to the accused. The trial judge was merely complying with the formal desirability of allowing counsel to appear but was in fact denying to the accused partially the substantive effect of such representation; and to adopt what was said in *R v Din* (mentioned above), the accused 'was entitled to feel strongly that justice did not appear to have been done'. On the principle that a trial must be fair to an accused in every respect, the Court of Appeal found that the refusal of the judge to allow the recall of the witnesses was, in the circumstances of the case, a miscarriage of justice. It pointed out that the importance of the fair trial of persons charged with criminal offences was recognized as one of the fundamental rights of the individual by the Constitution of Guyana. *Inter alia,* Art 10(2) guaranteed to anyone charged with a criminal offence the right to adequate time and facilities in order to prepare his defence and the right to be defended either in person or by a legal representative of his own choice. It also guaranteed that the person charged 'shall be afforded facilities to examine in person or by his legal representative the witnesses called by the prosecution before the court'. This guarantee provided in Art 10(2)(e) of the Constitution was but a restatement of the common law right referred to by Lord Maugham in *Galos Hired v R* (mentioned above).

In *Donovan Ceasar v State,* Criminal Appeal No 8 (1997), decided on 14 April 1999, the appellant had been convicted for the offence of rape and was sentenced to 15' years imprisonment. He appealed his conviction and counsel appearing for him urged on his behalf that the refusal of the trial judge to grant an adjournment to the appellant, who was unrepresented at the trial, in order to enable him to retain and instruct an attorney-at-law of his choice without delay to represent him at the trial was wrong, unlawful and unconstitutional. Counsel referred to paragraphs (c) and (d) of Art 144(2) of the 1980 Constitution which provided that the accused person:

(c) Shall be given adequate time and facilities for the preparation of his defence.

(d) Shall be permitted to defend himself before the court in person or by a legal representative of his own choice.

The defence of the appellant was one of consent. From the record, the case was called in court on the 4 February 1997. The indictment was read to the appellant, who pleaded not guilty. After the jury had been empanelled the appellant made a request for an adjournment of 2–3 weeks in order to retain counsel as he was waiting on his relatives abroad to send him some money for that purpose. Counsel appearing for the State informed the trial judge that the appellant had attended court on several occasions previously and that he was quite aware that the matter would be coming up for hearing very shortly.

The trial judge granted an adjournment of two days. On the resumption of the matter two days later the appellant made no further request and the trial proceeded. At the request of the Court of Appeal, counsel who appeared for the State laid over with the Court of Appeal a statement pertaining to matters occurring before the 4 February 1997. The statement revealed that after having been warned by the police to attend court the appellant did so on the 20 January 1997 when he was informed that the trial would be coming up very shortly and that he should return to court on the 28 January 1997. He attended court on that day and was told to return on 4 February 1997 when the trial would be commencing. Counsel for the appellant did not dispute these facts. The appellant had been committed for trial in October 1995.

Counsel for the appellant urged upon the Court of Appeal that the period of two days granted by the trial judge to enable the appellant to retain an attorney-at-law was quite inadequate and that that had rendered the trial an unfair one. (See *Gajraj v State* (1978) 27 WIR 119, *per* Haynes Ch, p 138.) Counsel for the appellant further urged upon the Court of Appeal that the appellant was at a great disadvantage in that he was unable to effectively cross-examine the witness called by the State at the trial and he referred to Lord Denning, MR, in *Pett v Greyhound Racing Association Ltd* [1968] 2 WLR 1475, p 1476.

Kennard Ch, in delivering the decision of the Court of Appeal himself referred to Viscount Maughn in *Galos Hired v R* [1944] AC 149. He noted, however, that the appellant had been aware, at least since 20 January 1997, a period of about two weeks before the trial actually started, that his matter would be heard very shortly. He should have made every effort before then to retain counsel bearing in mind that he had been committed for trial since October 1995 – a period of about 15 months before the date of the trial. He cited the following remarks of Sir Joseph Luckhoo in the Jamaican case of *R v Pussey* (1970) 12 Jamaica LR 243 (referred to in R Robinson (1985) WIR 37). Sir Joseph had said at p 247:

> While we fully appreciated that the Constitution of Jamaica enjoins ... that every person who is charged with a criminal offence must be permitted to defend himself by a legal representative of his own choice, if he so desires, yet the trial of an accused person cannot be delayed indefinitely in the hope that he will by himself or otherwise be able to raise at some indeterminate time in the future sufficient money to retain the services of counsel.

Kennard Ch noted that in the instant case the trial judge, in exercising his discretion to grant an adjournment for a period of only two days, must have considered the interests of the State as well. The victim at the time of the incident had lived in one place but by the time the trial had come on she had moved to another area in a different part of the country. 'This was certainly an important factor for the trial judge to consider as it is known that we have a "floating" population and it is very difficult at times to locate witnesses to attend trials.' He continued:

> An appellate court will not interfere with a discretion which had been exercised by a trial judge save in exceptional circumstances (see *Chaitlall v State* (1985) 39 WIR). We do not feel that the trial judge had exercised his discretion in an improper manner when he granted the appellant an adjournment of only two days in order to enable him to retain the services of an attorney-at-law when regard is had to all the circumstances of the case.

The learned Chancellor then discussed the Australian case of *McInnis v Queen* (1979) 143 CLR 575, which he considered had laid down the test that whether a miscarriage of justice had occurred should be determined by whether refusal of an adjournment had resulted in the appellant losing a chance of acquittal. The court in that case, according to the learned Chancellor, had concluded that in view of the strong case against the appellant no miscarriage of justice had occurred and consequently the appeal was dismissed. Kennard Ch then proceeded to hold as follows:

> In the instant case we would hold that even if the trial judge had erred in refusing to grant the adjournment requested, in view of the strength of the case against the appellant no miscarriage of justice had occurred and, therefore, the appeal must be dismissed and conviction and sentence affirmed.

We would offer the comment that a future court, in determining whether the interests of justice had been met in a case such as this one, might well find itself obliged to consider two issues of principle:

(a) Since the trial judge did decide to grant an adjournment, were two days reasonable for the appellant to select and instruct counsel?

(b) Would two days have been enough for a counsel found by the appellant to have studied the case and prepare the appellant's defence?

It would be hard to answer either of these questions in the affirmative and a future court might indeed be persuaded to hold that the adjournment granted by the judge should have been longer, say of a week's duration. At issue was a sentence of 15 years' imprisonment – no light matter.

## Regulation of the Guyanese legal profession

Attorneys-at-law in Guyana are officers of the court, subject to the final authority and control of the law and the courts in all matters pertaining to their conduct and practice. As Lord Denning put it: 'A barrister has a duty to the court that is paramount ... He owes allegiance to a higher cause ... the cause of truth and justice.' (*Rondel v Worsley* [1969] 1 AC 191.)

Matters pertaining to the conduct of attorneys-at-law not expressly regulated by the Constitution, legislation, and international norms are, in the final analysis, to be pronounced upon by the courts. Where codes of conduct by professional associations of attorneys-at-law are lacking or inadequate, they are to be spelled out by the courts.

The basis for the courts' control of the conduct of attorneys-at-law is the Constitution of Guyana, legislation, international human rights norms binding on Guyana and the common law as received in Guyana and interpreted and applied by the High Court. In Guyana, when the professions of barrister and solicitor were fused, attorneys-at-law continued to be governed by the rules of the common law save as affected by the Constitution, legislation or international human rights norms binding on Guyana. Attorneys-at-law in Guyana thus continued to be governed by the rules of the common law applicable to barristers and solicitors, depending on the nature of the legal services they provide in particular cases.

In *Re Lennox Arthur and Calvin Hermanstyne,* Civil Appeal No 34 (1970), Luckhoo Ch had considered the significance of the Legal Practitioners Ordinance, Cap 30, as it related to the rights of barristers and solicitors to practise in the courts. In the course of his judgment, he pointed out that prior to the Legal Practitioners Ordinance of 1931, methods of practice had developed between solicitors and barristers which were very inconsistent over the years. Barristers were encroaching on the work of solicitors and vice versa, and the whole state of the law was in a very unsatisfactory position. The legislature thought that the time was right to lay down in no uncertain manner how barristers should be entitled to practise and how solicitors should be entitled to share in litigation that came before the courts. The Chancellor made the following statement about the Legal Practitioners Ordinance:

> Its scheme and design was clearly to circumscribe comprehensively how and in what manner barristers and solicitors should be permitted to practise. It set out to settle by devious compromises their historical competing claims, by creating, to use the words of the Solicitor General, 'a curious professional hybrid'. The right to participate in the work of certain types was made open to both branches; in certain instances exclusive to each, and in others partially permissible to both, with residual provision for the implication that the practice in England would govern situations not expressly catered for.

> I would therefore accept the submission of the Solicitor General that the 1931 Ordinance was the first law to define the extent to which a barrister could act as a solicitor; that it was clearly intended to be a comprehensive regulation of this previously vexed question; that its entire purpose would be subverted by holding that something or the other was saved ...

In other words, an attempt was made to codify the law in 1931 as the legislature intended it to be, and except some subsequent ordinance or statute expressly provided to the contrary. Consequently, a barrister was entitled to practise as a solicitor in the bringing of an application under the under the Constitution of 1961, which meant that all ordinances or statutes subsequent to 1931 would be similarly affected.

In *Commissioner of Inland Revenue v Isahack*, Civil Appeal No 54 (1971), decided in 1975, counsel for the appellant drew to the court's attention s 42(1) of the Legal Practitioners Ordinance, which read as follows:

> Notwithstanding anything to the contrary in any ordinance or rule, a barrister or solicitor shall be entitled to act alone and have audience:
>
> (a) in any cause or matter in a magistrate's court or other inferior court or tribunal.

And also to s 44, which reads as follows:

> Notwithstanding anything to the contrary in any ordinance or rule, a barrister shall be entitled to practice as a solicitor in respect of all proceedings including the issuing of writs of summons or other processes, in any of the matters specified in s 42 hereof ...

To that, Luckhoo Ch held, the Court of Appeal would wish to have read what is said in s 19(1): 'A person practising as a solicitor and whose name is enrolled aforesaid shall be deemed to be an officer of the court'; and sub-s (2): 'A barrister who practises as a solicitor shall, in so far as he so practises, be deemed to be a solicitor within the meaning of this section.' The Court of Appeal was satisfied that a barrister had the right to act as a solicitor in this matter, and the Board of Review was wrong in excluding his right to so act.

## Professional competence of counsel

In *Oswald Lewis v RJ Eleazer*, Civil Appeal No 26 (1995), Persaud JA regretted that the issue of the competence of counsel who had appeared in the High Court had not arisen for discussion before the Court of Appeal. He noted that it was an issue that the American courts had been taking in their stride and that the English courts had been tending to do likewise and to allow appeals where a litigant might not have been properly represented. He recalled the following cases: *R v Mills* [1995] 1 WLR 511; *R v Clinton* [1993] 1 WLR 1181; *R v Crossdale* [1995] 1 WLR 864. He also recalled the local case *Seetal, Bharat and Pooran v R* (1960) 2 WIR 515. In the last case, the Federal Supreme Court had expressed regret that certain matters which defence counsel, had he studied the depositions, might have known, were not used by the defence to impugn the reliability of the identification evidence. The court frowned upon the failure of the more senior counsel in the case to attend and to conduct the defence and commented that 'such a failure even in a civil case would be regrettable, but where the client is faced with a serious criminal charge it is difficult to excuse the absence of counsel for any cause other than physical necessity'. The Federal Court added: 'It is unusual for this court to entertain an appeal because of the lack of professional skill with which the defence was conducted. Obviously the administration of justice would be greatly embarrassed if this was regarded as a valid ground of appeal, *unless the circumstances were very exceptional.*' As an example of such circumstances, the court held that were it to be satisfied without further enquiry that it was unsafe to convict on the identification of the witnesses it would have quashed the conviction.

Persaud JA regretted that in the instant case the Court of Appeal had not had the benefit of discussion on this topic. He went on: '[The topic] is an interesting one which some enterprising counsel will surely canvass at some future date. Then and only then will the court come to grips with the problem. Suffice it to say that the Federal Court did not shut out discussion but left it open on the question of exceptional circumstances.'

## Representation

In *Kemelia Ramgobin v Premnauth GD Persaud,* Bernard JA in chambers had to deal with the case of an attorney-at-law filing the appeal who had not appeared at the hearing of the matter before the lower court. Order 6, Rule 1 of the Rules of the High Court states:

> Every solicitor who shall be engaged in any action shall be bound to conduct the same if desired by the plaintiff or defendant, as the case may be, for whom he shall be engaged, unless allowed by the court or a judge to cease from acting therein, until the final determination of the action whether in the court of first instance or on appeal.

Order 6, Rule 2 provides for a party changing his attorney upon filing notice of such change in the Registry and serving a copy of such notice upon the opposite party.

The attorney who filed the appeal contended that the High Court and the Court of Appeal proceedings were separate and distinct, and referred to Order 2, Rule 1(1) of the Court of Appeal Rules which states that all appeals shall be by way of rehearing and shall be brought by notice signed by the appellant or his legal representative. He submitted that the legal representative need not be the lawyer who represented the appellant in the court below.

Having examined Order 6, Rule 1 of the High Court Rules, Bernard JA held that an attorney-at-law having been authorized to act on behalf of a party to an action continues to do so until the final determination of the action in the Court of Appeal unless he or she is discharged or another solicitor or attorney is appointed by the requisite notice of change of attorney. The words 'whether in the court of first instance or an appeal' at the end of Order 6, Rule 1 unequivocally suggested that an attorney's obligation to represent a party to an action continued up to the appellate stage. She continued:

> It cannot be disputed that a party can change his solicitor or attorney in our context at any time during the pendency of an action, but the relevant rules must be complied with, eg, Order 6, Rule 2 – a notice of change must be filed in the Registry and service effected on the other parties to the action. If this is not done the solicitor or attorney on record continues to be regarded as the solicitor. A solicitor or attorney who acts for a party without authority does so at his own peril unless his acts are later ratified by that party.

In the instant case, there was nothing on record to indicate that the appellant had adopted the second attorney as his *new* attorney-at-law. Had he filed an authority subsequent to the filing of the Notice of Appeal, this might have been regarded as a ratification and might have related the authority back to the filing of the Notice of Appeal. It would perhaps have been regarded as an irregularity rather than a nullity. This not having been done, the Notice of Appeal filed is a nullity as no Notice of Change of Attorney-at-Law was filed either before or after the filing of the Notice of Appeal, and it is now too late for it to be done. In the circumstances the application is dismissed.

In *State v Nolan Collins*, Criminal Appeal No 1 (1977), before Hon Mr CJE Fung-A-Fatt, P, JC Gonsalves-Sabola JA and GAG Pompey, additional Justice of Appeal, the appellant, a former member of the Guyana Police Force had been convicted at the Demerara High Court on 16 December 1976 for the offences of (a) wounding with intent and (b) discharging a loaded firearm with intent. On count (a) the appellant was fined $500.00 or in default six months imprisonment, and on count (b) he was reprimanded and discharged and ordered to pay compensation, in the sum of $500.00 to the virtual complainant. The appellant complied with the orders of the learned trial judge and subsequently left the jurisdiction.

On the hearing of the appeal, the appellant did not appear, and senior counsel's *locus standi* was questioned. He urged the court that there were over 40 misdirections in the judge's summing up and there was every possibility of the appeal being allowed. But there was no evidence that the appellant had instructed him to proceed with his appeal. The appeal was struck out for want of prosecution. (*R v Flowers* [1966] 50 CAR 22 was cited with approval.)

## Fees

It had been a hallowed principle of the common law, as received in Guyana, that barristers could not sue to recover their fees. This rule went back to Blackstone: 'A counsel can maintain no action for his fees, which are given not as a salary, but as a mere gratuity which a counsellor cannot demand without doing wrong to his reputation.'

In the Scottish case of *Batchelor v Mackersy and Pattison*, 3 R 914, Lord President Inglis laid down the position of counsel as follows:

> An advocate, in undertaking the conduct of a cause in this court, enters into no contract with his client, but takes on himself an office in the performance of which he owes a duty, not to his client only, but also to the court, to the members of his own profession, and to the public. From this it follows that he is not at liberty to decline, except in very special circumstances, to act for any litigant who applies for his advice and aid, and that he is bound in any cause that comes into court to take the retainer of the party who first applies to him. It follows also, that he cannot demand or recover by action any remuneration for his services, though in practice he receives *honoraria* in consideration of these services.

The Bar of England and Wales continues to maintain the rule that barristers do not enter into a contract by accepting professional instructions. (Code of Conduct of the Bar of England and Wales, 27 January 1990, Annex D, paras 19–20 (as amended 22 October 1990.) See David Pannick, *The Advocates*, 1993, Oxford: OUP, p 274.

In Guyana, however, the Court of Appeal has accepted that a barrister may sue to recover unpaid fees. This was the basis of the decision in *Derek Jagan v Karran Ganpat et al*, decided in 1999.

Even if attorneys-at-law may conclude contracts with their clients in respect of fees, the courts should exercise particular care to ensure that a client is on a footing of equality in entering into such a contract. As a minimum, the courts should insist on a written contract, expressed in simple and clear terms, so as to make absolutely sure that the client was not in any way befuddled by the attorney.

Section 21 of Cap 4:01 of the Laws of Guyana had precisely this point in view by providing that:

> No special agreement otherwise valid in law between a barrister or solicitor and his client as to the amount or manner of payment for the whole or any part of any past or future services, fees, charges or disbursements done by the barrister or solicitor shall be good and valid in law unless it is in writing.

In any event, the right of Guyanese under the Constitution and international human rights norms of access to counsel means the right of access to counsel at reasonable fees. Under the precepts of the common law and the practice and usage of Commonwealth jurisdictions, fees chargeable by attorneys-at-law are subject to the test of reasonableness, to be enforced by the courts of Guyana. In the event of disagreement by clients with fees charged by attorneys-at-law, the courts are to indicate procedures of recourse open to clients as part of the good administration of justice if such procedures are not maintained by the Bar Association. In the final analysis, the reasonableness of the fees of attorneys-at-law is to be determined by the courts.

Section 18 of Cap 4:01 of the Laws of Guyana expressly lays down that:

> A solicitor shall not recover any costs, fees, charges or disbursements for any business done by him until he has applied for and obtained a certificate of the Registrar as to the actual amount due in respect thereof upon taxation and has rendered account thereof to the party to be charged.

The term 'taxation of costs' is a technical term meaning determination of the amount of fees or costs by the courts. Section 20 of Cap 4:01 of the Laws of Guyana further provides that:

> (1) No barrister or solicitor of the court shall be entitled to any process issuing thereout for the recovery of fees from a client of the amount of any bill of costs, other than a bill of costs relating wholly to matters in respect of which a tariff of costs has not been by law prescribed, unless the bill has been taxed, and a copy of the bill so taxed has been delivered to the client to enable him to pay it seven days previously to the issuing of process.

The section continues:

> (2) In any proceedings in a court in which the amount of any bill of costs is sought to be recovered or is disputed, that court or the judge before which or whom those proceedings are pending shall decide whether the fees charged relating to matters for which no tariff of costs has been by law prescribed are excessive, or are a fair and adequate remuneration for the work done and services rendered, and shall reduce or allow them accordingly.

Rule 15 of the Solicitors' Practice Rules of England and Wales (1991) requires solicitors to operate a complaints handling procedure and ensure that clients are told whom to contact if they have a problem with the service provided. The Solicitors' Practice Rules also contain detailed provisions regarding the determination of fees, the processing of complaints about them, the operation of procedures for challenging the amount of fees and getting them determined by the Law Society or the courts in the final analysis.

The Law Society recommends that information about all these matters be given in writing, so that clients have the fullest and clearest possible information. On the issue of fees, a Law Society specimen letter from solicitors to their clients recommends the following language on fees chargeable:

> Our charges will be calculated mainly by reference to the time spent by me and by other solicitors and executive staff dealing with this matter. This includes advising, attending on you and others, dealing with papers, correspondence,

telephone calls, travelling and waiting time. I attach a list of this firm's staff and their charge rates and the rates for routine letters and telephone calls.

## What is a fair and reasonable fee

In England and Wales, solicitors may charge their clients only a 'fair and reasonable fee', taking into account all the circumstances. Non-contentious fees are covered by the Solicitor's Remuneration Order 1972. This provides that in assessing what is 'fair and reasonable', the following should be taken into account:

(i) the complexity of the matter or the difficulty or novelty of the questions raised;

(ii) the skill, labour, specialized knowledge and responsibility involved;

(iii) the time spent on the business;

(iv) the number and importance of the documents prepared or perused without regard to length;

(v) the place where and the circumstances in which the business or any part thereof is transacted;

(vi) the amount or value of any money or property involved;

(vii)whether any land involved is registered land within the meaning of the Land Registration Act 1925; and

(viii)the importance of the matter to the client.

Clients should, as already mentioned, be given written guidance at the outset of the case.

A solicitor in England and Wales cannot sue for money owed without giving the client formal notice of his/her right to apply for a remuneration certificate from the Law Society or to have the bill taxed by the court. The recommended wording is as follows:

> This constitutes notice of your right under paragraph (1) of Art 3 of the Solicitors' Remuneration Order 1972 to require me within one month of the receipt hereof to obtain a certificate from the Law Society stating that in their opinion the costs charged are fair and reasonable or, as the case may be, what lesser sum would be fair and reasonable. Also there are provisions in ss 70, 71 and 72 of the Solicitors Act 1974 relating to taxation (determination) of costs which give you the right to have the bill checked by an official of the High Court.

In court cases (contentious cases) the court can check a solicitor's bill. In non-court cases the bill can be referred to the Law Society, which will decide whether it is fair and reasonable. The Law Society will issue a remuneration certificate setting out what it regards as the proper fee. If either side is still dissatisfied the fees may be reviewed by the courts, which will settle the costs.

Solicitors must send a written bill, which must be detailed. In a 1955 case Lord Denning said a non-contentious bill:

> ... must contain a summarized statement of the work done, sufficient to tell the client what it is for which he is being asked to pay. A bare account 'for professional services' between certain dates, or for 'work done in connection with your matrimonial affairs' would not do. The nature of the work must be stated, such as advising on such a matter, instructing counsel to do so and so, drafting such and such a document, and so forth.

In Guyana work on a code of conduct for attorneys-at-law is still in gestation (see Appendix B). Until it is promulgated the only way to determine what the rules are is through the High Court.

In *Dereck Jagan v Karran Ganpat et al*, the appellant/plaintiff, an attorney-at-law and senior counsel, had instituted proceedings claiming from the respondents the sum of $25 million for legal services. Under cross-examination he said that there had been an agreement with the respondents/defendants that the $25 million were charged whether he won or lost the case or if it were settled before proceedings were commenced. The trial judge believed the defendant that no such agreement had been concluded and dismissed the claim with costs to the defendants. Upon appeal, Civil Appeal No 96 (1998), the Court of Appeal held that it would not interfere with the finding of fact by the trial judge.

Chancellor Kennard was incredulous of the appellant's contention that a contract existed:

> I ask myself: what man would agree to such an arrangement? The appellant is asking us to believe that this was the arrangement the parties had. It would be asking us too much to accept that there was an agreement for payment of the $25(M) dollars even if the claims were unsuccessful and the respondents received nothing at all ... The appellant's evidence that the first-named respondent had agreed to pay him the large sum of $25(M) as his fees in the matter even if the claim was unsuccessful, is so improbable that it would tax the credibility of even the most trusting mind.

## Disciplinary proceedings

The United Nations Basic Principles on the Role of Lawyers provide that, on the basis of codes of professional conduct for lawyers established by the legal profession through its appropriate organs or by legislation, charges or complaints made against lawyers in their professional capacity must be processed expeditiously and fairly under appropriate procedures. Disciplinary proceedings against lawyers shall be brought before an impartial disciplinary committee established by the legal profession, before an independent statutory authority, or before a court, and shall be subject to independent judicial review. Disciplinary proceedings are to be determined in accordance with the code of professional conduct and other recognized standards and ethics of the legal profession and in the light of the Basic Principles of the United Nations.

In Guyana a great deal of uncertainty persists as to what codes of conduct and regulatory regime attorneys-at-law are subject to. Cap 4:01, Part II of the Laws of Guyana contains procedures for dealing with issues of discipline, including the establishment of a legal practitioners committee. Any application by a client or other person aggrieved to require a legal practitioner to answer any allegations made by such a client or person against the legal practitioner, or to strike the name of the legal practitioner off the roll of the court, shall be made to the Registrar and shall be verified by affidavit (s 24). The Registrar shall forthwith transmit the application to the legal practitioners committee for investigation and determination in accordance with the procedures and standards laid down in Part II.

Guyana still has a far way to go in these matters. In England and Wales there are detailed laws and codes including: The Code of Conduct of the Bar of England and Wales (27 January 1990); the Solicitors Act, 1974; the Solicitors' Practice Rules, 1991, made by the Law Society under the Solicitor Act, 1974; and the Solicitor Account Rules, 1991. There is also a Solicitors' Complaints Bureau, a Solicitors' Disciplinary Tribunal and a Professional Conduct Committee of the Bar Council. Furthermore, there is a Legal Services Ombudsman: Complainants who are not happy with the way the Solicitors' Complaints Bureau or the Professional Conduct Committee of the Bar Council has handled their complaint may refer the matter to the Legal Services Ombudsman, who is neither a solicitor nor a barrister.

At issue is a matter of the greatest importance for the future liberties of Guyanese: the role of the legal profession and the relationship between lawyers and the public. A sacred principle is at stake, namely that lawyers shall at all times act as officers of the court, subject to the authority of the High Court, rendering a public service, namely the pursuit of justice. The rule of law requires a fiercely independent, ethical profession.

## CONCLUSION

In Appendix B below, we reproduce a Code of Conduct approved by the Guyana Bar Association in 1985. It was difficult to obtain a copy of it, as it has not yet been officially approved by the Ministry of Legal Affairs and is not distributed among lawyers. The copy reproduced is the nearest to the final text obtained from an office-holder of the Bar Association. For a start, the Code of Conduct should be officially promulgated and given wide circulation among the legal profession and the general public. This is crucial for the enhancement of the rule of law to which we shall now turn.

# CHAPTER 3

# THE RULE OF LAW

## INTRODUCTION

In this chapter we look at the jurisprudence of the Court of Appeal on matters related to the rule of law. But fairness demands that we record that since 1980 Guyana has operated under an illegal constitutional groundnorm that has held sway over the Courts.

## THE ILLEGAL CONSTITUTIONAL GROUNDNORM

There is little doubt that the Constitution of Guyana (1980) is a nullity for the reasons stated hereunder and that the Independence Constitution previously in force, the groundnorm of independent Guyana, remains valid and should be reinstituted on the basis of the legal doctrine of prospective limitation, in respect of future actions of the legislature of the executive.

Under Art 73 of the preceding Independence Constitution (1966), the procedures for amending certain provisions included the holding of a referendum. On April 1978, Constitution (Amendment) Bill No 8 of 1978 was introduced in Parliament with a proposal to change Art 73 of the Constitution so as to remove the requirement for holding a referendum and to enable provisions of that kind to be amended by a Bill supported by not less than two-thirds of all elected members of the National Assembly. The stated purpose of the amendment in the words of the then Prime Minister was that '[A]fter the Constitution has been so amended, it will be competent for Parliament to replace the existing Constitution and to replace it by another without the necessity of a referendum.'

A broad-based civic organization known as the Concerned Citizens' Committee was formed to coordinate the efforts of a number of non-party groups opposed to the Bill. Its composition included:

- the Lawyers' Committee;
- the Architects' Committee;
- the Committee of Medical Practitioners;
- the Committee of Concerned Educators;
- the University of Guyana Staff Association;
- the Clerical and Commercial Workers Union; and
- the National Association of Agricultural, Commercial and Industrial Employees.

The Guyana Council of Churches was represented by an observer on the committee.

The Committee of Lawyers opposed the Constitutional Amendment Bill, 1978, on the following grounds:

(1) The Constitution is the supreme law of the land. Lawyers therefore have a special interest in it, as does every citizen.

(2) The referendum seeks to deprive the people of their right to approve or disapprove any new constitution.

(3) It takes away the people's right to have a say in the changing of the supreme law of the land.

(4) It will put absolute power to alter the Constitution in the two-thirds majority in Parliament.

(5) A new constitution that the people do not like can be imposed on them.

(6) The power in the two-thirds majority Parliament is enough; to enlarge it would be dangerous.

(7) Any new constitution should be approved by the people through national elections.

(8) The Bill is an attempt to side-track national elections due this year.

(9) The life of Parliament, elections, the Constitution itself and the jurisdiction of the High Court in certain matters would be left completely in the hands of a two-thirds majority in Parliament.

(10) The Bill is asking us to sign a blank cheque and put out future in the hands of a dying Parliament.

(11) The referendum will be a referendum to end all referenda.

(12) No nation or people should ever surrender their rights:

'The Bill aimed to destroy democracy as Guyanese knew it. The legal profession opposed it. It invites all Guyanese to do the same.'

The campaign against the Bill united a wide spectrum of political views and ideology on a common platform. Membership of the Committee in Defence of Democracy (CDD) included:

- the Civil Liberties Action Council;
- the Guyana Agricultural Workers' Union;
- the Guyana Peace Council;
- the Liberator Party;
- the Organization of Working People;
- the People's Democratic Movement;
- the People's Progressive Party; and
- the Working People's Alliance.

In effect, the Bill sought to hold a referendum which would abolish the requirement for any further referendum to be held before changes in the entrenched provisions of the Constitution could be made. The power to make such changes would be vested in a two-thirds majority of Parliament. The Bill was first published on 1 April, had its first reading on 3 April, and was passed in Parliament on 10 April. Thus there was little understanding and no discussion of the Bill before its passage through Parliament. A later procedural Bill provided that the referendum should be held on the 10 July 1978.

The government of the day unilaterally assigned the symbols of a house to the YES vote and a mouse to the NO vote. The symbol of the mouse was repudiated by opposition groups as degrading, intimidatory, prejudicial and inimical to the fair and impartial conduct of the referendum. Guyanese complained that '[T]he mouse is a symbol that the average human being finds offensive'.

Because of a failure by the government of the day to meet minimum demands for the conduct of a referendum, both the Committee of Concerned Citizens and the Committee in Defence of Democracy (CDD) advised the Guyanese people to boycott the referendum. The United Force, the only opposition political party outside of the CDD also called for a boycott.

In the absence of minimal assurances concerning the fairness and legality of the referendum exercise, the Committee of Concerned Citizens organized an external monitoring exercise of polling stations. In view of the legislation then recently enacted removing the right to appeal against referendum results, such an exercise became especially necessary.

The Committee of Concerned Citizens published *A Report on the Referendum Held in Guyana, 10 July 1978*, in which it denounced the referendum as a massive fraud on each and every Guyanese and on the Guyanese people as a whole. Based on its monitoring of the referendum, the Committee of Concerned Citizens estimated the national turn-out of voters at 14.01% compared with the official figure of 71.45%. The Committee announced:

> The inescapable conclusion to be drawn from this survey is that the official results of the referendum have no possible basis in the reality of July 10th: They are massively fraudulent.

The mouse degraded and continues to degrade every Guyanese. The massively fraudulent referendum of 10 July 1978 degraded and continues to degrade every Guyanese and violated in a fundamental way the imperative rule of the United Nations Universal Declaration of Human Rights that 'the will of the people shall be the basis of the authority of Government'. It likewise violated the imperative norm of the contemporary international public order and law that all peoples are entitled to the right to self-determination (Art 1 of the International Covenant on Civil and Political Rights and Art 1 of the International Covenant on Economic, Social and Cultural Rights, both adhered to by Guyana).

The massively fraudulent referendum of 10 July 1978 discriminated politically against the majority of the Guyanese people and the Bill that enacted the Constitution of 1980 continues to do so until it is set aside and the Independence Constitution is reinstated.

In the *Seeram Teemal* case, Civil Appeal No 43 (1982) (p 24), RH Luckhoo JA propounded the doctrine that, 'A duty devolves upon the courts to pronounce on the validity of executive action when it is challenged, to determine whether such action goes beyond constitutional power. The first allegiance of the courts is to the Constitution'. The jurisprudence of highly respected Commonwealth courts, such as the Indian Supreme Court, has long established that the function of judicial review includes review of the constitutionality of acts of the legislature, including in respect of constitutional amendments and enactments. In the first place, the Indian Supreme Court has long held that a constitutional amendment must be within the range of permissible amendments and must not be such as to do away with the very essence of a constitution. In the second place, the Indian Supreme Court has held that the processes of constitutional amendment within the legislature are subject to review from the standpoint of legality and due process.[1]

The jurisprudence of the Guyana Court of Appeal is that acts which are shocking to the conscience of the Guyanese nation or to the international community at large will be struck down. (See Churaman JA as added to by Kennard C in Chapter 6, below.)

The 1978 'referendum' shocked and continues to shock the conscience of the Guyanese nation and is repugnant to Guyanese. The 1980 Constitution is the decaying symbol of that repugnance and must be expunged from the constitutional and legal order of Guyana. The legal basis for this is set out below.

## COMMONWEALTH JURISPRUDENCE ON CONSTITUTIONAL VALIDITY

Recently, there has been significant clarification of the law regarding constitutional validity in a number of Commonwealth jurisdictions, including Grenada, Trinidad, Lesotho, South Africa, Fiji and Guyana. The case law from many of these Commonwealth jurisdictions was reviewed extensively in a recent Fijian case that engaged the attention, first, of the Fiji High Court and then of its Court of Appeal that we shall look at below.[2] But, first, let us look at the Caribbean experience in Grenada.

1 See Basu, DD, *Shorter Indian Constitution*, reprint, 1999, Nagpur: Wadhwa & Co, p 368.

2 *Chandrika Persaud v Republic of Fiji*, 16 November 2000; *Republic of Fiji v Chandrika Persaud*, 1 March 2001.

## The Independence Constitution as the groundnorm

The Grenadan experience offers significant clarification of the foundations for considering a situation such as that in Guyana. In a recent essay, Dr Francis Alexis, a leading Caribbean author on constitutional law, summarized the jurisprudential lessons of the Grenadan experience as follows:[3] Grenada's groundnorm at independence (like that of Guyana) was the Independence Constitution. That constitution was the supreme law of Grenada and the yardstick to measure other laws for their validity. The Constitution could only be changed through special procedures for its lawful amendment, including special parliamentary majorities and referendum requirements.

Following the Maurice Bishop take-over of power in Grenada, from 19 March 1979 to October 1983, the law prevailing was that of the Provisional Revolutionary Government, a body which had vested in itself, by People's Law No 2 of 1979, 'all executive and legislative power'. After the American military intervention, the Governor-General returned Grenada to constitutional government and, by the Constitution of Grenada Order 1984, restored virtually all sections of the Grenada Independence Constitution. Return to constitutional validity thus took place, notwithstanding the previous irregularities.

## Judging revolutionary legality

The question subsequently arose before the courts in Grenada as to the legality of institutions during the Provisional Revolutionary Government (PRG). In *Mitchell v Director of Public Prosecutions and Another* (1986) LRC (Const) 35, Haynes P defined the principles of revolutionary legality as follows:

> For a revolutionary government to achieve *de jure* status, that is, to become internally a legal and legitimate Government, the following conditions should exist: (a) the revolution was successful, in that the Government was firmly established administratively, there being no other rival one; (b) its rule was effective, in that the people, by and large, were behaving in conformity with and obeying its mandates; (c) such conformity and obedience was due to popular acceptance and support and was not mere tacit submission to coercion or fear of force; and (d) it must not appear that the regime was oppressive and undemocratic.

3 Alexis, F, 'Grenada goes grundnorm', in Kodilnye, G and Menon, PK, *Commonwealth Caribbean Legal Studies*, 1992, published by Butterworths on behalf of the University of the West Indies, pp 59–79. On the fundamental rules of the Commonwealth association, with special reference to Kelsen's Grundnorm (see Latham, RTE, 'The law and the Commonwealth', in Hancock, WK, *Survey of British Commonwealth Affairs*, 1937, Vol I, pp 510–630. See also Brookefield, 'The Fiji revolutions of 1987' (1988) NZLJ 250.

Haynes P concluded that acceptable proof was lacking that the PRG had enjoyed such popular acceptance and support, as a result of which he could not find that the PRG regime had ever been actually a *de jure* government.

In the Guyana situation, there was no question of a coup, just the wholesale stealing of the referendum and elections. Gates J in *Chandrika Persaud v Republic of Fiji* (2000) expressly held that: 'The doctrine of necessity is not applicable to validate a change in the Constitution ...'

An issue that arose in Grenada and that would also arise in the Guyana situation concerned the validity of unconstitutional acts. In the *Mitchell* case (mentioned above), Haynes P held that necessity was a constitutional source of validation of unconstitutional acts. For this to occur the following requirements must be met:

- an imperative necessity must arise because of the existence of exceptional circumstances not provided for in the Constitution, for immediate action to be taken to protect or preserve some vital function for the State;
- there must be no other course of action reasonably available;
- any such action must be reasonably necessary in the interest of peace, order and good government; but it must not do more than is necessary or legislate beyond that;
- it must not impair the just rights of citizens under the Constitution;
- it must not be one the sole effect and intention of which is to consolidate or strengthen the revolution as such.[4]

In the Fijian case of *Chandrika Persaud v Republic of Fiji*, decided by Gates J on 16 November 2000, the applicant's originating summons had sought the following orders:

- that the attempted coup of 19 May 2000, was unsuccessful;
- that the declaration of a State of Emergency under the doctrine of necessity by President Ratu Sir Kamisese Mara was unconstitutional;
- that the revocation of the 1997 Constitution by decree by the Interim Military Government was unconstitutional;
- that the 1997 Constitution still remained in force;
- that the elected government was still a legally constituted government in view of the inability of the interim military government and Speight's group to reach an agreement on governing the country;
- that the elected government (The People's Coalition) was still the legitimate government;
- any relief that the court considered just and fair.

4 (1986) LRC (Const) 35, pp 88–89.

After an extensive review of the jurisprudence and literature, Gates J held as follows:

- The attempted coup of 19 May was unsuccessful.
- The declaration of the State of Emergency by President Ratu Sir Kamisese Mara in the circumstances then facing the nation, though strictly proclaimed within the terms of the Constitution, is hereby granted validity *ab initio* under the doctrine of necessity.
- The revocation of the 1997 Constitution was not made within the doctrine of necessity and such revocation was unconstitutional and of no effect. The 1997 Constitution is the supreme and extant law of Fiji today.
- The Parliament of Fiji, consisting of the President, the Senate, and the House of Representatives, is still in being. Its incumbents on and prior to 19 May still hold office; that is Ratu Sir Kamisese Mara, who had stepped aside, and who remains President as originally appointed by the Bose Levu Vakaturaga (Great Council of Chiefs); the Senators are still Members of the Senate; the elected Members of Parliament are still Members of the House of Representatives. The status quo is restored. Parliament should be summoned by the President at his discretion but as soon as practicable.
- Meanwhile, owing to uncertainty over the status of the Government, it will remain for the President to appoint as soon as possible as Prime Minister, the Member of the House of Representatives who in the President's opinion can form a government that has the confidence of the House of Representatives pursuant to ss 47 and 98 of the Constitution, and that the Government shall be the Government of Fiji.[5]

Upon appeal, the Fiji Court of Appeal, after extensively reviewing the jurisprudence literature and facts, made the following declarations in lieu of those made by Gates J:

- The 1997 Constitution remained the supreme law of the Republic of the Fiji Islands and has not been abrogated.
- Parliament had not been dissolved. It was prorogued on 27 May 2000 for six months.
- The office of the president under the 1997 Constitution had become vacant when the resignation of Ratu Sir Kamisese Mara took effect on 15 December 2000. In accordance with s 88 of that Constitution, the vice president may perform the functions of the president until 15 March 2001 unless a president is sooner appointed under s 90.[6]

5 Original judgment, concluding part.

6 Civil Appeal No ABU0078/2000S between 1 *The Republic of Fiji* 2 *Attorney General of Fiji, Appellants v Chandrika Prasad, Respondent,* decided by the Court of Appeal of the Fiji Islands on 1 March 2001. Original judgment, pp 48–49.

The decision of the Fiji Court of Appeal bears directly on the issues that have arisen as a result of the fraudulent referendum in Guyana in 1979. *The Court of Appeal of Fiji regarded the 1997 Constitution of Fiji as a reliable expression of the hopes and aspirations of the whole population* and saw this as relevant in determining whether there had been popular acquiescence in the Interim Civilian Government that came about as a result of the forcible removal of the lawfully elected government.

The Court of Appeal first discussed its jurisdiction to rule on whether the Constitution had been abrogated. It satisfied itself that it had such jurisdiction, having regard to the fact that the court owed its existence to that document, and proceeded to consider the constitutional doctrine of necessity, first developed in Grenada (mentioned above), which can give validity to otherwise unconstitutional action taken in the interest of public safety. The Court of Appeal agreed with the judge at first instance, Justice Gates, that this doctrine could not justify the abrogation of the Constitution, nor validate the Interim Civilian Government. The Court of Appeal, however, went on to consider court decisions and academic writings on the issue of acquiescence. After an extensive review, it held that a usurping government may be recognized as legal by exercising control over the State with the acquiescence of the people.

The Court of Appeal held that the Interim Civilian Government had the burden of proving that it was in firm control and that the people had truly acquiesced in it. It found that there was no question about control, but that there was no direct evidence of acquiescence produced by the government, and the court was left to infer this from affidavits by officials indicating that all branches of government were proceeding normally, and citizens were acting in conformity with its requirements.

The court did not accept such passive acceptance as persuasive evidence of acquiescence, having regard to the short time the government had been in control and its suppression of public demonstrations of dissent, evidenced in the material produced by the respondent. The Court of Appeal also referred to the numerous affidavits by people and organizations expressing disapproval of the Interim Civilian Government, and to the fact that the elected government was ready to take over and was awaiting the outcome of the appeal.

The Court of Appeal concluded that the Interim Civilian Government had not proved that it had the acquiescence generally of the people of Fiji. Accordingly, it could not be recognized as the legal government. The Court of Appeal then proceeded to consider how far its conduct of affairs aimed at maintaining normal government during the period it exercised power could be recognized as valid.

## Jurisdiction of court to pronounce on constitutional validity

In *Republic of Fiji v Chandrika Persaud,* the Fiji Court of Appeal discussed the important issue of the jurisdiction of the court to pronounce on constitutional validity. The Court of Appeal noted that each of the members of the court had been appointed under, or had had his appointment renewed, under either the 1990 or 1997 constitutions. Each had taken the oath of office prescribed by one or other of those constitutions. None of them had taken an oath of office under the Judicature Decree 2000 of the Interim Civilian Government. That decree had stated that nothing should affect their continuance in office as judges of the Court of Appeal and it had not required them to take new oaths. The Interim Civilian Government had raised no difficulties about the judges (who were from the region) travelling to Fiji to hear this case: it had provided administrative and security services.

What, then, was their position as judges asked by the Interim Civilian Government to decide on the appeal whether the 1997 Constitution had been successfully abrogated? Had the Court of Appeal the jurisdiction to decide whether a new regime, set up in defiance of the 1997 Constitution, had become legal and thus entitled to rule the country?

The Court of Appeal had no hesitation in holding that the answer to these questions was in the affirmative. They based their view on the finding by Lord Reid in *Madzimbamuto v Lardner-Burke* [1969] 1 AC 645 to the effect that courts, including those created by a written constitution, are authorized and required to decide when and if a revolutionary regime has become lawful. Lord Reid, in that case, said at p 723:

> With regard to the question whether the usurping government can now be regarded as a lawful government much was said about *de facto* and *de jure* governments. Those are conceptions of international law and in their Lordships' view they are quite inappropriate in dealing with the legal position of a usurper within the territory of which he has acquired control .... But the position is quite different where a court sitting in a particular territory has to determine the status of a new regime which has usurped power and acquired control of that territory. It must decide. And it is not possible to decide that there are two lawful governments at the same time while each is seeking to prevail over the other.

The Fiji Court of Appeal held:

> It is sufficient to observe that such a jurisdiction has been exercised by judges in other cases. We consider that not only is it appropriate for us to consider the seminal issues raised by this appeal, but that it is our duty as judges of Fiji to do so.
>
> The exercise of jurisdiction is rendered all the more sensible because the Interim Civilian Government, by appealing, has effectively invited this court to

decide whether the 1997 Constitution survives. By preserving the role and status of the court, it has acknowledged that the court has survived any attempted revolution which may have affected the legislative and executive branches of government.

In a situation where there has been a purported overthrow of a constitution but where the court system has survived virtually unscathed, the court has two options, as the cases show. First, it can say that the usurping government, by abrogating the Constitution or by changing it in an illegitimate manner, has succeeded in changing permanently the previous legal order and that the new order is legally valid. There is always the danger that such a finding is seen as giving the stamp of legitimacy to a usurper. As against that perception, a court cannot be blind to reality, however unfair or unfortunate that reality may be.

The other option for the court is to declare the usurpation invalid. Under this option, a revolutionary change to the legal order will be declared to have been ultimately unsuccessful. This result can occur even if the usurper had been acting under the doctrine of necessity – eg, as a result of events which were so drastic as to call for the suspension of the Constitution and/or the imposition of martial law. Under this scenario, when the crisis is over, the Constitution emerges again.

Even when the doctrine of necessity does not apply, but there was a purported change in the legal order and an illegitimate overthrow of the Constitution, the new order may not ultimately be recognized as the legal government unless the usurper proves various matters ... including, notably, acceptance of the new regime by the general populace.[7]

## The duty of the judiciary upon the occurrence of extra-constitutionality

In *Chandrika Persaud v Republic of Fiji*, Gates J affirmed that judges were required to uphold lawfulness and to apply justice. Upon being appointed they swear both the oath or affirmation of allegiance to the Republic of Fiji and the oath of affirmation for the execution of judicial office (s 135 of the Constitution). The judicial oath in Fiji was two-pronged. First, the judge swore to uphold the Constitution, and secondly, he swore that he would do right (that is, would do justice) to everyone in accordance with the laws and usages of the Republic (that is, he would not go against the law or make a perverse decision or one not in accordance with the law). Finally, he would so act, with courage, without bias, without favouring anyone and without malice or spite towards anyone. A judge's first duty was to uphold the Constitution. Because a judge might be called upon to pronounce on the legality of executive action when an instance of supra-constitutionality occurs, it was wiser counsel for a judge, indeed for the Bench of Judges, to make no public statement on the matter.

7 Original judgment, pp 23–25.

In the case of *Makenete v Lekhanya* (1993) 3 LRC 13, Ackermann JA at p 56c declared:

> A peculiar duty is ... cast upon the court to remain open to argument when subsequently called upon to adjudicate in a dispute regarding the legitimacy of the new regime.
>
> A judge's strength and value lies in continuing to hold office and to carry out his or her duties with integrity, even-handedness, boldness and courage.
>
> If the judiciary is deserving of any respect, it must at least aim for these precepts.
>
> What does even-handedness mean when the judicial oath enjoins the judge to uphold the Constitution? Events will no doubt place the Constitution into one of three categories, namely 'abrogated', 'still in being' or 'wait and see'. One must commence from the presumption, however, that the Constitution is still in being and not subverted.
>
> The onus of impugning the validity of the Constitution lies on those seeking to suggest it is no longer operative. In *Premier of Kwazulu-Natal and Others v The President of the Republic of South Africa and Others,* Constitutional Court of South Africa Case No CCT 36195 (unreported), 29 November 1995, Mahomed DP had said at p 47: 'There is a procedure which is prescribed for amendments to the Constitution and this procedure has to be followed. If that is properly done, the amendment is constitutionally unassailable.'

In *Chandrika Persaud* (mentioned above), Gates J noted that it had been unchallenged that the Fiji Constitution had not been amended by the new regime in the way expressly provided for in Chapter 15. The doctrine of necessity was not applicable to validate a change in the Constitution either. That left only a consideration by the court as to whether the interim government had established a proper claim to have succeeded the previous regime on the doctrine of effectiveness. Such a doctrine would clearly take some time, perhaps over months if not a year or two, before it could be established with certainty.

He added that the courts had pronounced frequently on the presumption in favour of the Constitution. In *Madzimbamuto* (mentioned above), Lord Pearce had said at p 732c:

> The judges under the 1961 Constitution therefore cannot acknowledge the validity of an illegal government set up in defiance of it. I do not agree with the view of Macdonald JA that their allegiance is owed to the rebel government in power. Judges could not carry on, his Lordship said at p 742B, without acknowledging some formalities and acts that had an illegal origin.

In *Makenete,* Ackerman JA quoted extensively from Fieldsend AJA sitting in the Court of Appeal in *Madzimbamuto RAD* case (1968) 2 SA 24, pp 429–30; (1968) RLR 203, p 385) with full approval at pp 65–66:

> The courts become the pivot on which the constitutional arrangements of the country turn for the bench can and must determine the limits of the authority

> of both the executive and the legislature. The consequence follows that the bench of judges is a guardian of the constitution ...
>
> Judges appointed to office under a written constitution, which provides certain fundamental laws and restricts the manner in which those laws can altered, must not allow rights under that constitution to be violated. This is a lasting duty for so long as they hold office, whether, the violation be by peaceful or revolutionary means. If, as in South Africa, the courts were obliged to stand resolutely in the way of what might be termed a legitimate attempt to override the Constitution, *a fortiori* must a court stand in the way of a blatantly illegal attempt to tear up a constitution. If to do this is to be characterized as counter-revolutionary, surely acquiescence in illegality must equally be revolutionary. Nothing can encourage instability more than for any revolutionary movement to know that, if it succeeds in snatching power, it will be entitled *ipso facto* to the complete support of the pre-existing judiciary in their judicial capacity.
>
> It may be a vain hope that the judgment of a court will deter a usurper, or have the effect of restoring legality, but for a court to be deterred by fear of failure is merely to acquiesce in illegality. It may be that the court's mere presence exercises some check on a usurper who prefers to avoid a confrontation with it.
>
> I am in full agreement with these views and in particular with the warning that a court ought not to shirk its constitutional duty because it fears that its orders may not be executed by the usurper.
>
> Clearly, Gates J continued, the judges at the outset of an extra-constitutional occurrence must uphold the Constitution until evidence and argument are placed before them impugning successfully the operation of that Constitution.

That was the approach taken by Fijian judges in three recent cases. The judges had applied the Constitution and, in doing so, correctly applied the lawful presumption of continuing legality applying long-established law in consonance with their judicial oaths.

Gleaned from the recorded cases and from what had happened in Fiji in the early days of the military takeover, Gates J made the following observations on the role of the judiciary in such crises:

- Judges should remember their oaths of judicial office to uphold the Constitution. The presumption is that the Constitution remains unimpugned until pronounced otherwise in court.
- Extra-constitutional occurrences or subversions if not intended to be temporary will not displace the Constitution for some period of time. Judges should continue to uphold the Constitution meanwhile. Even in cases where the doctrine of necessity applies, time will need to pass before validity *ab initio* can be granted to acts committed under the doctrine.
- Unless there has been a 'Glorious Revolution' to remove an undoubted tyrant, or to end a regime whose record 'was one of turmoil' (*Mokotso*, p 167) followed by 'clear acceptance, jubilation and acclaim' for the revolution, the judges should await the filing of cases and production of

evidence and arguments for consideration of validity under all other heads of claims. (See *Pakistan Petitions* Case (mentioned above) generally.)

- It is not the oath taken or regime under which an appointment is made that colour a judge's role on legitimacy. A judge is expected to act at all times impartially, fairly, with integrity and to uphold all the laws of the land independently of the regime existing at the time of his or her appointment. A judge may called upon to curb the excesses of a revolutionary regime acting arbitrarily or outside the law.
- Judges should remember the importance of the constitutional separation of powers and not to intrude into political matters. To do so compromises the independence of the judiciary. In particular the president can be advised to seek his own counsel and constitutional adviser. Such persons would have been made available to the president readily and urgently through the auspices of several of the overseas missions of Commonwealth countries represented in Fiji.

It would be inappropriate, as happened here in Fiji, for three judges of the High Court to provide written opinions to His Excellency and oral advice on political paths out of the impasse. It is unwise also to tender advice on the grant of immunity as this is bound to feature in future criminal prosecution or civil litigation. (See *Lennox Phillip and Others v DPP and Another* [1992] 1 AC 545; *Attorney General of Trinidad and Tobago and Another v Lennox Phillip and Others* [1995] 1 AC 396.)

Even more unwise and dangerous a judicial precedent was the tendering of advice on the proroguing of Parliament, the appointment of an acting prime minister and the dismissal of the Government. These were not appropriate judicial functions:

- Similarly judges should not compromise their neutrality by taking an active part in advising an usurping regime. Nor should they assist in drafting decrees for the usurper. Such may attract the criticism that they were aiding and abetting the abrogation of the Constitution, indeed were acting with indecent haste to see the Constitution gone, such assistance being in obvious conflict with their judicial oaths of office. The cynical will say they hoped for something in the new regime. Such views undermine the public's confidence in the judiciary.
- It is well known the same judges assisted in the drafting of the Administration of Justice Decree 2000 (Interim Military Government Decree No 5 of 2000). That decree was subsequently repealed by the Judicature Decree 2000 (ICG Decree No 22):

  In the Decrees of notoriety were the raising of the retirement age of the Chief Justice and that of the puisne judges of the High Court and the unfathomable abolition of the Supreme Court. None of this conduct provided buttress, in the opinion of the nation as evidenced in the press, to the institutions of the courts and the judiciary, and such drafting should never have been entered upon.

> There was no power to abolish the Supreme Court. No necessity compelled its abolition. It existed under the Constitution and it remains Fiji's final Appellate Court still.

## When is there a new legal order?

In *Republic of Fiji v Chandrika Persaud,* the Fiji Court of Appeal, noting that there had been a purported overthrow of the Constitution and its replacement by the establishment, first, of military rule and, secondly, of the Interim Civilian Government, discussed whether what happened could be characterized as a 'revolution' or not. The Court of Appeal cited with approval the following definition of 'revolution' in Brookefield:[8]

> For the purposes of a constitutional theorist (though one with practical concerns as well), a revolution may be widely defined as the overthrow and replacement of any kind of legal order, or other constitutional change to it – whether or not brought about by violence (internally or externally directed) – which takes place contrary to any limitation or rule of change belonging to that legal order.

The Court of Appeal observed that not all revolutions were successful. Nor were all revolutions on the grand scale of the French Revolution or the Bolshevik Revolution in Russia. Nor were all revolutions 'glorious', in the sense of ending the reign of a tyrant or replacing a repressive regime. Nor did all revolutions involve bloodshed.

In the Fijian situation at hand, there had been a purported change in the legal order when the Commander decided to abrogate rather than suspend the Constitution on 29 May; he reinforced this change when he later chose to install the Interim Civilian Government which had purported to govern ever since. The Interim Civilian Government had clearly shown that it wished to implement a new or significantly altered constitution by setting up a body to seek submissions on constitutional 'reform'.

The Court of Appeal noted that various formulations were given in the cases of what must be proved to validate a new legal order in place of the previous one. None of the authorities were binding on the court. Some seemed over-influenced by the writings of the Austrian jurist, Hans Kelsen, whose theories on one view might too readily reward a usurper. (See Das, 'Governments and crisis powers', *Cornell International Law Journal,* Winter 1994.) Many of the authorities were decided before the modern shift towards insistence on basic human rights in a raft of international treaties and, more importantly for present purposes, the 1997 Fiji Constitution.

The Court of Appeal observed that the starting point for any consideration of authority on this point was the Privy Council decision in *Madzimbamuto v*

8 *Op cit,* Brookefield, fn 3.

*Lardner-Burke,* which held as illegal the regime of Ian Smith in Southern Rhodesia set up under the 'Unilateral Declaration of Independence'. The majority decision of the Southern Rhodesian Appellate Court was reversed. Although its decision was given almost three years after Smith's usurpation of legal power and he was to remain in power for some nine further years, the Privy Council considered that various formulations about the effect of an abrupt political change referred to in cases cited to it from Pakistan and Uganda did not apply. The British Government, acting for the lawful sovereign, was taking steps to regain control and 'it is impossible to predict with certainty whether or not it will succeed' (Lord Reid, *Madzimbamuto,* p 724).

Lord Reid had said at pp 723–24:

> It is an historical fact that in many countries – and indeed in many countries which are or have been under British sovereignty – there are now regimes which are universally recognized as lawful but which derive their origins from revolutions or *coups d'état*. The law must take account of that fact. So there may be a question how or at what stage the new regime became lawful.
>
> A recent example occurs in *Uganda v Commissioner of Prisons ex p Matovu* (1966) EA 514. On 22 February 22 1966, the Prime Minister of Uganda issued a statement declaring that in the interests of national stability and public security and tranquillity he had taken over all powers of the Government of Uganda. He was completely successful, and the High Court had to consider the legal effect. In an elaborate judgment, Sir Udo Udoma CJ said:
>
>> Our deliberate and considered view is that the 1966 Constitution is a legally valid Constitution and the supreme law of Uganda; and that the 1962 Constitution having been abolished as a result of a victorious revolution in law does no longer exist nor does it now form part of the Laws of Uganda, it having been deprived of its *de facto* and *de jure* validity. (p 539.)
>
> Pakistan affords another recent example. In *State v Dosso* (1958) 2 PSCR 180, the president had issued a proclamation annulling the existing Constitution. This was held to amount to a revolution. Muhammed Munir CJ said at p 184:
>
>> It sometimes happens, however, that a Constitution and the national legal order under it is disrupted by an abrupt political change not within the contemplation of the Constitution. Any such change is called a revolution, and its legal effect is not only the destruction of the existing Constitution but also the validity of the national legal order.
>
> Their Lordships would not accept all the reasoning in these judgments but they see no reason to disagree with the results. The Chief Justice of Uganda (Sir Udo Udoma CJ) said at p 533: 'The Government of Uganda is well established and has no rival.' The court accepted the new Constitution and regarded itself as sitting under it. The Chief Justice of Pakistan (Sir Muhammed Munir CJ) said at 185: 'Thus the essential condition to determine whether a Constitution has been annulled is the efficacy of the change.' It would be very different if there had been still two rivals contending for power. If the legitimate

Government had been driven out but was trying to regain control it would be impossible to hold that the usurper who is in control is the lawful ruler, because that would mean that by striving to assert its lawful right the ousted legitimate Government was opposing the lawful ruler:

> In their Lordships' judgment that is the present position in Southern Rhodesia. The British Government, acting for the lawful sovereign, is taking steps to regain control and it is impossible to predict with certainty whether or not it will succeed. Both the judges in the General Division and the majority in the Appellate Division rightly still regard the 'revolution' as illegal and consider themselves sitting as courts of the lawful sovereign and not under the revolutionary Constitution of 1965. Their Lordships are therefore of opinion that the usurping Government now in control of Southern Rhodesia cannot be regarded as a lawful government.

The Fijian Court of Appeal proceeded to an extensive consideration of other cases:

(i) *Vallabhaji v Controller of Taxes* (1981), unreported, 11 August, Court of Appeal of the Seychelles.

A taxpayer had claimed that he should not have been assessed for tax under decrees made by what he claimed had been an illegal regime. There had been a bloodless coup in the Seychelles in 1977 which had abrogated the Constitution. A year later, the usurping regime had issued decrees levying the tax of which the appellant complained. The court held that the decrees were valid and enforceable: the extra-constitutional regime had acquired validity through the consent of, or acceptance by, the people. 'Acceptance, consent or its equivalent remain a touchstone' said President of the Court, Sir Michael Hogan.

Mustafa JA at p 20 had said:

> I am of the opinion that a coup Government which continues in office and existence must be viewed as a whole, and if it has become legitimate and valid, then such legitimacy relates back to its inception, that is, it becomes legitimate and valid *ab initio*. Similarly, if it does not acquire validity or legitimacy, it remains invalid and illegitimate, subject to savings for necessity. I do not think such a Government can be divided into legitimate and illegitimate portions, the dividing line in this instance being, according to Mr Heald, the time when it established a constitution based on public consultation. I think that one has to accept a successful revolution as valid from its inception if it has remained in office for a sufficient period of time and has the consent and backing of the people, express or implied. On this basis, the coup Government has acquired legitimacy and validity and the decrees it enacted in 1977 and 1978 are valid and enforceable.

Hogan P at p 14 had said:

> We have the advantage of not having to decide this case *in mediis rebus* (in the middle of the events) after an interval of some four years, during which the new revolutionary regime has enjoyed unchallenged authority and maintained

> stable and effective government in the Seychelles, with little or no interruption in the ordinary life of its citizens. But, even if I did not have the benefit of this hindsight, I believe I would have come to the conclusion, from the smoothness and efficacy of the revolutionary transition, that the new regime had, by 28 June 1977, received such widespread and unqualified acceptance and consent that it was, already, a legal authority at that time. Even if I were wrong in this assessment because, for example, there had been insufficient time for the habit of obedience to become manifest, when a regime is firmly established and accepted as legitimate, this legitimation is extended back to cover legislation enacted by the regime from the inception of its context.

At another point, Hogan P said that fair elections probably provide the most convincing proof of acceptance of a regime but that obedience, when manifested, has also been recognized as a form of ratification. Then later:

> In any event, whether the term chosen is success or submission, consent or acceptance, efficacy or obedience, there appears to be a consensus or at least a strong preponderance of opinion that *once the new regime is firmly or irrevocably in control it becomes a lawful or legitimate government and entitled to the authority that goes with that status* [emphasis added].

(ii) *Mitchell v Director of Public Prosecutions* (mentioned above), a decision of the Court of Appeal of Grenada.

In 1979, Maurice Bishop led a coup which overthrew the government established under the Constitution. He suspended the Constitution and took executive and legislative power, although the Queen remained Head of State and the Governor-General remained in office. On 19 October 1983, Bishop and some of his ministers were killed. The head of the military assumed power. Six days later, armed forces of the United States and some Caribbean states invaded Grenada and arrested the military leaders. On 31 October 1983, the Governor-General issued proclamations assuming executive power and declaring a State of Emergency. About a year later, he brought back the 1973 Constitution. New elections followed and the legislature enacted a law which confirmed the validity of laws passed between March 1979 and November 1984, eg, the time during which the Constitution had been suspended.

The leaders of the military coup were charged with murder but claimed that the High Court had no jurisdiction to try them since the court had been created by the Bishop regime in a manner contrary to the 1973 Constitution. Further, that the Act validating the legislation of the Bishop regime was invalid because it effected a change to the Constitution by ordinary legislation and not by the means mandated by the Constitution.

In the High Court, the Chief Justice found that the court was valid and had jurisdiction, though admittedly extra-constitutional. This ruling was on the basis of the doctrine of necessity. On appeal, Haynes P and Peterkin JA held that the High Court was 'temporarily valid' on the grounds of necessity until the current government took steps to reinstate the court contemplated by the

1973 Constitution. Liverpool JA concurred on the necessity point but held that the Bishop regime had become the 'legitimate and lawful government'.

Haynes P formulated the 'efficacy' test in these words at pp 71–72:

> I would hold that for a revolutionary government to achieve *de jure* status, that is, to become internally a legal and legitimate government, the following conditions should exist: (a) the revolution was successful, in that the Government firmly established administratively, there being no other rival one; (b) its rule was effective, in that the people by and large were behaving in conformity with and obeying its mandates; (c) such conformity and obedience was due to popular acceptance and support and was not mere tacit submission to coercion or fear of force; and (d) it must not appear that the regime was oppressive and undemocratic.
>
> In my view unless all four of these conditions exist, no court in a democratic country should pronounce a revolutionary regime legitimate. Every one of them, (a), (b), (c) and (d), raises a question of fact ...
>
> I do not think these are unduly stringent conditions; (a) and (b) can exist without popular acceptance and support, because of submission to force or fear of it or weakness. This court should not take an approach which might encourage power-seeking politicians or over-ambitious army officers to believe that; if by force of arms they can gain and retain governmental powers for a few years, their government will become consequentially lawful and legitimate. We must bear in mind the warning of Fieldsend AJA, in *Madzimbamuto v Lardner-Burke* that 'nothing can encourage instability more than for any revolutionary movement to know that if it succeeds in snatching power it will be entitled *ipso facto* to the complete support of the pre-existing judiciary in their judicial capacity. It may be a vain hope that the judgment of a court will deter a usurper, or have the effect of restoring legality, but for a court to be deterred by fear of failure is merely to acquiesce in illegality'. Hence the importance of conditions (c) and (d).
>
> A revolutionary regime should not be accorded legitimacy by this court unless it is satisfied that, on the whole, the regime had the people behind it and with it. Legality should be achieved only if and when the people accept and approve, for in them lies political sovereignty, and the court so finds. This approval they may give *ab initio* or subsequently. Length of time might or might not be sufficient to infer it. It might be expressed or tacit approval. But it is that which should give legitimacy to a successful and effective revolutionary regime. The support of a real majority is sufficient. This could be shown by its majority vote at a general election or a referendum or a majority percentage at polls.

Later at p 73 he said:

> I do not think this court can properly act on a bare statement of fact or opinion of popular support, however credible and knowledgable the source is and whatever is the basis of it. Proof of the fact by judicial notice may be admissible. But the weight to be given to it is another matter. I would hold that what is needed here is proof of particular facts or circumstances from which the court itself can infer popular support. In my view the proof here was insufficient.

(iii) *Mokotso v HM King Moshoeshoe II* (1989) LRC (Const) 24, a 168-page judgment of Cullinan CJ in the High Court of Lesotho.

Lesotho became independent in 1966 as a constitutional monarchy with a Westminster-style constitution. When the Prime Minister was defeated at the first general elections in 1970, he seized control, suspended the Constitution and assumed dictatorial powers. For the next 16 years, this extra-constitutional regime remained in power and was notorious for abuses of freedoms. In 1986, the military forces staged a coup as a result of which the King, acting on the advice of the Military Council, assumed legislative and executive authority. The courts were to retain their jurisdiction.

The court took 'judicial notice' of the 'notorious fact' that the 1970 coup had been successful. Such a finding seems hardly surprising given that this regime, however unlovely, had remained in place for 16 years. The court then held that the government established by the 1986 coup was firmly established and functioning effectively. It relied on the affidavit of the Attorney General that the government had effective control. The judge took 'judicial notice' of several matters, eg a 'formidable body of legislation'; that the judiciary was functioning effectively; that the vast majority of the people were behaving in conformity with the government's administration; and that peace and stability 'now reign'. The judge then held that the 1986 revolution had been popular, noting the factors above and the jubilation in the streets which greeted news of the coup. He said at p 165 of the judgment that the applicant did not 'adduce a scintilla of evidence to suggest that there was a general air of discontent'.

The Fijian Court of Appeal considered it important that Cullinan CJ had considered that the burden of proof of legality rested upon the new regime. It quoted his comments at pp 132–33 of the judgment which end with his formulation of the test for efficacy:

> ... the burden of proof of legitimacy must always rest upon the new regime. No presumption of regularity can operate in the regime's favour: indeed, there must be a presumption of irregularity, if I may put it that way. If, then, a revolutionary regime is unpopular or oppressive, it is likely that it will meet with initial resistance, perhaps even physical resistance, and the people will not conform. During any such period of resistance, of course, neither of the first two conditions formulated by Haynes P will then be satisfied. Ultimately, however, the situation must resolve itself, one way or the other. If the people ultimately acquiesce, then the new regime is entitled to recognition by the courts.
>
> The situation is comparable even where there has been no initial rejection, but none the less, the people's acquiescence in the matter is not a willing one. In the situations depicted, it would seem to be that the burden of proof of legitimacy must be all the greater. This perhaps is another way of saying that a longer period would be required for the habit of obedience to become manifest. Nonetheless, such considerations cannot affect the principle that once the court

is satisfied as to the establishment of such habit, then it must grant recognition to the new government. I would accordingly express the test to be applied as follows:

A court may hold a revolutionary government to be lawful, and its legislation to have been legitimated *ab initio*, where it is satisfied that (a) the government is firmly established; there being no other government in opposition thereto; and (b) the government's administration is effective, in that the majority of the people are behaving, by and large, in conformity therewith.

The Fijian Court of Appeal observed that the facts of *Mokotso* differed from the *Chandrika* case in many respects, particularly:

(i) In *Mokotso*, there was no evidence of discontent with the new regime; rather, the evidence pointed to wide public acceptance. Here, as we shall summarize later, there is evidence of general discontent with the present regime and with the purported abrogation of the 1997 Constitution.

(ii) International approval attended the overthrow of the 16 year rule of Chief Jonathan by the 1986 coup. On the evidence the same cannot be said of the reaction of the international community to the purported overthrow of the 1997 Constitution. Rather the opposite.

(iii) *Mokotso* is valuable but we consider that the Chief Justice's formulation of the efficacy test is too narrowly expressed. Haynes P's 'extra conditions' in *Mitchell* cited earlier have been criticized as unable to be 'reconciled with the facts of history'. (See Ackermann JA in *Makenete v Lekhanya* (1993) 3 LRC 13, p 63.) It may be that Haynes P went too far in his condition (d) (ie, it must not appear that the regime was oppressive and undemocratic) because, as Brookefield opined (mentioned above, at p 28), the condition goes to the legitimacy of a regime and not its legality. The distinction does not always appear to have been fully understood in some of the authorities cited to us.

(iv) *Makenete v Lekhanya* (1993) 3 LRC 13 was a decision of the Lesotho Court of Appeal after the regime recognized as legal in *Mokotso* had itself been overthrown by the defence forces in 1990. The regime, whose birth was said in *Mokotso* to have been attended by great public rejoicing, had thus lasted a bare four years. The Court of Appeal of Lesotho upheld Cullinan CJ at first instance, finding that there had been another new legal order established by the 1990 regime which had satisfied the various tests of efficacy.

The Fijian Court of Appeal considered the following comments of Ackermann JA at pp 56–57 to be of some guidance, particularly when the court has to consider the length of time since a change took place in coming to a decision on a new regime's efficacy:

As pointed out by Lord Reid in *Madzimbamuto*, there are situations where 'the law must take account of (the) fact that there are now regimes which are universally recognized as lawful but which derive their origins from revolutions or *coups d'état*. The question is 'how or at what stage the new regime became lawful'. At the one end of the scale, therefore, there is the case of a regime, born out of a revolution or *coup d'état*, which has been entrenched for so long and has been accepted voluntarily as legitimate for so long by the people, that the court 'must take account of that fact'. Here, it seems to me, the facts have indeed become normatively prescriptive. At the other end of the scale there is the case of a regime whose usurpation of power and acquisition of control of the territory in question is so tenuous that it cannot be said that the revolution is successful or the administration's control firmly established or its rule effective where a court is bound to decide (as did Fieldsend AJA and the Privy Council in the *Madzimbamuto* case) that the usurper is not the lawful government. Here, too, the facts are normatively prescriptive. The problem, as Lord Reid pointed out, is that 'there may be a question how or at what stage the new regime became lawful'. *This would relate to the middle ground between the two poles, where the task of adjudication becomes complex and difficult and where the totality of the circumstances must be anxiously scrutinized and where isolated facts must not be allowed to become 'prescriptive'* [emphasis added].

The Fijian Court of Appeal commented that there have been cases where courts have upheld the success of a usurpation on the grounds of control by the new regime and acceptance of control by the populace, despite the regime having some unattractive characteristics. Where courts have held coups invalid, the new regime has often responded by a drastic curtailment of the power, independence and jurisdiction of the courts. The resignation of judges on conscience grounds in these situations opens the way for the usurpers to pack the courts with sympathetic judges. To its credit, the Interim Civilian Government in the *Chandrika* case had adopted a very responsible stance. At the end of the hearing Counsel for the Interim Civilian Government had said that in the event of the 1997 Constitution being upheld by the courts, it would use its best endeavours to promote a return to constitutional legality.

The Fijian Court of Appeal noted that Counsel for Chandrika Persaud had urged the court to add to its formulation of the efficacy test an additional criterion to those of Haynes P, namely, whether the new regime acknowledges basic human rights as evidenced by international obligations assumed by the nation. The court did not think it necessary to include a requirement that a usurping regime had to show adherence to international human rights treaties. The 1997 Constitution was made in Fiji for Fiji by the Parliament and people of Fiji. It contained many of the rights and freedoms mandated by international instruments. It protected the rights of the indigenous people and entrenched some of those rights. The extensive consultation undertaken by the Reeves Commission that preceded its adoption in Parliament provided strong evidence that the 1997 Constitution reflected the will of the great majority of the people of Fiji. It was permissible when assessing the test for efficacy in this context to take into account the evidence which suggested contentment with, or acceptance of, the 1997 Constitution by the population at large. Such acceptance militates against the proposition that there had been general acquiescence in its abrogation.

In formulating its understanding of the common law of Fiji on the efficacy question, we are conscious that it was sitting as judges of a Fiji court.

Consequently, statements by judges, which may have been appropriate for other countries where a 'revolution' may have come about in a variety of ways, need not be adopted here. As we have emphasized, this case is unique in that it is the Interim Civilian Government itself that seeks a ruling on the legality of its regime, only some seven months after it was established. Nor is Mr Prasad like the appellants in the Seychelles and Grenada cases who sought to manipulate the legal aftermath of a coup to avoid, in one case, payment of tax and, in the other, a trial for murder. By contrast, Mr Prasad is just an ordinary citizen seeking a return to normality.

We see the 'efficacy' test, in the context of the common law of Fiji, as follows:

- The burden of proof of efficacy lies on the *de facto* government seeking to establish that it is firmly in control of the country with the agreement (tacit or express) of the population as a whole.
- Such proof must be to a high civil standard because of the importance and seriousness of the claim.
- The overthrow of the Constitution must be successful in the sense that the *de facto* government is established administratively and there is no rival government.
- In considering whether a rival government exists, the enquiry is not limited to a rival wishing to eliminate the *de facto* government by force of arms. It is relevant in this case that the elected government is willing to resume power, should the Constitution be affirmed.
- The people must be proved to be behaving in conformity with the dictates of the *de facto* government. In this context, it is relevant to note that a *de facto* government (as occurred here) frequently re-affirms many of the laws of the previous constitutional government (eg criminal, commercial and family laws) so that the population would notice little difference in many aspects of daily life between the two regimes. It is usually electoral rights and personal freedoms that are targeted. As one of the deponents said, civil servants such as tax and land titles officials worked normally throughout the coup and its aftermath. Their functions were established and needed no ministerial direction. We derive little proof of acquiescence from facts of that nature.
- Such conformity and obedience to the new regime by the populace as can be proved by the *de facto* government must stem from popular acceptance and support as distinct from tacit submission to coercion or fear of force.
- The length of time in which the *de facto* government has been in control is relevant. Obviously, the longer the time, the greater the likelihood of acceptance.
- Elections are powerful evidence of efficacy. It follows that a regime where the people have no elected representatives in government and no right to vote is less likely to establish acquiescence.
- Efficacy is to be assessed at the time of the hearing by the court making the decision.

## Proof of facts and burden of proof

Gates J in *Chandrika Persaud v Republic of Fiji* noted that, inevitably, the affidavits submitted would not present all of the facts before the court. The wide-ranging history of the matter and of its numerous events and the logistical difficulty in presenting opinions and views representative of the people of Fiji and of its various groups, religious and ethnic, meant that he had to take a more generous approach as to what were notorious facts than might be appropriate in an ordinary case. To do so would be in accord with the approach taken above – constitutional cases where events were numerous, fast flowing and fluid. It was an approach that was necessary in such cases in order to see justice done both to the litigants and also to the wider public, which had a proper interest in their outcome.

Nevertheless, he considered that in relation to proof of whether there had been popular acceptance of the abrogation of the Constitution or to the overthrow of the elected Parliament or the forcing out of office of the president, the court would require full and proper proof. He recalled that in *Mitchell and Others v Director of Public Prosecutions and Another* (1986) LRC (Const) 35, a case dealing with a similar extra-constitutional situation in Grenada. Haynes P in the Court of Appeal at p 72f had set out the approach of the courts to such issues as follows:

> A revolutionary regime should not be accorded legitimacy by the court unless it is satisfied that, on the whole, the regime has the people behind it and with it. Legality should be achieved only if and when the people accept and approve for in them lies political sovereignty, and the court so finds. This approval they may give *ab initio* or subsequently. Length of time might or might not be sufficient to infer it. It might be expressed or tacit approval.
>
> But it is that which should give legitimacy to a successful and effective revolutionary regime. The support of a real majority is sufficient. This could be shown by its majority vote at a general election or a referendum or a majority percentage at polls. In court it can be proved by agreed statements of fact (as in *Valabhaji*) or by affidavits (as in *Matovu*). And these modes are not exhaustive. If a constitution was abrogated, a new one should be substituted forthwith as happened in both of those cases.

Such an onus, Gates J held, could not be discharged without proper affidavits or an agreed statement of facts. It was insufficient for a court to have to rely solely in deciding such an issue on the taking of judicial notice of notorious facts. He supported the following statement of the law of Haynes in the *Mitchell* case, p 73g:

> I do not think this court can properly act on a bare statement of fact or opinion of popular support, however credible and knowledgeable the source is and whatever is the basis of it. Proof of the fact by judicial notice may be admissible. But the weight to be given to it is another matter. I would hold that what is needed here is proof of particular facts or circumstance from which the

> court itself can infer popular support. In my view the proof here was insufficient.

In *Mokotso and Others v HM King and Others* (1989) LRC (Const) 24, Cullman CJ had accepted an affidavit from the acting Attorney General deposing that the laws promulgated by the government were enforced and obeyed throughout the Kingdom of Lesotho and that the decisions of the courts were enforced by the government. The efficacy of the change was marked by the acceptance of the people, which acceptance was spontaneously popular, unqualified and widespread. The matter was not seriously challenged. However, in the *Chandrika* case those issues were seriously challenged, and Gates J commented that the deponent, Mr Qetaki, the Attorney General, could hardly put himself forward as a neutral witness or independent observer.

## Legal interest

Gates J held, in *Chandrika Persaud*, that the loss of democratic rights enshrined in the supreme law was such that any citizen of Fiji would be able to argue:

(i) that he or she had suffered a grave loss of rights and freedoms;

(ii) that to approach the courts would be a rightful path to redress such grievances (indeed, it may be the only remedy open to him); and

(iii) that to bring such proceedings could not be considered an abuse of process or the work of a mere busybody.

## Usurpation of power constitutes treason

In the *Chandrika* case, Gates J referred to the consequences of a constitutional usurpation of power. Section 190 of the Fijian Constitution stated that: 'This Constitution may be altered in the way set out in this chapter and may not be altered in any other way.'

The purpose of such a provision, Gates J observed, was to ensure due and careful consideration before the supreme law of the land was changed, including the safeguard of a two-thirds majority of both houses, 60-day lapses between the second and third readings of Bills so as to allow for proper debate, and provided certain veto provisions were not exercised against the Bill. He commented:

> It was obvious that an usurpation of the power of Parliament, that is the Parliament consisting of the President, the Senate and the House of Representatives, by subverting or abrogating the Constitution did not amount to an amendment within the supreme law.

A challenge made in this way was, rather, an unlawful act. He asked:

> What laws therefore could come to the rescue of those who would otherwise be guilty of treason by such usurpation?

He answered:

> When one considered the amount of incursion and damage caused to the lives of the ordinary people of Fiji as a result of the attempted civilian coup of the George Speight group and the extra-constitutional disengagement then affecting Fiji nationally and internationally, it was not difficult to see why such acts should be visited with the most serious charge in the Penal Code, namely treason.

## Legality of intervening acts

In *Republic of Fiji v Chandrika Persaud,* the Fiji Court of Appeal having concluded that the 1997 Constitution remained in force throughout, addressed the question of the extent to which the decrees, executive acts and decisions of the administrations since 19 May 2000 were to be recognized as valid. It noted that this point had been discussed in the Privy Council in *Madzimbamuto v Lardner-Burke* [1969] 1 AC 645, but the majority had found it unnecessary to decide the question. At p 726, Lord Reid had referred to decisions of the Supreme Court of the United States dealing with the situation after the American Civil War, in the former Confederate States and had cited *Horn v Lockhart* (1873) 17 Wallace 570, 580 (84 US), where the court had said:

> We admit that the acts of the several States in their individual capacities, and of their different departments of government, executive, judicial, and legislative, during the war, so far as they did not impair or tend to impair the supremacy of the national authority, or the just rights of citizens under the Constitution, are, in general, to be treated as valid and binding. The existence of a state of insurrection and war did not loosen the bonds of society, or do away with civil government, or the regular administration of the laws. Order was to be preserved, police regulations maintained, crime prosecuted, property protected, contracts enforced, marriages celebrated, estates settled, and the transfer and descent of property regulated precisely as in time of peace. No one that we are aware of seriously questions the validity of judicial or legislative acts in the insurrectionary states touching these and kindred subjects, where they were not hostile in their purpose or mode of enforcement to the authority of the National Government, and did not impair the rights of citizens under the Constitution.

In *Madzimbamuto* Lord Pearce had said at p 32:

> I accept the existence of the principle that acts done by those actually in control without lawful validity may be recognized as valid or acted upon by the courts, with certain limitations, namely (a) so far as they are directed to and reasonably required for ordinary orderly running of the State, and (b) so far as they do not impair the rights of citizens under the lawful ... Constitution, and (c) so far as they are not intended to and do not in fact directly help the usurpation ...

The Fiji Court of Appeal adopted this statement as an expression of the law applicable to Fiji.[9]

## The doctrine of necessity

In *Chandrika Persaud v Republic of Fiji,* Gates J discussed the legal doctrine of necessity. He considered that a useful starting point was Haynes P's conclusions, after an exhaustive review of all the cases on necessity and extra-constitutional situations in the *Mitchell* case, p 88h *et seq*:

> (3) I would lay down the requisite conditions to be that:
>
> (i) an imperative necessity must arise because of the existence of exceptional circumstances not provided for in the Constitution, for immediate action to be taken to protect or preserve some vital function to the State;
>
> (ii) there must be no other course of action reasonably available;
>
> (iii) any such action must be reasonably necessary in the interest of peace, order, and good government; but it must not do more than is necessary or legislate beyond that;
>
> (iv) it must not impair the just rights of citizens under the Constitution;
>
> (v) it must not be one the sole effect and intention of which is to consolidate or strengthen the revolution as such.
>
> (4) It is for this court to pronounce on the validity (if so) of any unconstitutional action on the basis of necessity, after determining as questions of fact, whether or not the above conditions exist. But it is for the party requiring the court to so to ensure that proof of this is on the record.
>
> (5) Such validation will not be a once-and-for-all validation, so to speak, it will be a temporary one, being effective only during the existence of the necessity. If and when this ends, the right constitutional steps must be taken forthwith, that is, within a reasonable time.
>
> (6) I am not at all attracted to the principle of 'condonation' invented and applied in *Jilani v the Government of the Punjab.* I can find no support for it either in the classical maxims or in the cases or in the writings of the jurists ancients and modern. In my view, necessity, when it applies, must legitimize or not legitimize: I find it difficult to conceive of a judicial jurisdiction to pardon an illegality. To pardon should be the prerogative of the executive. I would not adopt this principle of 'condonation' on the basis of necessity as law in Grenada.

On the question of onus of proof of regularity or lawfulness, Gates J recalled that Cullinan CJ in *Mokotso* (*supra*) at 132 had said:

> .... the burden of proof of legitimacy must always rest upon the new regime. No presumption of irregularity can operate in the regime's favour; indeed there must be a presumption of irregularity ....

9 Original judgment, pp 47–48.

He further recalled that Ackermann JA in *Makenete v Lekhanya* (1993) 3 LRC 13, a case from Lesotho, had said, p 65b:

> I likewise agree that the onus of providing that a government is entitled to recognition as lawful notwithstanding its revolutionary origins lies on the government claiming such recognition and in particular when it relies on such recognition as a defence to an individual's claim that it has acted in breach of the previous constitutional order. I also support the view that a court ought not lightly to uphold such a defence or uphold it on insubstantial grounds or persuade itself to uphold it precipitately on the evidence of rapid military or executive success which might give a misleading impression of 'effective' government control in the narrow sense of the word.
>
> The courts have recognized the existence of a law of necessity. Such a law permits emergency action to be taken validly in times of extreme crisis, such action being in normal circumstances illegal.
>
> But if such action is taken, it must be transient and a proportionate response to the crisis [see de Smith and Brazier: *Constitutional and Administrative Law* 7th edn, 1994, pp 73–74]; and the *Mitchell* case at p 88e wherein Haynes P said:
>
> > ... whether we read it into the written Constitution of 1973 as an implied constitutional provision thereof or regard it as a purely extra doctrine, this court should adopt and adapt necessity as a constitutional source of validation of unconstitutional acts and legislation in fit cases.
>
> Whatever is done, however, should be done in order to uphold the rule of law and the existing constitution. Necessity cannot be resorted to in order to justify or support the abrogation of the existing legal order. The doctrine is valid only to protect not to destroy.

Gates J drew upon Brookefield who, in an article on 'The Fiji Revolutions of 1987' in the *New Zealand Law Journal* (1988) at p 250, had summarized the principle as:

> The power of a Head of State under a written Constitution extends by implication to executive acts, and also legislative acts taken temporarily (that is, until confirmed, varied or disallowed by the lawful Legislature) to preserve or restore the Constitution, even though the Constitution itself contains no express warrant for them.

Gates J held that the doctrine did not permit necessity to be used as a means of subverting the existing constitutional structure either by abrogating the existing legal order or by bypassing the path laid out for lawful amendment. It may in a fit case allow for a short-lived temporary suspension. He recalled that Lord Pearce, in his dissenting view in the Privy Council in *Madzimbamuto v Lardner-Burke* [1969] 1 AC 645, p 732E, had advised her Majesty over the unilateral declaration of independence by Rhodesia as follows:

> I accept the existence of the principle that acts done by those actually in control without lawful validity may be recognized as valid or acted upon by the courts, with certain limitations namely (a) so far as they are directed to and reasonably required for ordinary and orderly running of the State, and (b) so

> far as they do not impair the rights of citizens under the lawful (1961) Constitution, and (c) so far as they are not intended too and do not in fact directly help the usurpation and do not run contrary to the policy of the lawful Sovereign. This last, ie (c), is tantamount to a test of public policy.

Fieldsend AJA in the court below had said:

> The act must not be intended to, or in fact in its operation directly, further or entertain the inspiration (1968) 2 SA 284, p 441.

Gates J drew upon US legal precedents. Following the outbreak of the Civil War in the USA, the Supreme Court of the United States held that a limited validity might be accorded to the actions of the southern confederacy. Chase CJ stated for the court at p 733:

> It is not necessary to attempt any exact definitions within which the acts of such a state must be treated as valid or invalid. It may be said perhaps with sufficient accuracy, that acts necessary to peace and good order among citizens, such, for example, as acts sanctioning and protecting marriage and the domestic relations, governing the course of descents, regulating the conveyance and transfer of property, real and personal, and providing remedies for injuries to person and estate, and other similar acts, which would be valid if emanating from a lawful government must be regarded in general as valid when proceeding from an actual, though unlawful government, and that acts in furtherance or support of rebellion against the United States, or intended to defeat the just rights of citizens, and other acts of like nature, must, in general, be regarded as invalid and void.

Gates J concluded that the doctrine of necessity could come to aid Commodore Bainimarama in resolving the hostage crisis, imposing curfews, maintaining road-blocks and ensuring law and order on the streets. However, once the hostage crisis had been resolved and all other law and order matters contained, if not entirely eradicated, the Constitution, previously temporarily on ice or suspended, would re-emerge as the supreme law demanding his support and that of the military to uphold it and to buttress it against any other usurpers. The doctrine of necessity could not be used to give sustenance to a new extra-constitutional regime (*Moketso*, p 122). Nor could it provide a valid basis for abrogating the Constitution and replacing it with a Constitutional Review Committee and an Interim Civilian Government. Necessity did not demand any of that.

Commodore Bainimarama had made his intentions in dealing with the emergency situation very clear. They were to preserve law and order, 'to save the State from further destruction and to ensure the safe release of the hostages in Parliament', 'to restore normality', 'our whole nation was on the brink of total anarchy and the safe release of the hostages was the primary and paramount concern'. Subject to an analysis of the effectiveness of the doctrine, it could be concluded that there was no foundation, cause or genuine desire to remove the 1997 Constitution. Nor was there evidence that Fiji had been affected by a state of affairs when 'there was no real democracy because the country, by large, was under one-man rule', 'where the judiciary was ridiculed', 'where an attempt was made to politicise the Army', 'where the representatives of the people are accused of massive corruption', 'disqualification suits abounded for corrupt practices', and when the economy was highly precarious, bank loan defaults rampant and there was generally no accountability or transparency of government. Such a situation leading to constitutional deviation could be validated for a transitional period on the ground of State necessity (see Short order of Judgment of Supreme Court of Pakistan on Petitions challenging the provisional constitutional order and proclamation of emergency *per* IH Khan CJ in a decision made in 2000). No such demonstrably desperate situation faced Commodore Bainimarama concerning the state of health of the body politic and social fabric of Fiji. There was thus no need to pass any decrees purporting to abrogate the 1997 Constitution. Nor at the end of the hostage crisis was there need, in order to shore up the Constitution and preserve the fabric of society, to have the government of the day dismissed. These were unconstitutional and unnecessary acts unprotected by the doctrine of necessity.

Nor was it necessary to seek to dilute rights in the Constitution granted to its inhabitants by the people's democratically elected representatives. Any decree in which it was sought to do so would be unlawful at least to the extent, such as for example s 19(7)(g) of the Interim Military Government Decree No 7, the Fundamental Rights and Freedoms Decree 2000, purporting to narrow the meaning of equality in s 38 of the Constitution. Similarly there was no need to prorogue the Parliament of Fiji, even more so since the Emergency Powers Act required Parliament to be recalled if a proclamation was to be made (s 4 of the Emergency Powers Act 1998; s 188 of the Constitution).

## The doctrine of effectiveness

In the *Chandrika* case, Gates J held that in view of the factual situation, the doctrine of effectiveness did not apply. Commodore Bainimarama was clearly no usurper. Having acted as he thought best in a temporary but dire hostage crisis, he handed over power to a civilian caretaker administration. Necessity would permit him to suspend the Constitution just for so long as to allow him to free the hostages and to restore law and order. That concluded his role. An examination of his regime for effectiveness did not arise (see generally *Mitchell* and *Mokotso*).

However, Gates J asked what was the status of what remained, namely, the interim administration of Prime Minister Laisenia Qarase? Those, for the most part, worthy, talented and public-spirited persons, had been drawn into a government on a misunderstanding of what was possible following on from the emergency of the hostage crisis. But the rule of law meant that the suspended state of affairs and the Constitution returned to life after the stepping down of a responsible military power and after the conclusion of its work for the restoration of calm for the nation. The nation had much for which to be grateful to the military, and may yet have further need for its assistance to maintain stability.

However, there was no constitutional foundation of legality for the interim government or for the Constitutional Review Committee. The military was therefore invited and recommended by the court to ensure a smooth and amicable handover of government to that which will soon be chosen by the incoming Prime Minister, following the court orders.

## Evidence of control and acquiescence

In *Chandrika Persaud v Republic of Fiji*, Gates J considered whether, on the evidence presented, the court could be satisfied that: (a) the Interim Civilian Government was firmly established and there was no rival government; and (b) the people were behaving in conformity with the dictates of the Interim Civilian Government in such circumstances that their acquiescence could be inferred.

In relation to the first requirement of control, Gates J noted that the violence and lawlessness that had ensued in the country following the events of 19 May had taken the country to the verge of anarchy. The Interim Military Government had successfully undertaken the task of restoring order. On 2 November, an attempt by elements of the army to take control was effectively put down. There was no evidence of an effective organized resistance or an attempt to displace the Interim Civilian Government by force. That did not mean that there was not a 'rival government'.

Affidavits filed by the former Prime Minister, Mahendra Chaudhry, and former members of his cabinet claimed that the Peoples Coalition was ready and willing to resume office under the 1997 Constitution. Adi Kuini Speed, in her affidavit, had said that the Coalition still had the support of at least 44 out of the 71 seats in the House of Representatives and thus a comfortable majority, enough to form a government. In addition to this, two proceedings had been instituted in the High Court by members of the Coalition challenging the abrogation of the 1997 Constitution.

The first was commenced on 8 August 2000 by Ratu Isireli Vuibau, the former Assistant Minister of Fijian Affairs, Mr Deo Narayan and Dr Gounder, both former members of Parliament who supported the People's Coalition Government. The defendants included Ratu Mara, the Commander, and Ratu Josefa Iloilo, the Interim President. Dr Gounder deposed that the plaintiffs had brought the action also on behalf of other duly elected members of Parliament, ministers, and assistant ministers whose names would be filed in court. The second, of 13 October 2000, was by Anand Kumar Singh, the former Attorney

General. The defendants included Alipate Qetaki, the Interim Attorney General, the Commander, and Ratu Josefa Iloilo. This was evidence that demonstrates that there was a rival government seeking through the courts to assert its authority to govern.

So far as the second requirement, that of acquiescence, was concerned, counsel for the Interim Coalition Government had relied on the continuing functioning of the administration of government throughout the attempted coup and its aftermath, for inferring acquiescence of the people in the Interim Civilian Government and the abrogation of the 1997 Constitution. Gates J considered that this factor afforded little proof of acquiescence.

In his affidavit of 14 September, the Commander had said:

> ... that the interim government headed by Prime Minister Qarase has effective control and acceptance by the majority of Fiji's people and the administration has acquired legitimacy by such widespread acceptance by the people of Fiji.

Gates J held that the court could not properly act on a bare statement of belief by the Commander that there was widespread acceptance by the people, when there was a serious challenge to this claim in the evidence filed for Mr Prasad. 'What is required is proof of facts from which the court can infer widespread public support for the Interim Civilian Government and acquiescence in the purported abrogation of the 1997 Constitution.' The Interim Civilian Government had adduced no such evidence. Its evidence came almost exclusively from persons holding official positions. Five volumes of affidavits had been filed on behalf of Mr Prasad to prove that people in Fiji by and large did not support the Interim Civilian Government.

This evidence suggested that a significant proportion of the people of Fiji believe that the 1997 Constitution embodied and protected the ideals and aspirations of the different ethnic groups in Fiji. The material also indicated a widespread belief that there had been no proper justification for its abrogation.

The Interim Civilian Government faced an almost impossible task in demonstrating real acquiescence on the part of the people when the evidence filed on behalf of Mr Prasad showed that emergency legislation remained in force, and had been used to inhibit public expression of dissent. However, the press appeared to be free to publish views opposing the Interim Civilian Government.

A human rights delegation sponsored by the Commonwealth Human Rights Initiative had visited Fiji between 27 August and 5 September 2000 and had consulted with more than 25 civil society organizations and community groups in Suva, Nadi and Lautoka, regional areas and Vanua Levu. They had concluded at page seven of their report:

> After consulting civil society organizations, in particular civil society groups who represented sections of the indigenous Fijian community, it became clear that there is little public support for the military backed interim administration.

The courts had also recognized the continued existence of the 1997 Constitution. Between 23 August when Gates J heard the case and 15 November 2000 when he delivered his decision, four judgments were given by judges of the High Court which proceeded on the basis that the 1997 Constitution remained in force (see *Prakash v Native Land Trust Board, BR Kwon v Suva City Council; Singh v State;* and *Doyle v Doyle*).

The Fiji Court of Appeal took the view that, in the light of the large volume of additional material put before the court, the appeal had become a rehearing, to be decided on the current situation. It held that the burden of proving that the 1997 Constitution had been superseded lay on the Interim Civilian Government, and the standard of proof was a high one, having regard to the great public importance of the issues involved. Counsel for the Interim Civilian Government accepted that he had to satisfy the court that the citizens of Fiji truly acquiesced in the new constitutional arrangements and the Interim Civilian Government, in order to justify the conclusion that it had become the legally valid government. The affidavits filed on its behalf were directed at showing that it was in full control and that all branches of government were working normally. They made no reference directly to acquiescence, and it was left to the court to decide what conclusions should be drawn from them on that subject. People would have noticed little difference between this and the former constitutional regime in many aspects of their daily lives which they carried on as before, but such passive compliance was hardly a persuasive indication of true acquiescence in a government which had been in power for only about seven months and severely restricted public protest. The affidavits produced on behalf of Mr Prasad demonstrated that substantial sections of the community did not accept the legitimacy of the interim government or acquiesce in it. It should also be remembered that the elected government had said it would await the outcome of this appeal before taking any further steps.

In the absence of any convincing evidence of real acquiescence, the Court of Appeal held that the Interim Civilian Government had not discharged the burden of proving acquiescence and had accordingly failed to establish that it was the legal government of Fiji. The purported abrogation of the 1997 Constitution had not been justified and it remained in place. The court made declarations to this effect and of the current status of Parliament and the president.

In the case of Guyana, the doctrine of necessity is inapplicable in regard to the fraudulent revolution of 1979. What took place was outrageous and massive fraud. Furthermore, the doctrine of acquiescence would place a burden upon those defending the fraudulent referendum of 1979 to prove to the court that the majority of the Guyanese people had acquiesced in it. This is a contention that would hardly be entertained by the Guyanese people.

## *Ultra vires* the Constitution

In Guyana, in the *Esther Perreira* case, Justice Claudette Singh, on 15 January 2001, held that legislative Act 22/97 was *ultra vires*, null and void Arts 59 and 159 of the Constitution inasmuch as it required the possession of a voter identification card in order to vote. Consequently, the 1997 elections had not been conducted in accordance with the provisions of the Representation of the People Act Chapter 1:03 and Arts 59 and 159 of the Constitution of Guyana.

In her consequential orders the judge ordered: '... that fresh National and Regional elections shall be held ... on or before 31 March.' She further ordered 'that of necessity to uphold the rule of law, to prevent the creation of a legal vacuum with grave consequential chaos and in the interests of effective government, the President and his Cabinet, as presently constituted, shall perform their respective functions of office, not under or by virtue of the declared unlawful National and Regional elections but under and by virtue of the Order of this Court from the date of this order until the date on which fresh elections as aforesaid are held on or before 31 March, subject to the following limitations:

(i) No legislation shall be introduced in Parliament except those required for the proper and timely holding of fresh ... elections and or in compliance with the terms of the Herdmanston Accord.

(ii) No substantial contracts for the execution of public works shall be awarded without the permission of this court.

(iii) The State-owned media shall only be used for election purposes through paid advertisements.

The order permitted Parliament to function for the necessary and limited purposes of passing the above legislation and 'any further working out of the terms of the Herdmanston Accord' and it shall stand dissolved by nomination day.

Regional assemblies and regional administrations were permitted to function up to the new elections. All national and regional executive acts performed after 15 December 1997, 'which would otherwise be lawful were it not for their invalidity due to the decision of the court are temporarily validated until such time as newly elected ... representatives can validate, amend, modify or revoke them according to law, of necessity and in order to uphold the rule of law to preserve obligations and other legal effects as if they had arisen under the provisions of valid enactments ...'.

All legislative enactments including subsidiary legislation and by-laws made between 15 December 1997, and the date of the order were granted temporary validity until the new legislature validates them.

## Electoral legality

In findings directly relevant to a consideration of the fraudulent referendum of 1979, Justice Singh had held in her judgment that it was for the court to consider the evidence in relation to the unlawful acts and omissions and to say whether the evidence established that the elections were flawed and whether those flaws were sufficient to declare the elections void (judgment, p 4). The question to be considered had been well put by Bollers CJ in *Petrie v Attorney General* (1968) GLR 504, p 519: 'Whether there is some general illegality either affecting the whole election or the election held in some particular place, or in the absence of a general illegality, whether there has been some specific illegality, being either an act or an omission which affects the results of an election' (judgment, p 6).

In another significant passage in her judgment, Justice Singh said that it would follow that if the law governing the conduct of an election had not been substantially complied with then there would have been no election and the size of the majority would be irrelevant (judgment, p 9) Furthermore, the standard of proof on the petitioner was one of a preponderance of probability in relation to whether the unlawful act or omission did affect the result (judgment, p 11).

Justice Singh cited with approval the following passage from Ray J in *Bennett Coleman v Union of India* (1973) AIR 106, p 119:

> The true test is whether the effect of the impugned action is to take away or abridge fundamental rights. If it be assumed that that direct object of the law or action has to be a direct abridgement of the right of free speech by the impugned law or action it is to be related to the directness of effect and not to the directness of the subject matter of the impeached law or action. The action may have a direct effect on a fundamental right although its direct subject matter may be different.

Justice Singh held that: 'An Act coming into being after the 1980 Constitution would be stillborn to the extent that it is inconsistent with any provision in the Constitution.' What she nowhere considered was the validity of the 1980 Constitution itself, something that it would have been essential to do. The following passage from p 26 of her judgment admirably states the imperative for a consideration of the validity of the 1980 Constitution because of the massively fraudulent 1979 referendum:

> ... no political party can arrogate unto itself the power to barter away or waive the constitutional right of members of the electorate. The voice of members of the electorate to speak through the ballot cannot be silenced by arrogant agreements among political parties. Even Parliament cannot do so since the voice of members of the electorate to speak through the ballot is a constitutional right under Art 59.

Why was this voice of the court never raised in Guyana against the fraudulent referendum of 1979 and the resulting illegal constitution of 1980?

# FRAUDULENT ELECTIONS AND OPPRESSION THROUGH LAW

Following Guyana's independence in 1966, the government's control of the country under the Presidency of Forbes Burnham could not, under any circumstances, be described as democratic. The US Administration had orchestrated the ouster of the professed Marxist/Leninist leader, Dr Cheddi Jagan, from power in 1964.

## Rigged elections 1968–89

It has been documented by impartial international observers that the 1968 elections in Guyana were massively rigged by the introduction of the 'overseas vote'. The rigging of the elections permitted the People's National Congress (PNC) party, led by Dr Forbes Burnham, to win a majority of votes and to become the dominant party in the country, thus displacing the People's Progress Party, headed by Dr Jagan, to second place.[10]

The United States Department of State (hereinafter referred to as 'Department of State') 'Country Reports on Human Rights Practices, 1982', publicly acknowledged that the elections of 1964 'were the last relatively free national elections held in Guyana'.[11]

External support for the PNC/United Front coalition government came about because the latter initially professed to uphold the same western ideals, such as a free market economy. Of particular importance was Burnham's partnership with the United Force party led by Peter d'Aguiar, which was for free enterprise. This partnership convinced the US of the PNC's 'free enterprise' spirit; support for democracy and its belief in free and fair elections. Only time was to prove the falsity of such pronouncements. These were only a means to an end. Burnham's ambition was to obtain power (by whatever means it took) and if that meant denouncing Jagan's leftist views, even though his deep convictions were the same, he did so. Ashton Chase summed up Burnham's character in the following statement: '... Burnham was a pragmatist and realized that leftist views would be unacceptable by the West so he played the "game" until he assumed the role of the head of the Guyana Government when he began to put into operation his plans.'[12]

Following independence in 1966, the PNC government began manipulating the electoral system in order to ensure Burnham's permanency as head of the country. Its first victim was the Electoral Commission, which

10 'Guyana: fraudulent revolution', *Latin America Bureau*, London, 1984, p 10.

11 Department of State, 'Country report on human rights practices, 1982', February 1983, p 532.

12 Chase, A, *A Nation in Transit: Burnham's Role*, 1994, Georgetown: Paunik, p 18.

had been an independent body responsible to oversee that elections were carried out freely and democratically. During the two years leading up to the 1968 elections, the PNC/UF coalition government sponsored and successfully passed through the National Assembly fundamental changes in the existing electoral system.[13] Given the voting pattern along racial lines, Burnham knew that he could never secure outright victory, so his first priority was to 'fix' every aspect of the voting system in preparation for the 1968 elections. The Electoral Commission, which in any democracy ought to be an independent institution, became the first victim. It was transformed into a political tool of the ruling party (PNC). Then followed changes in the methods of voting, which included voting by 'proxy', postal votings and the use of overseas votes. The irregularities which ensued during the 1968 elections were captured by Granada TV (UK), in two documentary films: *The Trail of the Vanishing Voters* and *The Making of a Prime Minister*. These two films exposed the electoral fraud, particularly the abuse of the overseas votes. They found that the voters' registration list in Britain listed 44,000 names of which only 10,000 were genuine. Voters on the list had been shown to be living at non-existent addresses: in vacant lots, cemeteries, horse pastures, boarded-up butcher shops, to mention only a few. It had been reported that 95% of the overseas votes went to the PNC. In response to the results, Granada's film director said:

> Obviously I don't know what happened in Guyana, but as far as Britain is concerned, the compilation of the register was a totally dishonest and corrupt operation, and, as we have clearly established, the great majority of the people listed do not exist. This I would think is unprecedented for a Commonwealth country, as far as I know; and it's you know, a pretty awful and disgraceful episode.[14]

Opinion Research Centre,[15] a reputable London firm, corroborated the story of the fraud scheme carried out by the use of 'overseas' votes. It reported that at least 75% of the entries on the UK part of the electoral register were incorrect. Taking into consideration the voting pattern of previous elections within the country, the result had given a clear indication of election rigging by the PNC. The gravity of what occurred in the 1968 election had been captured by Randolph Cheeks, a member of the UF, who had been minister of local government in the coalition government of 1964–68, and who summed up the situation thus: 'Fraud is a mild word to describe the motions which Guyana went through on 16 December 1968.'[16]

---

13 Americas Watch, 'Political freedom in Guyana', 1968, p 12.

14 PPP brochure: 'Towards free and fair elections', p 14.

15 Cited in the reports of Americas Watch, 1985, p 26, and UK Parliamentary Human Rights Group, November 1985, p 32.

16 *Op cit*, Americas Watch, fn 13, p 30.

The elections of 1973, 1980 and 1983 under Forbes Burnham and those of 1985 and 1989 under Desmond Hoyte were similarly rigged. The PNC Government's use of the army during the elections to secure ballot boxes became a common practice. Repeated complaints of election riggings and lobbying of international, regional and non-governmental organizations, and influential private groups by the opposition parties and individuals, both at home and abroad, led to the visit of the International Observer Team headed by Lord Avebury, Chairman of the UK Parliamentary Human Rights Group, to Guyana to observe the 1980 elections.

It reported that:

> We came to Guyana aware of the serious doubts expressed about the conduct of previous elections there, but determined to judge these elections on their own merit and hoping that we should be able to say that the result was fair. We deeply regret that ... the election was rigged massively and flagrantly. Fortunately, however, the scale of the fraud made it impossible to conceal either from the Guyanese public or the outside world. Far from legitimizing President Burnham's assumption of his office, the events we witnessed confirm all the fears of Guyanese and foreign observers about the state of democracy in that country.[17]

It was therefore common knowledge that the regime that ruled Guyana between 1968 and 1989 was not a democratic one. Nevertheless, because the regime started out as one opposed to communism, the US Government supported it and maintained that support throughout the period of the Cold War. Even when the regime subsequently declared itself superficially as a Marxist-oriented one, in order to strengthen its hold on power, successive US governments continued to support it because the alternative was considered to be the truly Marxist/Leninist-inspired party of Dr Jagan.

## Acknowledgment of rigged elections and human rights violations, 1968–89

From a historical point of view the annual reports on human rights published by the US Department of State since 1978 provide one of the best sources of evidence on the attitude of governments in Washington toward the non-democratic regime that ruled in Guyana between 1968 and 1992. The US, having decided on Burnham to head the post-independence government of British Guiana/Guyana, backed the government from 1968 to 1989 despite well documented claims made throughout this period about the government's abuse of power. It is appropriate to mention here that in 1968, in preparation for the elections, the voters' registration list and the identification cards for

17 'Something to remember', the report of the International Team of Observers at the elections in Guyana, December 1980, cited in *op cit*, fn 10, p 83.

Guyanese had been closely supervised by a US company, Shoap Registration System International.[18] The US, having succeeded in the ouster of Jagan from power, began to show unfailing support for the new leader.

The *Country Report on Human Rights Practices*, published in 1978 (the first one) and that of 1979, backed the government, despite evidence of fraudulent elections in 1968 and 1973 by Forbes Burnham. The charges made by the opposition of irregularities were dismissed as being the usual function of an opposition party. On the charges of corruption by government officials, the US declared themselves to be satisfied with Burnham's enforcement campaign, which they claimed had been aimed at correcting the alleged abuses. Due notice was taken of the PNC's change toward Marxist ideology.[19] The report for 1981 stated that:

> ... the Executive President, Forbes Burnham, has dominated the nation's political life. His Government ... draws its principal support from among the approximately 40% of Guyanese of African descent and has declared itself a socialist party, operating on Marxist-Leninist principles with the goal of making Guyana a non-aligned Socialist Cooperative Republic.[20]

The same report noted that, after the elections of 1980, international observers and many Guyanese had charged: '... and with apparent justification, that the elections were conducted fraudulently and cannot be considered a free and fair test of public opinion.'[21]

The 1981 Department of State report admitted that in 1980 the PNC Government had amended the Constitution whereby Forbes Burnham became the 'Executive President' and bestowed upon himself extensive powers. The government thereafter dominated all sectors of the political spectrum. The result in effect was a dictatorship, a government accountable to no other authority but itself. The paramountcy of the party was declared. This meant that the party, and by implication, the government, was above the law. Such a system was certainly not democratic, but a dictatorship.

The 1982 Department of State report stated:

> Guyana maintains the structure of a multi-party parliamentary republic within the Commonwealth, but the ruling People's National Congress and its leader, President Forbes Burnham, have imposed a racially-oriented, minority government on the nation. The 1982 report by Freedom House, a US organization, classified Guyana as 'partly free'.
>
> The predominantly Afro-Guyanese party and President Burnham have consolidated power, to a great extent, through such non-democratic means as electoral fraud, harassment of the opposition, and interference with the

18 'The Caribbean and Atlantic: Guyana', *Annual Survey of Commonwealth Law*, p 95.

19 Department of State, *Country Report on Human Rights Practices, 1978*, p 266.

20 Department of State, *Country Report on Human Rights Practices, 1981*, p 267.

21 *Op cit*, Department of State, fn 11, p 270.

> judiciary. Officially, the party operates on Marxist-Leninist principles with the goal of making Guyana a non-aligned cooperative socialist state ... The 1980 Constitution, which established an executive presidency dominating the legislative branch, was a practical acknowledgment of Burnham's long-time political dominance and personal power.[22]

The electoral system was not the only aspect that suffered abuses under the PNC Government of which the US was aware but either did nothing to stop them, or only reported them in a matter-of-fact manner in the annual Department of State reports. It had been alleged by the opposition party that many civil and political rights of the International Covenant on Civil and Political Rights (1966) had been violated in Guyana, which should have been protected under the Guyana Constitution of 1980.

Could there be some credence to these charges when considering the Department of State report for 1981, which reported on 'an apparent increase in police use of lethal force' in Guyana in 1980?[23] The Guyana Human Rights Association (GHRA) in January 1981 had cited some 19 instances during the preceding 18 months in which police had shot and killed suspects and no inquiries had been held to bring the criminals to justice.[24]

The 1983 and 1984 Department of State reports reported on the government's alleged interference with the judiciary in order to render justice favourable to party members, who undoubtedly, it had been claimed, had committed 'illegal' acts.

What actually took place in Guyana, according to the State Department report for 1984 was summarized as follows:

> ... the PNC Government ruled Guyana for 20 years, preserving the facade of parliamentary democracy without the substance. The party has employed the government apparatus to advance its aims to maintain political power in the hands of a ruling elite. Every election since 1964 has been marred by fraud and intimidation of the opponents of the PNC.[25]

## THE JURISPRUDENCE OF THE COURT OF APPEAL ON THE RULE OF LAW

It was in this environment that the Court of Appeal operated. What building blocks was it able to put down for the rule of law? To this we shall now turn.

---

22 *Op cit*, Department of State, fn 11, p 532.

23 *Op cit*, Department of State, fn 20, p 455.

24 *The Guyana Human Rights Association Report of January 1981*, p 451.

25 Department of State, *Country Report on Human Rights Practices*, 1984, p 563.

## The province of a judge

In *J Misir, Lackhan Lall and Seulall*, Civil Appeal No 38 (1990), decided on 30 June 1994, the trial judge, after all the evidence had been led, reserved his decision on 13 March 1989. His written decision was dated 1 November,1989, but for some reason not explained, it was not delivered until 30 March 1990 and then by another judge. The reason for what the Court of Appeal referred to as 'this unusual happening' was that the trial judge had by then ceased to be a judge, having retired from that office with effect from 25 November 1989. Counsel for the appellant contended that the fact that a judge other than the presiding judge read the decision was unconstitutional, null and void.

By a majority of two to one, the Court of Appeal held that the reading of one judge's decision by another was, in all the circumstances, 'a matter gravely wanting in constitutional rectitude and constitutional probity, and was accordingly contrary to law. It was a nullity' (Churaman JA). Bernard JA joined Churaman JA. However, George Ch took the view that what the second judge had done was merely to read the written reasons for decision and judgment of the trial judge, that had already been reduced into writing by him before he had demitted office; and in which he had decided all the factual and other issues. The challenge mounted against what had taken place amounted merely to an objection that the retired judge had personally failed to communicate the self same decision to the parties. No injustice had been done to any party and such an objection should not be allowed to prevail.

Churaman JA declared:

> ... what Perry J did not do, but should have done, was to enquire of the parties through Counsel whether or not they agreed to receive the written decision of Pompey J, he not being on that day a Judge of the High Court, albeit that the written decision bore a date when he was in fact the holder of the office.

He agreed with the submission of counsel for the appellant that the critical factor was that the consent of the parties to receive Pompey J's decision was a prerequisite to invest the decision with the necessary character of a constitutionally pronounced decision. The judgment of Bernard JA also turned on the consent issue.

## A tribunal established by law

*Neil Rafferty v Attorney General of Guyana; Orlando Adams*, Civil Appeal No 50 (1992), decided in 1993, gave rise to an interesting rule of law issue. The appellant, Neil Rafferty, and one John Mendes were the joint holders of claims in the Cuyuni Mining District. On 6 February 1986, the second respondent, Orlando Adams, challenged the continued validity of the claims. The appellant rejected the challenge and the resulting dispute eventually came on for hearing during March 1987 before Ms Reihl who was then, and at all material times, a magistrate. She had been appointed by the Commissioner of Mines by letter dated 17 February 1982 to be a 'hearing' officer for all disputes arising under the Mining Regulation. The letter recited that in making the appointment the commissioner was acting in pursuance of the power vested in him by virtue of Reg 81 of the Mining Regulations.

On 29 April 1988, Ms Reihl gave her decision. She upheld the challenge and under Reg 93 ordered that the appellant's claim be cancelled. Some three years later, on the 22 April 1991, the appellant filed a motion seeking a declaration that the decision of Ms Reihl was unconstitutional and void in that the hearing over which she presided was not a tribunal established by law as required by Art 144(8) of the Constitution. He named the Attorney General and the challenger Orlando Adams as respondents.

The substance of the appeal was that under the Constitution of Guyana an officer appointed to hear any dispute under the mining laws could only be validly appointed to such a position by the Judicial Service Commission acting under Article199 of the Constitution. Therefore as Ms Reihl had been appointed by the Commissioner of Geology and Mines her appointment was *ultra vires* the Constitution and void; and accordingly any decision that she gave was in violation of the provisions of Art 144(8) and was also void.

George first clarified that the naming of the Attorney General as a respondent was misconceived because the Geology and Mines Department had ceased to be a department of government and the State Liability and Proceedings Act was no longer applicable since the commission as a corporate body could be sued in its own name. He left open the question whether, had the commission been made a party, a case could have been made out for the view that it was a public authority in the context in which that expression had been used in *Maharaj v Attorney General of Trinidad and Tobago (No 2)* (1978) 30 WIR 310 or in *Thornhill v Attorney General of Trinidad and Tobago* [1981] AC 61.

The wrongful joinder of the Attorney General led the learned Chancellor to consider another issue: whether the appellant could proceed by constitutional motion against the second respondent alone. He noted that the procedure by way of motion for obtaining redress for a breach of any of the fundamental rights provided for under Arts 130–52 of the Constitution was permitted by virtue of the Fundamental Rights (Practice and Procedure) Act 1988. In the view of the learned Chancellor, having regard to the decisions of *Maharaj v Attorney General of Trinidad and Tobago* and *Thornhill v Attorney General of Trinidad and Tobago* the answer to this question must also be in the negative, for in challenging the continued validity of mining claims the respondent could not be said to have been exercising an executive function of a public nature. And further, and in any event, he could not be held liable for any wrongful or unlawful acts committed by the Commission of Geology and Mines, even if the Court of Appeal were to find that to be the case.

On the substantive issue, Art 144 of the Constitution is expressly concerned with the protection of the individual under the law, and the specific paragraph which it was contended had been violated, para (8), read as follows:

> Any court or other tribunal prescribed by law for the determination of the existence or extent of any civil right or obligation shall be established by law and shall be independent and impartial: anywhere proceedings for such a determination are instituted by any person before such a court or other tribunal, the case shall be given a fair hearing within a reasonable time.

The determination of disputes under the Mining Regulations, such as the one between the appellant and the second respondent, was provided for in Part XI of the Mining Regulations, the scheme of which was intended to create a tribunal for the impartial resolution of disputes concerning the mining claims challenged. The tribunal before which the dispute is to be heard is provided for in Reg 81, which reads as follows:

> All disputes by way of opposition to the issue of any licence and all disputes as to what land is or is not lawfully occupied or has or has not been lawfully located or any other disputes arising under these regulations shall be decided by the Commissioner or any officer appointed by him or the mines officer of the mining district in which the dispute arises.

George Ch noted that this regulation expressly empowered the Commissioner of Geology and Mines to hear a dispute himself. However, in the event that he decided not to do so, the regulation empowered him to appoint any officer, or alternatively, the mining officer of the district in which the dispute arose to hear and determine it. In this case the commissioner had appointed Ms Reihl and the question which arose during the hearing of the appeal was whether she was an officer within the meaning of the regulations.

Regulation 2 of the Mining Regulations provided that 'officer means and includes every district commissioner, assistant district commissioner, mines officer, officer of the Geology and Mines Commission, customs officer, all ranks of the Police Force, every other public officer or justice of the peace specifically appointed by the Minister to act under these Regulations and, when specifically referred to in any particular regulation, rural constables'. George Ch held that as a magistrate Ms Reihl was a public officer in that she was under the Constitution the holder of an office of emolument in the public service of Guyana; and by virtue of that office she was under s 13 of the Summary Jurisdiction Magistrates Act, Cap 3:05, a Justice of the Peace.

He noted, however, that in order to comply with the definition of 'officer' in Reg 2 she must in either capacity be 'specially appointed by the minister to act under the regulations', a matter about which there was no evidence. Still, he continued, the lack of evidence on this issue could be of little moment in the case at hand since her appointment by the minister had not been an issue before the judge who had heard the motion initially.

Aside from whether she had been appointed by the commissioner, the appellant's other contention was that as her appointment to hear disputes under the regulations had not been made by the Judicial Service Commission, her hearing of the dispute was a nullity and therefore her final order ineffective. In amplification of this contention, counsel for the appellant had argued that as Reg 81 had created either a court or a tribunal, then under the Constitution the only authority that was empowered to appoint persons to preside over such a body was the Judicial Service Commission that had been created under Arts 134, 198 and 199 of the Constitution.

George found this contention untenable. He noted that the only provision in the Constitution that was concerned with the appointment of judicial officers, other than judges or the Supreme Court of Judicature was Art 199, the relevant portion of which read as follows:

> (1) The power to make appointment to the offices to which this article applies and to remove and to exercise disciplinary control over persons holding or acting in such offices shall vest in the Judicial Service Commission.
>
> ...
>
> (3) This article applies to the office of Commissioner of Title, Magistrate and to such other offices (not being offices in respect of which provision for the making of appointment is made by any provision of this Constitution other than Art 20) connected with the courts of Guyana or for appointment to which legal qualifications are required as may be prescribed by Parliament.

George Ch then proceeded to hold as follows:

> It is clear from this provision that the only body that is constitutionally empowered to appoint a magistrate is the Judicial Service Commission. But no issue arises in the present case concerning the constitutionality of Ms Reihl's appointment as a magistrate. What is to be considered is whether it is also the function of the Judicial Service Commission to appoint the offices such as those of presiding or hearing officer in a mining dispute under the Mining Act. Aside from the offices of Commissioner of Title and Magistrate the only other offices to which the Judicial Service Commission is empowered to appoint are 'offices ... connected with the courts or for the appointment of which legal qualifications are required'. An 'officer' as defined in the Mining Regulations who is appointed to hear a mining dispute is not required to possess legal qualifications nor can his office, if indeed it can be described as such, be said to be in any way 'connected with the courts' for I understand the expression 'the courts' to mean the traditional civil courts of the country, eg the system of permanent courts established for the resolution of civil and criminal disputes. In my view it would be an unwarranted extension of the meaning of the expression to hold that it embraces any *ad hoc* tribunal that maybe set up for some specific purpose, such as for example a tribunal set up that is under the Commissions of Enquiries Act, Chapter 19:03, or indeed that envisaged for the resolution of mining disputes. And in any event it is for Parliament to prescribe the additional offices to which Art 199(1) would be applicable. Accordingly, the appointment of a hearing officer is not a constitutional appointment.

Having held that the appellant had failed to establish any link between the appointment of Ms Reihl and a breach of his right to a fair trial by an independent tribunal, George Ch also held that both the claim and the procedure used had been misconceived and he dismissed the appeal with costs to the respondents.

## A public office

In *Clement Johnson v Attorney General of Guyana*, Civil Appeal No 21 (1992), the meaning of a 'public office' arose once again, as it had arisen earlier in *Evelyn v Chichester* (1970) 15 WIR, 410 and *Gordon Yaw v Correia* (Guyana Court of Appeal, Case No 12/1973). In the *Clement Johnson* case, George Ch cited approvingly the following four questions posed by Luckhoo Ch in the *Yaw* case for determining whether a person was in the employ of the government, held a public office, and could be regarded as a public officer:

> In order to determine, therefore, whether a 'public office' has been constituted under Arts 125(1) and 96(1) [of the 1966 Constitution] a useful method of ascertainment might be to examine the question in this way:
>
> (1) Is there an 'office' established in the sense afore described with a sufficient degree of permanence and continuity, and which exists apart from the holder? If so, (2) Has an appointment been made to that office in accordance with Art 96 (1)? If so, (3) Is it an office of emolument? If so, (4) Is it an office which involves service with the Government of Guyana in a civil capacity?
>
> When each of these four questions can be answered in the affirmative, then the person who holds the said 'office' could be counted a public officer. In other words, there must be an office (a) held by a person appointed by or on behalf of the Public Service Commission, (b) to serve the State, (c) for an emolument; all of which must be duly satisfied before the person serving could be regarded as a public officer.

## Judicial conduct

In *Bata Shoe Co Guyana Ltd v Commissioner of Inland Revenue*, Crane JA addressed the issue of a judge referring in his judgment to the Budget Speech of the Minister of Finance, particularly the minister's discussion of the motive behind proposed legislation, and the judge's reference to the Attorney General's statement as 'well taken' with him that the spinning out of the appeal procedures by appellants might well result in empty coffers. The judge referred to such appellants as 'tax dodgers and assorted recalcitrant and conscienceless defaulters'. Crane JA declared:

> Speaking for myself, I am substantially in agreement with the ... criticisms that have been levelled against the trial judge for the things he said and for paying regard in the manner he did to the parliamentary history of the matter before

> him, eg, the budgetary proposals and the Minister's remarks relating to the *motive* behind prospective legislation, obviously as a means of exploring the meaning of it ... The better opinion is that judges should eschew such a course.
>
> I cannot too strongly agree with learned counsel for the appellants that it was quite wrong for the judge not only to have referred to the intention behind prospective legislation as having emanated from the lips of the Minister of Finance and the reasons for the enactment of that legislation, but, above all, to have expressed in no uncertain terms his approval, that in the circumstances stated by the Minister, Parliament was justified in imposing whatever conditions it considered just on the right to appeal in order to frustrate the intention of tax dodgers who are not fairly sharing their burden of taxation and who can delay payment of taxes for inordinately long periods by frivolous appeals all of which lead to short collection of revenue and, moreover, to have openly expressed the opinion that 'this is as it should be'.

In *Rambeharry v Ressouvenir Estates Ltd,* Law Reports of Guyana (1971), there was a claim for workmen's compensation in which the medical evidence called on behalf of the workman conflicted with that given on behalf of the employer. It was disclosed at the trial, however, that the employer's doctor had referred the workman to a specialist for treatment, and that at the time of his giving evidence, the workman was still being treated by the specialist. But neither side sought leave to call the specialist. The magistrate before whom the matter was being heard did not see fit to call the specialist, but gave judgment on the medical evidence before him. It was held on appeal that in the interest of justice, the magistrate ought to have exercised his power under the Evidence Ordinance s 88 and called the witness, provided that an opportunity was given to cross-examine him. The matter was referred to the magistrate for that purpose .

In *Sugrim Jeaman v Ressouvenir Estates Ltd,* Law Reports of Guyana (1969), the appellant applied for and was granted compensation by a magistrate on the ground that he had received an injury to his ear in the course of his employment as a cane cutter. On appeal, the Full Court held that the finding by the magistrate in favour of the appellant was unreasonable having regard to the medical evidence upon which, it was held, there was no conflict and reversed the magistrate's decision. The Court of Appeal held that the finding by the magistrate was not unreasonable. It also held that the Full Court was not entitled to make a finding on an issue not raised in the pleadings or evidence.

## Due process

In *Abdool Saleem Yassin and Noel Thomas v Attorney General of Guyana,* Constitutional Appeal No 40 (1996), decided on 30 August 1996, the appellants had been convicted for murder and sentenced to death by hanging. They successfully appealed their conviction and a retrial was ordered by the

Court of Appeal. The attorney-at-law representing the No 2 appellant at the first trial and first appellate proceedings at the Court of Appeal, was later appointed Attorney General of Guyana in October 1992. In December 1992 the retrial of the appellants was completed and both were again found guilty by the jury and sentenced to death by hanging. They again appealed to the Court of Appeal which dismissed their appeal this time around, and affirmed the sentence of death by hanging.

The appellants thereafter filed a constitutional motion where they sought a declaration that the death penalty was unconstitutional, or, alternatively, that the undue delay of their execution ought to result in a commutation of their death sentences to one of life imprisonment. This motion was dismissed by the first instance judge. The appellants appealed the decision of this judge, and their appeal to the Court of Appeal was dismissed. However, at this appellate proceeding certain admissions by the Attorney General were made as to what transpired at the proceedings when the Advisory Council of the Prerogative of Mercy Committee had met in December 1995. He admitted that he was the minister designated by the president under Art 188(2) of the Constitution and by Art 189(1) became Chairman of the Advisory Council on the Prerogative of Mercy created by Art 189. He also stated that the council considered the cases of the appellants and although he took his place as its chairman, he made recommendations to the president in his capacity as the designated minister under Art 190(1). Thereafter, the president directed that the law should take its course.

Based primarily on these admissions of the Attorney General, the appellants yet again instituted a further constitutional motion, this time seeking declarations that the sitting of the Advisory Council on the Prerogative of Mercy on December 1995 was unconstitutional being contrary to Arts 188–90; the recommendations of the Attorney General to the president were unconstitutional and the Advisory Council's decision void; and that their execution by hanging should be stayed until the Advisory Council was properly constituted and had pronounced on the case. Their main argument was that the Attorney General ought not to have sat on the Advisory Council of December 1995, nor should he have recommended to the president as he was in a serious conflict of interest position, he being defence counsel for the No 2 appellant at the first trial and appellate proceedings.

The judge at first instance in relation to this motion dismissed the said motion on the ground that proceedings in the Advisory Council on the Prerogative of Mercy were not justiciable. The appellants appealed to the Court of Appeal arguing that since the Advisory Council was created by the Constitution, and also since the council's advice to the designated minister could influence the right to life of the appellants, the proper constitution of that body was reviewable by the courts, further that the serious conflict of interest which arose out of the fact that the Attorney General had made recommendations to the president when he was in possession of our ought to be in possession of confidential information from the No 2 appellant, who he represented, ought to have led him not to sit as a member on the Advisory Council and not to have recommended to the president. They contended that this impropriety in the procedure of Arts 188–90 was justiciable.

The Attorney General countered that Arts 188–90 of the Constitution conferred no fundamental rights to the appellants; that the prerogative of the president to grant or not to grant mercy is purely discretionary and hence should not be a matter which the court should review; that even if it were justiciable, he having been appointed the designated minister by the president was bound by necessity to sit in the Advisory Council and to recommend to the president.

The Court of Appeal held that Arts 188–90 of the Constitution are prerequirements which must be complied with before a condemned person is deprived of his life. Any substantial breach of the provisions of these Arts 188–90 could amount to a contravention of the Constitution, more particularly Art 138(1), the Article on the right to life.

George Pres declared:

> Under the Constitution, the pronouncement of a sentence of death by a court competent to do so for an offence for which that sentence is permitted, does not lead to the automatic execution of the convicted person. In other words, he cannot thereafter at a convenient date suffer execution, for there are Arts 188 to 190 to be complied with. In other words, until the requirements of those Articles are adhered to, no execution can take place. The condemned person cannot be therefore lawfully deprived of his life. For the procedures under Arts 188–90 form an integral part of the law as it related to the lawful deprivation of one's life; for it is only after its provisions have been complied with and the President has decided not to intervene that the sentence can be lawfully executed. Viewed from this perspective, it can indeed be said to be an integral part of the criminal justice system. Accordingly, the efficacy of Art 138(1), the right to life, would be stultified unless it is read to include words such as 'and after the President has decided that he would not exercise his powers under Art 188(1)' after the word 'convicted'.
>
> And I propose to read it. Therefore, if there is a substantial procedural breach of the provisions of Arts 188 to 190 it would also amount to a breach of Art 138(1) and could be the subject matter of successful proceedings–as the President would not have properly decided not to intervene – under the breach-redress Art 153.

The Court of Appeal further held that the actual exercise of the prerogative of mercy, namely whether the president should commute a death sentence or not, is outside the pale of judicial review and hence non-justiciable. However, the court has jurisdiction to review the manner in which the decision is reached especially so when the manner of how it is to be reached is spelt out in Arts 188–90 of the Constitution. George Pres stated:

> Provided the processes set out in Arts 188 to 190 of the Constitution are complied with, the exercise of the Prerogative by the President would be outside the pale of justiciability.

The Court of Appeal held, additionally, that the fact that the Attorney General sat in the Advisory Council of the Prerogative of Mercy and recommended as the designated minister to the president was improper in the context of him being previously defence counsel for one of the appellants. It created a serious conflict of interest situation, (which is not mitigated or negatived by his not participating in the actual proceeding in the Advisory Council), and which led to procedural unfairness and impropriety. George (Pres) stated:

> The relationship of lawyer and client and in particular the privilege attendant on such a relationship has long been recognized. It is based on a recognition of the need for free, frank and intimate communication by the client to his legal adviser, and the privilege from disclosure of such communication is the client's. Therefore a lawyer should never allow himself to be placed in the position in which there can be a conflict or the likelihood of conflict between the sacrosanct nature of the information he received from his client, and his loyalty and the consequent need for frankness to another.
>
> This is just the kind of situation in which the Attorney General found himself. To be true to his position as Chairman of the Advisory Council would require his participation in its deliberations. His omission to do so is a silent admission that he must have felt some unease to sit in deliberation over the ultimate fate of condemned persons whose acquittal he had previously espoused. And then under Art 190 in his capacity as Chairman he was required to express his own deliberate opinion, an opinion that would not necessarily represent the view of the Council. It was in my view, a procedural impropriety that the constitutional provision could not have contemplated and judicial fairness would not countenance.
>
> The honesty and frankness of the opinion that he is expected to express to the President may well be in conflict with the requirement of confidentiality that his former relationship engenders.

Fitzpatrick JA declared:

> There was a clear conflict between the duties of Mr De Santos [the Attorney General] to his erstwhile clients, having represented them at earlier stages of their attempts to avoid the ultimate penalty, and his duties as Attorney General and the Minister designated by the President in respect of the proceedings of what is called the Mercy Committee and the tendering of his personal opinion to the President.

Carl Singh (Add J) stated:

> In the instant case, in that *interregnum* between the affirmation of sentence by this court and the Presidential decision that the law should take its course, the constitutional process to determine whether the appellants were to be deprived of their lives or not became tainted with the involvement of the Attorney General through his presence on the Advisory Council which considered the appellants' case ...

> His presence on the Advisory Council nullified all those constitutional procedures relating to consideration for the exercise of the prerogative of mercy for the appellants and renders unenforceable the President's decision that the sentence of death be carried out.

The Court of Appeal held, finally, that the Attorney General's plea of necessity – namely, that onward from his appointment by the President as designated minister until such appointment was revoked, he had no alternative but to act in conformity with the constitutional dictates that flowed from it – did not apply in these circumstances because alternative arrangements could have been made, namely, a reconstituted Advisory Council with a new designated minister. Fitzpatrick JA stated:

> The rule of necessity is recognized in the common law as an exception to the general rule that a biased or prejudiced adjudicator must disqualify himself from participating in a proceeding (see *Flick on Natural Justice*, 1979 edition, pp 138 [*et seq*] on the American cases; also, *DeSmith's Judicial Review of Administrative Action*, 4th edn, by JM Evans, pp 276 and 277).
>
> But the rule of necessity itself has its limitations. One suggested limitation is that the rule does not apply if the disqualification of a member of the group responsible for acting will still leave a forum capable of acting. Another is where an alternative forum exists. Another is where actual bias can be shown (which does not apply here). For the above exceptions see *Flick* at pp 140 and 141.
>
> DeSmith also states: 'But the rules of necessity ought not to be mechanically applied if its enforcement can be an affront to justice' (p 277). The author goes on to make an interesting proposition: 'It may be right for a court to scrutinize the actual conduct of a proceeding closely if the rule cannot wholly be circumvented.' And the deciding factor is: 'If it is possible to constitute a different tribunal unaffected by interest or bias, no difficulty arises.'
>
> It is possible to do so here. Article 188(2) refers to the designated minister as being 'such Minister as may from *time to time* be designated by the President' [my emphasis].
>
> This hardly indicates an appointment of a permanent nature. The words 'time to time' imply an element of transience that contemplates another minister being designated by the President where the circumstances warrant.
>
> And, although the Attorney General is always required to be a member of the Advisory Council (Art 189(1)(b) he is not always the designated minister. Indeed, in England the responsible minister is the Minister of Home Affairs.
>
> I am certain that if, as the government's principal legal advisor, the Attorney General had advised the President that in the circumstance another minister should be designated to chair the council in its consideration of the convictions of Messrs Yassin and Thomas, the President would have had no difficulty whatever in doing so. And as an ordinary member of the council, the Attorney General could have excused himself from attending the relevant meeting.
>
> In the circumstances, the rule of necessity does not apply.

The Court of Appeal thus allowed the Appeal and declared that:

(1) The Attorney General, as the former legal adviser of the appellants in the self same charge for the offence of murder, which engaged the attention of the Advisory Council on the Prerogative of Mercy, ought not to have presided as its chairman.

(2) His presence as the chairman of the council at which the sentences of the appellants were considered vitiated those deliberations.

(3) The opinion expressed by him to the President in that capacity was null and void.

(4) The decision of the President that he would not intervene must be vacated.

## Establishment of a magistrate's jurisdiction

In Criminal Appeal No 7 of 1975, between Tula Ram, Det Const 7325, and Vishnu Ramdass, Crane JA had to deal with the following issue: In what circumstances can a magistrate be justified in inferring from the facts of a case before him that the matter has been proved to be within his jurisdiction? He recalled that in the administration of justice, a magistrate is statutorily enjoined to have regard to the law which invests him with both civil and criminal jurisdiction. That law is to be found in ss 31 and 32 of the Summary Jurisdiction (Magistrates) Act, Cap 3.05, and, in so far as relevant to the question under consideration, it provides as follows:

> 31 The court in each district shall, in civil causes and matters within that district, have the jurisdiction and powers prescribed in, and shall exercise such jurisdiction and powers in the manner provided by, the Summary Jurisdiction (Petty Debt) Act.
>
> 32(1) Subject to the provisions of this and of any other written law, of the court in each district shall, within its district, have full jurisdiction and power –
>
> (a) to hear and determine all complaints or information for summary conviction offences, including complaints or information for the recovery of fines, penalties, or forfeitures not specially assigned by written law to the High Court.

Crane JA observed from the above that magisterial jurisdiction in Guyana is territorial and that a magistrate has no common law jurisdiction (see *Sadler v Wight* (1938) LRBG 1); he has only such jurisdiction as the law confers on him which he must exert so strictly within the confines of his district as delimited by the Magisterial Districts (Boundaries) Order. (See O 15/1956, Subsidiary Legislation, Cap 3:05, p 34.)

The facts at issue in the instant case were provided by the sole prosecution witness, the virtual complainant, a 12 year old girl called Sursattie Ramnauth. In her attempt to prove that the commission of the offence fell within the court's jurisdiction, she replied to a leading question from the police prosecutor that the incident which caused the defendant/respondent to make use of threatening language (to kill her) 'took place at Strathspey, East Coast, Demerara, in the East Demerara Magisterial District'. In this answer, there was an obvious attempt to establish jurisdiction by both indirect and direct proof.

Under cross-examination, however, Sursattie admitted that she did not know what 'magisterial' meant, nor did she know where the cases of offenders were tried when they were charged for committing offences at Strathspey. As mentioned earlier, she was the only prosecution witness, and after her testimony was concluded, counsel for the defendant submitted there was no evidence to show the offence was committed within jurisdiction. The magistrate did not agree, however; he convicted the defendant and fined him $100 with an alternative of two months' imprisonment for having made use of threatening language to Sursattie whereby a breach of the peace may be occasioned.

Crane JA held:

In his reasons for decision, the magistrate referred to the prosecution's attempt to prove jurisdiction by means of a leading question, eg, by a mode that is admittedly uncommendable to anyone reading the record of these proceedings. The means was by a question put to Sursattie whereby (in the words of the magistrate), she was 'led to say that Strathspey is in the East Demerara Magisterial District'. Surprisingly, in spite of this, he considered jurisdiction proved for two reasons, viz, (i) that there was no evidence that Strathspey was anywhere else than in the East Demerara Magisterial District, and (ii) that the inference was compelling that the offence took place within that district because 'the witness was unshaken that Strathspey is on the East Coast of Demerara'.

On appeal, the Full Court did not agree with the above reasons, and after reviewing local authorities from *Humphrey v Crooks* (1914) LRBG 41, to *Stoll v D'Oliviera* (1968) 13 WIR 208, that court concluded, *inter alia*, that the conviction of the defendant/respondent must be set aside since the inference that jurisdiction had been proved ought not to have been drawn in the particular circumstances of this case.

The point on which the decision in this appeal must ultimately turn is the weight of the evidence derived from the means or method of proof employed, viz, the leading question which enabled the court to draw the inference that the village of Strathspey was within its jurisdiction, eg, the East Demerara Magisterial District.

It has been contended by counsel for the appellant that jurisdiction must be proved beyond reasonable doubt and that nothing short of that standard ought to suffice. But, as it seems to me, jurisdiction being a fact must be proved like any other; the standard of proof in relation to it must depend on the nature of the proceedings before the court. In all criminal trials, the general standard is proof beyond reasonable doubt; whereas, in civil cases it is proof on a balance of probability. I, for myself, can see no good reason why these two standards of proof should not obtain.

The conclusion which must be drawn from both principle and the decided cases then is that proof of locality to found jurisdiction has always been the same as it is in England and continues to be the practice in our magistrates' courts; there is no set formula of words to be used in so doing, and such proof may be simply established either by a direct statement that the locality is within the magisterial jurisdiction, or inferentially. But there is no absolute requirement for a direct statement that the locality is 'within this or that magisterial district'. No hard and fast rule can be laid down as to what words should be used. Of course, the name of the locality must be stated. The place must be accompanied by some descriptive word or words so as to prove to the magistrate that the offence was committed within his district. But whatever accompanying words are used, it will always be a question of fact whether proof has been established to his satisfaction so that he can safely infer from the description given that the complainant or plaintiff has brought the offence or suit within his magisterial district.

I am decidedly of the opinion that at the close of the case for the prosecution, the magistrate ought to have acceded to the submission of learned counsel that jurisdiction had not been proved and dismissed the complaint.

## A judge's decision must be made on the evidence

In *F Ramsahoye and Ramjit Singh and Persaud Singh*, Civil Appeal No 16 (1969), decided on 3 April 1970, the appellant/plaintiff, who had been Attorney General of Guyana, claimed that he had paid the defendants to purchase cattle on his behalf and to care for the cattle in return for the benefit of the milk. The respondent/defendants denied the claim and said that the plaintiff had paid them by way of commission for having introduced to him certain people who had requested the plaintiff, in his capacity as Attorney General, to assist in the stifling of certain prosecution. The latter allegation was, however, never pleaded and was not put to the plaintiff in cross-examination. An issue that also arose was whether the receipts involved had been tampered with while in the custody of the plaintiff. Here again, this was not put to the plaintiff, so that he had no opportunity of answering it. As Persaud JA noted in deciding on the appeal 'It was only when the learned judge came to write his decision that this matter was ventilated'. He added:

> I am not saying that the learned judge could not have made such a finding; not by any means. It was quite open to the judge to make a finding of fact, but such a finding must have evidence to support it ...
>
> All in all, the judge seems to have made findings not based entirely on the evidence, and even when there was some evidence he seems to have assessed the weight of that evidence erroneously. He omitted, in my view, to make findings which he would have made. I refer specifically to the finding as to the purpose for which the money was advanced. I feel that this was the crux of the case, the heart of the matter, and it is not satisfactory for a judge to refrain, in those circumstances, from coming down clearly on one side or the other. As I say, this was the main issue raised by the pleadings and I feel the judge was

> required to make a finding on this issue. He failed to do this, and rather based his judgment exclusively on the documents which he found to be tampered with, and in respect of which he expressed the view that it is more likely that they were tampered with when they were in the custody and control of the plaintiff which, as I said ... clearly indicates that the plaintiff was either a party to the tampering, or he himself did the tampering ...
>
> Consequently ... I would allow this appeal. The nature of the evidence being what it is, however, I feel that the best course to adopt in this matter is to order a re-trial ...

## An appeal is from the lower court's decision, not its reasons

In *Vibert de Santos v Francis Approo,* Criminal Appeal No 90 (1969), decided on 15 December 1970, EV Luckhoo Ch dealt with a magistrate's reasons for decision and underlined that an appeal is not from a magistrate's reasons, but rather from his or her judgment. He cited with approval the following passage by Duke J, in *Codlall Hardeen v Ramcharran* (1946) BGLR 35, p 42:

> A magistrate is, however, required by law to state his reasons for any decision against which an appeal is being brought ... it has been laid down by this court, in the general interests of justice, that an appeal under the Summary Jurisdiction (Appeals) Ordinance, Chapter 16, is from the decision of the magistrate and not from his reasons of decision. If the decision of the magistrate is right, it will be upheld by this court, even if this court prefers to base its judgment on circumstances not specifically stated by the magistrate in his reasons. It is not unusual for two or more judges, although they may approach the consideration of a case from entirely different points of view, to arrive at the same result.

## Non-retroactivity

In *Kadar Lall Gobind v HS Cameron et al,* Civil Appeal No 35 (1968), decided on 30 December 1970, Persaud JA dealt with the question whether time which began to run before the enactment on 31 December 1952 of the Title to Land (Prescription and Limitation) Ordinance, Cap 184 can be counted in favour of the appellant towards the compliance of s 3 of the Ordinance. He held that the weight of the authorities was against retroactivity of the ordinance. He cited with approval the following passage from Luckhoo CJ in *Basiran v Brown* (1960) LRBG 232 :

> I do not see that retroactive effect is being given to the provisions of s 13 of the Title to Land (Prescription and Limitation) Ordinance, Cap 184, by holding that title to land is extinguished if some portion, however short, of the period of twelve years, is subsequent to the 31 December 1952. Such a construction of the provisions of s 13 would neither impair nor diminish any vested interest existing before those provisions were enacted.

Persaud JA also cited with approval the following passage by Adams J (Ag) in *Basir v Goolcharan* (1961) LRBG 528, p 533:

> Even if the defendant could not establish 30 years' possession, provided that she could prove, as she has done, sole and undisturbed possession, user or enjoyment for not less than 12 years, part of which fell after 1952, she would be entitled to a declaration of title, if claimed, because the right of every other person to recover the land had expired or been barred and the right of every such person thereto had been extinguished by virtue of the cumulative effect of ss 5 and 13 of the Ordinance.

Persaud JA also cited the case of *Tackorie v Port Mourant Ltd* (1954 LRBG 108), decided soon after the enactment of the ordinance in 1952. He noted that prior to 1952, the courts of Guyana had been unanimous in deciding that adverse possession of 12 years barred the legal owner from recovering his land, but it did not extinguish his title. The Full Court in that case had said (p 110) that 'the distinction was no mere legal conundrum for it meant that if the owner of the legal title could obtain possession of his land other than by action, the adverse possession is of no avail to the stranger'. It was held that s 13 of the ordinance not only operated as a bar to the remedy for possession, but extinguished the title of the owner, to that extent introducing a new doctrine into the law of immovable property 'and it would be abhorrent to common sense and offend one's sense of natural justice if it were to be held that a person in adverse possession for 12 years prior to 1952 had succeeded in extinguishing the title of the true owner'.

Persaud JA continued:

> As I have already indicated, the balance of legal opinion is weighted against retroactivity, and even though the respondents themselves may not have been able to bring an action for possession – as prior to 1952 there was s 4(2) of the Civil Law of British Guiana Ord (Cap 7) to prevent them from doing so – if the petitioner can establish 30 years' uninterrupted possession *nec vi nec clam, nec precario,* he would be entitled to succeed.

## Exercise of judicial discretion

In *Bhupal Persaud, Det Const 7402 and 1 Daneshwar Ramsumeer, 2 Thakur Persaud, 3 Loaknauth c/d Cuttie,* Criminal Appeal No 37 (1980), the issue before the Court of Appeal was the exercise of the judicial discretion of magistrates. At the Wakenaam Magistrates' Court, a request had been made by the prosecutor for a postponement in order that he might produce two persons as witnesses at the next sitting of the court as they were vitally necessary for the conduct of the prosecution's case. The reason given for requesting the adjournment was that one of the witnesses Dharamdeo Mohan had not yet been served with a subpoena to attend court, and that another, Detective Inspector Jagmohan, was busy attending another court in Georgetown as a witness. The magistrate ordered each of the names of the absent witnesses to be called out three times, and when no reply was forthcoming, he recorded 'Case for Prosecution' in his note-book. The matter was then dismissed on a no-case submission by defence counsel.

On appeal to the Court of Appeal by the Director of Public Prosecutions under s 32(a) of the Court of Appeal Act Chap 3:01 as amended by s 8 of the Administration of Justice Act 1978, it was contended that the decision was erroneous in point of law in that the learned magistrate exercised his discretion injudiciously when the he dismissed the case on improper and/or insufficient grounds. The Court of Appeal allowed the appeal and the case was remitted to be dealt with *de novo* by another magistrate.

Crane Ch declared:

> Failure of the magistrate to grant the prosecution at least one adjournment to produce both the absent witnesses was a denial of justice and an error of law of his own creation. Everyone knows how busy magistrates are; they work continuously under sustained pressure. It is understandable they are very anxious to dispose of their cases so as to present reasonably good returns to the Chief Justice each month, but they are not to do so at the expense of justice.[26]

## Evidence

In *Bibi Sahieman Yassin and David Joseph*, Civil Appeal No 63 of 1984, Churaman JA had to deal with a situation in which the trial judge admitted in evidence a document but did not keep it in the custody of the court. Upon appeal the document could not be found. The learned Judge of Appeal declared: 'All admissible evidence, real and documentary ... must be received and preserved for use in the superior courts.'

## Visit to *locus in quo*

In Criminal Appeal No 36 of 1980, *Mahindra Persaud c/d Vishnu; Bernard da Silva and Kennard Barran, Det Cpl 9189*, decided on 22 June 1981, the central issue which had to be determined was in what circumstances a magistrate should conduct a view of the *locus in quo*?

The facts of the case were that the appellants had been charged under s 57 (a) of the Criminal Laws (Offences) Act Chapter 8:01 with the indictable offence of wounding with intent to maim disfigure or disable one Yagendra Kishore. The magistrate elected to hear the matter summarily and convicted the defendants.

26 Much the same problem arose in *State v Douglas James*, Criminal Appeal No 4 (1980), Court of Appeal.

It had been the defence contention that the virtual complainant sustained his injury through an accidental fall from a steep perpendicular drop about seven inches on the parapet from the bitumen surface of the public road. The learned magistrate in his memorandum of reasons said he paid a visit to the scene of the incident and saw for himself that nowhere on the Maria's Lodge public road was there any perpendicular drop of seven inches on to the parapet from the bitumen surface of the road. This led to a ground of appeal that the learned magistrate erred in conducting a view all by himself in the absence of, and without the consent of, either party and that by so doing the trial was vitiated.

The appeal was allowed, and the conviction and sentence set aside.

Crane Ch said:

> Every court of trial has a discretionary power to conduct a view of the *locus in quo*. It is a power that is inherent in every court and one which it must necessarily exercise in appropriate cases subject to certain precautions in the interests of justice, particularly when conducting it with a jury, care must be taken to see no one approaches, and/or puts any improper suggestions to them. A magistrate of course sits without a jury. He performs at one and the same time both magisterial and jury functions; nevertheless, in the light of the authorities, no view can ever be said to be properly conducted by a judge or magistrate if the person charged is not given an opportunity to be present with his attorney-at-law if he is represented, and if the prosecution and such witnesses for the prosecution and the defence as may be deemed material are not also invited to attend.[27]

## CONCLUSION

We set out the Commonwealth jurisprudence on an illegal constitutional groundnorm at the suggestion of lawyers in Guyana. We also set out the record on irregular elections so that one could see the context in which the judges had to operate. Nevertheless, when one looks at the actual cases, one could see the judges striving for the rule of law in technical areas of the law. Sensitive areas were another matter, as we shall see in the next chapter on Fundamental Rights.

27 In this case the local authority of *Williams v Sancho* (1917) LRBG 137 was cited with approval. Other local authorities referred to are *Karamat v Queen* (1955) LRBG 213; [1956] 1 All ER 415; 40 CAR 13; *Tameshwar v Queen* (1957) LRBG 56; 2 All ER 41; CAR 161; AC 476.

# CHAPTER 4

# FUNDAMENTAL RIGHTS

## INTRODUCTION

The Reverend John Smith is one of the heroes of freedom in Guyana and the world. He helped inform the slaves in Guyana about their rights. He was persecuted and denied justice before the courts. The record of his trial was a travesty of justice. It was Massah's law, Massah's court, Massah's jurisprudence and the total denial of justice.

After independence in 1966 and until the restoration of democracy in 1992, Guyana would again experience Massah's law, Massah's court, Massiah's jurisprudence and the denial of justice. This was brought out excruciatingly in an earlier chapter. How would the Guyana Court of Appeal, the highest court in the land, deal with this situation? Was the court a champion of freedom? Or was it a pliant tool in the face of oppressive government, as has been seen all too often in many countries. Alas, one must conclude that the latter was nearer the mark and the law as well as the courts became instruments in the deliberate denial of justice, as will be seen presently.

## MASSAH'S RULE, 1966–92

### *Bata Shoe Co Guyana Ltd v Commissioner of Inland Revenue*[1]

During a time when democracy was snuffed out from the land and a government gave itself whatever electoral majority it wished, the Income Tax (Amendment) (No 2) Act 1970 was enacted and provided that a taxpayer who desired to appeal against an assessment by the Commissioner to the Board of Review must first deposit with the commissioner a tax equal to two-thirds of the tax disputed. To appeal to a judge in chambers the appellant was required to deposit with the commissioner a tax equal to the whole amount of the tax in dispute. The amendment was challenged by the Bata Shoe Company on the ground that it was an encroachment on their right to address themselves to the appropriate court or tribunal for the determination of their civil rights or obligations. Massiah J, who would later join the Court of Appeal and become Chancellor before resigning and becoming Attorney General, held that there

1 (1976) 24 WIR 172.

was no constitutional right of appeal to which the plaintiffs could point and which they could properly say the amendment violated.

The Court of Appeal unanimously upheld his ruling. It is arguable in strict law that the court was right in its finding. But in the circumstances prevailing in the country, where the law was patently being used as an instrument of oppression, the ruling was a blatant denial of justice. Justice, after all, is what the courts are about. Massah's law, Massah's court, and Massah's (Massiah's) jurisprudence resulted in a flagrant denial of justice.

## *Frank Hope v The New Guyana Co Ltd*[2]

The Trade (Caribbean Free Trade Association) Amendment Order, 1971, prohibited a number of commodities from being imported without a licence granted by the competent authority. One of the commodities prohibited was newsprint. The Trade (Control of Import and Export) Amendment Order, 1972, also prohibited a number of commodities from being imported without a licence granted by the competent authority. Printing machinery and bookbinding machinery were among the prohibited commodities.

The New Guyana Co Ltd, newspaper publishers, challenged the constitutional validity of the two orders on the ground that they violated the freedom of expression guaranteed in the Constitution of Guyana. The trial judge, Veira J, held that both orders abridged the applicants' enjoyment of their freedom of expression guaranteed under Art 12 of the Constitution and that no evidence was led to show that they were reasonably required in the public interest.

The Court of Appeal unanimously reversed his decision. They held that the right to import newsprint paper, printing machinery and book binding machinery could not by implication be included in the freedom of expression. Massiah JA, now on the Court of Appeal, held in his judgment that: 'One result of acceptance of the construction for which the respondents contend would be an unwarranted and superogatory judicial enlargement of the area of fundamental rights beyond their clearly demarcated boundaries. Such enlargement would appear to be a matter entirely within the province of Parliament. It is clearly a subject beyond the competence of the courts.' Never mind that the newspapers could not be published for lack of newsprint; never mind that Parliament was the product of rigged elections. Justice was blindfolded. Massah's law, Massah's court, Massah's (Massiah's) jurisprudence and the denial of justice reigned again.

2 (1979) 26 WIR 233.

## *Ameerally v Bentham and Attorney General of Guyana*[3]

In this case it was argued that the criminal charge against Ameerally did not disclose an offence known to the law and that the appellants were entitled to the protection of the courts under the Constitution. However, the Court of Appeal held that the Constitution did not guarantee the appellants a fundamental right not to be charged for an offence unknown to the law. While they may have had a common law right not to be charged for an offense unknown to the law, that common law right had not been enshrined in the Constitution. Justice did not appear on the court's radar screen.

It is hard to resist the conclusion that the court was not only being blind to the requirements of justice but had crossed the line into spinelessness or complicity.

## *In Re Norris Williams and Cecil Salisbury*[4]

In this case the appellants requested a magistrate to refer a question of a contravention of a protective provision of the Constitution to the High Court for its determination but the magistrate made no ruling. The appellants petitioned the High Court for a writ of certiorari to direct the magistrate to refer the question to the High Court for determination.

On appeal Massiah JA held that the High Court had no power to grant such a writ because there was no reference by the magistrate to the High Court of any question of a contravention of a fundamental right or freedom. According to him, the proper procedure was to approach the High Court for a determination of a substantive constitutional question. Massah's law, Massah's court, Massah's (Massiah's) jurisprudence, and a denial of justice prevailed again.

## *Jaundoo v Attorney General of Guyana*[5]

This case involved a challenge to the compulsory taking of property. The applicant, by originating notice of motion, applied to the High Court under Art 19 of the 1966 Constitution, which prohibited the compulsory acquisition of property except under prescribed circumstances. The High Court dismissed the application on the procedural ground that an originating notice of motion was not the proper procedure and that the application should have been made by writ of summons. The Court of Appeal by a majority decision dismissed her appeal.

3 (1977) 25 WIR 272.

4 (1979) 26 WIR 133.

5 [1971] AC 972; 3 WLR 13.

The applicant appealed to the Privy Council (whose jurisdiction had not yet been rescinded). The Privy Council allowed her appeal and held that since neither Parliament nor the rule-making authority had by then made provision with respect to practice and procedure the method to apply to the High Court was unqualified. The right was wide enough to cover application by any form of procedure by which the High Court could be approached to invoke the exercise of any of its powers and an originating notice of motion was one of the ways by which the court could be approached.

For the Court of Appeal the applicant would have been denied access to justice on a formality. It was subsequently provided by statute that an application to the High Court may be made either by way of originating motion or by way of writ of summons.

## Assessment

Cases such as these help to explain the following submission of Professor Clive Thomas to the Select Committee on Constitutional Reform in 1996:

> The past three decades have been littered with breaches in, and the erosion of, the 'fundamental rights' of citizens of Guyana, as they are traditionally recognised in democracies. The courts have played no small role in this unfortunate situation, despite the catalogue of entrenched fundamental rights in the 1980 Constitution, which were carried over from the original Independence Constitution. The provision of 'exceptions' to these rights under the 1980 Constitution have also helped to pave the way for this outcome. Emergency legislation has been invoked without the prior declaration of a State of Emergency and has been used as a weapon clearly aimed at regime survival as distinct from protection of the State against serious security threats. The National Assembly has also failed to make any noticeable progress in the provision of court practice and procedures, for the enforcement of fundamental rights.[6]

# THE OPENING

Following the end of the Cold War, and with the push for democracy, Guyana began to open up, already in the second Presidency of President Desmond Hoyte. One could see a corresponding relaxation in the Courts, which we present below.

6 Taken from the text of the original submission. Copy provided by the Secretariat of the Select Committee.

## *Mohamed Ali v The Teaching Service Commission*, 14 May 1991

The appellant, a head teacher dismissed by the respondent commission, brought an action in the High Court in which he claimed an infringement of his constitutional right to a fair hearing guaranteed under Art 144 of the Constitution. He contended that contrary to the regulations, rules of natural justice and customary procedure, he was never charged with an offence nor given an opportunity to exculpate himself prior to his dismissal.

The Commission responded by alleging that the appellant had committed acts of gross misconduct rendering him unfit for the job and that the proceedings were misconceived in law. At the hearing, counsel for the commission submitted *in limine* that:

- The commission was not a suable entity.
- The commission was a statutory body and as such any person seeking redress against it must comply with the Justices' Protection Act, Chapter 5:07.

The trial judge upheld the latter submission and rejected the first. The appellant appealed the dismissal of the action.

George C delivered the judgment of the Court of Appeal which held that the authority given by Art 13 of the 1961 Constitution (now Art 153) to the Legislature to confer supplementary powers on the High Court must be construed as empowering procedures that facilitate rather than hinder the effective vindication of any rights and freedoms. It would amount to an unnecessary or illegal fetter on those rights to insist on compliance with the provisions of the Justices' Protection Act as a condition precedent to the institution of an action. The appeal was allowed and the matter was remitted to the trial judge for a continuation of the action.

Article 13 of the 1961 Constitution was similar in all material respects to Art 19 of the 1966 and 1970 Constitutions and Art 153 of the 1980 Constitution. The relevant portions read as follows:

> (1) If any person alleges that any of the provisions of this Part of this Constitution has been, is being or is likely to be contravened in relation to him then, without prejudice to any other action with respect to the same matters which is lawfully available, that person may apply to the Supreme Court for redress.
>
> (2) The Supreme Court shall have original jurisdiction –
>
> (a) to hear and determine any application made by any person in pursuance of the preceding paragraph; and for securing the enforcement of any of the provisions of this Part of the Constitution to the protection of which the person concerned is entitled: 'Provided that the Supreme Court shall not exercise its powers under this paragraph if it is satisfied that adequate means of redress are or have been available to the person concerned under any other law;

...

(6) A law of the legislature may confer upon the Supreme Court such additional or supplementary powers as may appear to be necessary or desirable for enabling the court more effectively to exercise the jurisdiction conferred upon it by paragraph (2) of this article and may make provision with respect to the practice and procedure of the court while exercising that jurisdiction.

Paragraph 1 empowered an aggrieved party to apply to the Supreme Court (now the High Court) for redress in the event of a perceived or anticipated breach of any of his rights as set out in Arts 1–12; and para 2 gives that court an original jurisdiction, a jurisdiction hitherto unknown, to hear and determine such issues. Paragraph 6 empowered Parliament to confer additional and supplementary powers on the Supreme Court in order to enable it to more effectively t exercise this jurisdiction and also to make provision with respect to the practice and procedure of the court in the exercise of that jurisdiction.

The Fundamental Rights (Practice and Procedure) Act 1988, No 13 of 1988 designated the writ of summons and the originating motion as the procedure for invoking the fundamental rights jurisdiction of the court.

The learned Chancellor held that the authority given to the Legislature to confer additional or supplementary powers on the High Court must be construed as empowering procedures that *facilitate* rather than hinder the effective vindication of any breach or perceived breach of any of the fundamental rights and freedoms provided for in the Constitution.

## (b) Election petitions

Article 163 of the 1980 Constitution of Guyana provides that the High Court shall have exclusive jurisdiction to determine any question whether an election has been unlawfully conducted or the result thereof has been or may have been affected by any unlawful act or omission. In *Stanley Singh v Esther Perreira;* and *Janet Jagan v Esther Perreira,* Notice of Motions Nos 97B and 98B of 1998, the applicants, Stanley Singh and Janet Jagan, applied for an extension of time to appeal the decision of the learned chief justice whereby she had granted leave to Esther Perreira on the 24 February 1998 to present an election petition. Kennard C noted that a matter of considerable constitutional importance had been raised of which there was no prior decision of the Court of Appeal, namely whether it is a condition precedent to the presentation of an election petition in the High Court that the intended petitioner must obtain leave of the High Court, and if leave is required how is the court to be approached for such leave, bearing in mind that there were at the time no provisions, statutory or otherwise, setting out the procedure to be adopted.

He cited with approval the following *dictum* of Lord Keith in *Attorney General of Trinidad and Tobago v Whiteman* [1990] 2 WLR 1202: 'The language of a constitution falls to be construed, not in a narrow and legalistic way but broadly and purposively as to give effect to its spirit.'

Kennard C noted that Art 163(3) by itself does not suggest that leave is necessary before an election petition is presented. That sub-Article gave the right to a citizen who applies to a judge of the High Court for leave to present an election petition to appeal to the Court of Appeal from a refusal to grant such leave. In addition, it gave to a citizen a right to appeal the order of a High Court judge who had granted to another citizen leave to institute proceedings by way of election petition. In the particular facts of the case at hand he asked the question: '... how can a person appeal the grant of leave to present an election petition if that person is not aware that leave has been granted,' and continued, 'Can it not be reasonably argued that leave of the Court to Appeal is necessary before an election petition is presented?'. In the particular facts of the case at hand he granted the applicants an extension of seven days within which to file the necessary appeals.

## Right to property

In Civil Appeal No 43 of 1994, decided in January 2000, the Court of Appeal had to deal four square with the right to property in the 1980 Constitution of Guyana. Kennard C and Prem Persaud JA held that: '... the power of Eminent Domain is an essential attribute of sovereignty and it connotes the legal capacity of the State to acquire private property for public purposes ... and there is no need to confer this authority expressly by the Constitution as it exists without any declaration to that effect.' Churaman JA entered a powerful and magisterially reasoned dissent which we discuss later.

# CONCLUSION

In this chapter we have presented only a snapshot of the cases in order to give an indication of the tenor of the Court of Appeal in dealing with human rights issues. We would conclude with one observation: the Guyana Court of Appeal must embrace the jurisprudence of international human rights law as superbly presented in Appendix A below: 'The Georgetown Conclusions on the Effective Protection of Human Rights Through Law.'

We shall turn now to some basic areas of the law as dealt with by the Guyana Court of Appeal, starting with sources of law.

# CHAPTER 5

# SOURCES OF LAW

## INTRODUCTION

In this chapter we present some cases of the Guyana Court of Appeal, touching on the sources of law in Guyana.

## SOVEREIGNTY

In Civil Appeal No 43 (1994), decided on 26 January, 2000, the majority opinion had recourse to the attributes of sovereignty in the following terms:

> The power of Eminent Domain then seems to be an essential attribute of sovereignty and connotes the legal capacity of the State to take private property of individuals *for public purposes*. Since it is an inseparable incidence of sovereignty there is no need to confer this authority expressly by the Constitution, and it exists without any declaration to than effect. But because it is used for *public purposes* there must be constraint within certain limits and there must be safeguards subject to which the right may be exercised.

In his powerful dissenting opinion, Churaman JA was scathing in his denunciation of what he considered a departure from the Constitution:

> One must keep in the forefront of one's mind that our Constitution does not, neither in Art 40 nor 142, speak of compulsory acquisition or deprivation of property for *public purposes*. It is important to bear this in mind for this reason pivotal to the reasoning of my brethren in the instant appeal is the argumentation in each judgment that 'public purpose' is an essential prerequisite for the right of the State to acquire private property, that is to say, the property must have been taken for some public purpose. With all due respect, our Constitution simply does not say so, and it seems to me, with deep respect, to be something of a confusion of thought to engraft upon our Constitution the essential prerequisite of the American concept of Eminent Domain in justification of the conduct of the Government of Guyana in this matter. Our Constitution is the supreme law of the country. It does not exempt the Government from the constraints imposed by the Constitution, by taking property for public purposes. However public the purpose, however noble the purpose, the Government – the executive – simply cannot take private property under the guise that it is being taken for public purposes.

## LEGISLATION

The Court of Appeal has proceeded on the basis of a presumption of the constitutionality of legislation and, in the words of Prem Persaud JA in Civil

Appeal No 43 (1994), decided on 26 January 2000: '... it is for those who contend otherwise to establish to the satisfaction of the court that it is unconstitutional, and it is for the party who attacks the validity of the legislation to show that it is arbitrary and unsupportable.' He cited in support of this view the American case of *Middleton v Texas Power and L Co*, 249 US 152, p 157, where the US Supreme Court said:

> It must be presumed that a Legislature understands and correctly appreciates the needs of its own people, that its laws are directed to problems made manifest by experience and that its discriminations are based on adequate grounds.

He also cited the local case of *Attorney General v Mohamed Alli* (1987) 41 WIR 176, p 189 where Chancellor Massiah (see Appendix E below) advised that: '... there must be borne in mind also that there exists a presumption in favour of the constitutional validity of an impugned enactment.' He further cited the following passage from Basu's *Commentary on the Constitution of India*, 5th edn, Vol l, p 199:

> The most important of the self-imposed limits upon the power of judicial review both in the United States and in India is the presumption in favour of the constitutional validity of a statute which is challenged as unconstitutional.

He further cited *Pillai v Mundanayake* [1955] 2 All ER 833 where Lord Oaksey dealt with a challenge to the constitutional legality of legislation in Sri Lanka as follows:

> The principle that a legislature cannot do indirectly what it cannot do directly has always been recognized by their Lordships' Board, and a legislature must, of course, he assumed to intend the necessary effect of its statutes. But the maxim *omnia praesumuntur rite esse acta* is at least as applicable to the Act of a legislature as to any other acts, and the court will not be astute to attribute to any legislature motives or purposes or objects which are beyond its power. It must be shown affirmatively by the party challenging a statute which is, on its face *intra vires*, that it was enacted as part of a plan to effect indirectly something which the legislature had no power to achieve directly.

## THE PRINCIPLES OF NATURAL JUSTICE

In *In the Matter of an Application by Kemp Roberts for a Writ of Certiorari v Attorney General of Guyana*, Civil Appeal No 35 (1991), decided on 5 July 1994, Barnard JA prayed in aid the principles of natural justice in the following passages from her judgment:

> The principles of natural justice cannot be circumvented by utilizing a short cut in achieving the desired objective of removing an employee from office. The errant constable or public servant is entitled to be heard before any disciplinary action is taken against him especially if such action is likely to affect his ability to earn a living in the future and any financial entitlements. Dismissal is not an option to be exercised lightly by those who exercise disciplinary control over

> others. To emphasize the need to apply the *'audi alteram partem'* rule before any tribunal or person in an administrative position exercises the option of dismissal. I refer to the *dictum* of Kelly CB in the case of *Wood v Wood* LR 9 Exch 190 at p 196: 'This rule is not confined to the conduct of strictly legal tribunals but is applicable to every tribunal or body of persons invested with authority to adjudicate upon matters involving civil consequences to individuals.'
>
> The principles of natural justice and more specifically the *'audi alteram partem'* rule was applied recently and addressed extensively by all the justices of this court in the case of *Kenneth Wyndham Barnwell ... Attorney General et al* (CA No 84/1991) which concerned removal from office of a judge of the High Court. This court was unanimous in its finding that the judge ought to have been given an opportunity to be heard by the Judicial Service Commission before that body represented to the President that the question of his removal ought to be investigated as provided for under the Constitution.
>
> For all of the reasons stated above, I find that the Commissioner of Police wrongly invoked his powers under s 35(1) of the Police Act, Cap 16:01 to discharge the appellant from the Police Force instead of utilizing the procedure laid down in the Police (Discipline) Act, Cap 17:01, and as such deprived the appellant of the right to be heard before he was dismissed. This rendered his actions void for failure to comply with the statutory provisions ...

## INTERNATIONAL STANDARDS

In Civil Appeal No 43 (1994), decided on 26 January, 2000 Prem Persaud JA had recourse to international standards in determining the legality and constitutionality of an order deferring the payment of a debt owed by the Government for 12 years:

> And judged by international standards also, the order of 1992 is not arbitrary, whimsical or fanciful. UN resolution 1803(xvii) stresses the primacy of the State's own laws. The relevant portion reads: 'Nationalization, expropriation or requisitioning shall be based on grounds or reasons of public utility, security or the national interest which are recognized as overriding purely individual or private interests, both domestic and foreign.'

## THE WRITINGS OF PUBLICISTS

The judgments of the Court of Appeal are replete with citations from learned treatises. In Civil Appeal No 43 (1994), decided on 26 January 2000, the majority, as was seen above, incorporated into the Constitutional and legal order of Guyana the American doctrine of Eminent Domain. Prem Persaud JA approached the matter thus:

> Learned Senior Counsel for the appellant raised the question of 'Eminent Domain' in presenting his case that the Order was properly enacted and not in breach of the respondent's constitutional rights. Eminent Domain is an American concept. *The Osborn's Concise Law Dictionary* (1993) defines it as a

> 'doctrine originating in the United States giving the government the right to take private property for public purposes. In international law the State is regarded as not only having power of disposition over the whole of the national territory, but also as being the representative owner of both the national territory and all other property found within its limits'.

As was seen above, the majority in that case held that the power of Eminent Domain was 'an essential attribute of sovereignty.

In approaching the question whether there was deprivation or compulsory acquisition of property, and if there was adequate compensation paid, Prem Persaud JA found 'a useful classification which assists in ascertaining the true nature of an expropriatory legislation' in *Cheshire and North's Private International Law,* 12th edn, and cited *in extenso* its fourfold classification of expropriatory legislation into (i) requisition; (ii) nationalisation; (iii) compulsory acquisition; and (iv) confiscation.

## CONCLUSION

The jurisprudence of the Court of Appeal on the Sources of Law would need to be carefully watched in the future as it is fundamental to the future development of the rule of law in Guyana. As we shall see in the following chapter, the Guyana Court of Appeal has been brilliant in its development of the criminal law in Guyana, notwithstanding the difficult political environment.

# CHAPTER 6

# CRIMINAL LAW

## INTRODUCTION

### The environment in which the courts have had to function

In the period 1968–92, as was seen in previous chapters, the legal system of Guyana was controlled by governments that rigged successive elections and used the law for narrow partisan purposes. This included even the criminal law. The Administration of Justice Bill 1978 was deemed 'obnoxious' by the Guyana Bar Association because it contained the following features:

(a) It removed in the majority of cases, the right of the accused to elect to be, and to be tried by a judge and jury.

(b) The jurisdiction of magistrates was enlarged to try most indictable offenses.

(c) The jurisdiction was amended to allow the upward and downward movement of judges of the High Court and the Court of Appeal on a selective basis.

(d) The Court of Appeal might enter a guilty verdict where the accused had been acquitted by jury.

(e) Any number of complaints may be heard by a magistrate.

(f) Funds allegedly obtained by fraud by convicted persons could be recouped from family and dependents.

The purpose of the Criminal Law Bill was to make it possible at the magistrate's discretion to try hybrid offences, eg indictable offences, summarily rather than by judge and jury. The Guyana Bar Association boycotted the courts in protest at the measure. The Organization of Commonwealth Bar Associations (OCCBA) condemned the Bill for:

(1) Its infringement of the citizen's right to trial by jury.

(2) Its introduction of the Criminal Law Bill as legislation calculated to have retrospective effect on pending criminal proceedings to annul decisions of courts of justice and to abrogate the civil liberties of the citizens of Guyana.

(3) Its hasty passage of important legislation in such a manner as to deprive the public and the legal profession a fair opportunity to examine and comment on such legislation.

The task of the courts in such an environment was not an easy one. Nevertheless one saw in the Guyana Court of Appeal traces of the majesty of the law.

## THE MAJESTY OF THE LAW

Nevertheless, it must be said of the Guyana Court of Appeal that while the political environment in which it had to deal during the first decades after independence was a testing one, with an environment of political and other corruption, the court nevertheless managed to maintain a high level of technical proficiency in areas such as the criminal law. One saw the majesty of law in motion in the following words of Chancellor Haynes in *State v Ronald Gajraj* (1978) WIR 138:

> This court does not sit to determine whether a convicted man is 'guilty' or 'not guilty' of the crime for which he was charged and convicted. That was the jury's function. What we usually sit here to do, in our criminal jurisdiction, is to review what happened at the trial and determine whether it was a fair one. It if was, we may dismiss the appeal. If it was not, we may quash the conviction: A trial in law may be unfair if it is not conducted in accordance with those cardinal rules of law and procedure laid down by judges for centuries, and I would say, by Parliament, to ensure that no one shall be found guilty of a crime he did not commit or to reduce as much as practicable the risk of this happening. Because these rules are made to protect the innocent, they place a fundamental and inescapable duty on this court, a duty we will never hesitate to perform. In this sensitive area the appearance of justice is part of the substance of it. And if because we have to insist that trials be conducted according to law guilty men may go free, this is an adversity society must bear if the innocent are to be protected.

In *State v Baichandeen* (1979) 26 WIR 228, the same Chancellor, one of the brilliant sons of the law in Guyana, expanded on his own pronouncement as follows:

> When a trial is not conducted according to law this court may be obliged, to use the description of Byrne J in *R v Patel* [1951] 35 CAR 62, p 66, to steer between the Scylla of releasing to the world unpunished an obviously guilty man and the Charbydis of upholding the conviction of a possibly innocent man. In such a case the court would lean to the more merciful course, since it is better to release the guilty than to run the risk of convicting the innocent.

# THE PROVINCE OF THE JURY

The Court of Appeal has given clear guidance on the province of the jury. In *Jennifer Swamy v State*, Criminal Appeal No 28 (1988), decided on 20 September 1991, the appellant was convicted of the offence of murder. At the trial, the evidence relied on by the prosecution was the impression of a palm print found at the scene of the crime. At the hearing of the appeal, the point considered was whether the trial judge had misdirected the jury as to the manner in which expert evidence tendered by the prosecution was to be regarded.

The evidence led by the prosecution was enough to establish a *prima facie* case against the appellant. The question of belief or disbelief of the evidence of a witness was, the Court of Appeal held, a matter for the jury, who could either accept or reject any witness's evidence, including one whom the trial judge deemed an expert.

The direction given by the trial judge to the jury, that they should not lightly disregard the opinion of the expert unless they had good reasons for doing so, was held to have been a clear misdirection, something that the Court of Appeal had already pronounced upon in *State v Baichandeen* as being misleading for several reasons: (1) it might have erroneously suggested to a jury that there was a rebuttable presumption in favour of the acceptability of expert evidence; (2) a juror might feel obliged to accept expert evidence which he lacked knowledge to find good reasons to disbelieve because no direction was given in relation to other witnesses who did not give expert testimony; (3) the juror might expect the defence to produce the good reasons for him not to accept the testimony; (4) the juror might assume expert evidence to stand in an exceptional position which required good reasons for disbelief, as opposed to reasonable doubt in the case of the ordinary witness.

In *State v Baichandeen*, the learned judge had told the jury in respect of the testimony of an expert witness:

> I accept him as an expert because of his post and experience and therefore, his opinion must be considered. But members of the jury you are not bound to accept his opinion because it is a question of fact, but you must have a good reason why you should not accept his opinion. If you can say his reasoning is bad, you need not accept his opinion but consider him a man with so many years of experience in the Fire Service.

In dealing with this direction, Haynes C said ((1979) 26 WIR 224):

> We think that this direction should not be given and would have been misleading even though put as a matter of fact and not of law. In the first place, it is the burden of the prosecution to establish good reasons why the evidence of any of their witnesses should be accepted and to put it this way is that you must accept the evidence of the prosecution witness unless you have good reason to disbelieve it – would or might at least suggest erroneously to a jury that there is a sort of rebuttable presumption in favour of the acceptability of

expert evidence. Secondly, if it is the right approach for a juror to say to himself: 'I must believe this witness, unless there are good reasons not to do so,' he might feel mistakenly that he was under some sort of obligation to accept expert evidence which he lacks the knowledge to find good reasons to disbelieve, more so, because no such direction was given in relation to the other witnesses, who did not give expert testimony.

Thirdly, he might well come to think that the defence should produce the good reasons for him not to accept the testimony, since it could hardly be the duty of the prosecution to do so.

Finally, what is the juror to do if he is in doubt about the reliability of the expert evidence? He might well feel this kind of evidence stands in an exceptional position, so that, although reasonable doubt about the evidence of the ordinary witness is enough for not acting on it, for expert evidence it would not be since only good reasons to disbelieve it would justify not acting on it. So this was a grave misdirection. If Norton's was the only evidence implicating the appellant, the conviction could not stand.

## THE CONSCIENCE OF THE GUYANESE NATION AND THE SENSITIVITIES OF THE WORLD

In *Yaseen and Thomas v Attorney General et al*, Civil Appeal Nos 19 and 20 (1996), Churaman JA addressed the issue of the normative standards that should guide the Courts of Guyana. He was dealing with the issue of delays in carrying out the death penalty. He stated the following:

> I dissent and dissent strongly, from any suggestion that a period of delay should be preordained as a fixed or inflexible one by which every case be measured and judged. Such an approach is, in my respectful view, too arbitrary, too rigid, and absolute in dealing with a concept as amorphous as delay. Each case must be determined on its own merits. In determining whether a period of delay is so prolonged or unconscionable as to conclude that the sentence of death ought to be commuted, the court is engaged in a balancing process. How long is too long? In my view the court must take account of the length of the delay, the diverse circumstances under which the delay arose, the reasons for the delay and any element of culpability that may be attributed to such delay ...
>
> And it is only too well known, the speed and efficiency of any appellate system, indeed the whole legal system, is closely determined by the quality of the support legal services a State is financially able and/or willingly to sustain ...
>
> In conclusion, on the more general question of delay, I am of the clear view that whether the delay in executing a sentence of death is so prolonged as to make the punishment when it comes inhuman or degrading in terms of Art 141 of the Constitution is a question which the judiciary must answer by posing to itself the further question whether such execution is likely to shock the conscience of the Guyanese nation. *That is the test I would propose*. Inhumanity

> and degradation in the context of punishment is something that reaches out to man's inner conscience. To concatenate the question to the nation's conscience will be, in my view, to sustain a link between contemporary community values and the penal system itself, and thus serve to bond the community with the due administration of justice which is itself intended to serve the community at large. It is this link between community values and the penal system which gives meaning to the expression 'the evolving standards of decency that mark the progress of a maturing society'. At the end of the day the judiciary must accept the responsibility of answering the question as profoundly philosophical as this by a reference to the nation's sense of moral values and standards of decency, and the nation's compassion for mankind. *In discharging this responsibility the judiciary should intercede to restrain the due process of the penal system if, but only if, an execution has been so long delayed that to implement it, when proposed, is likely to shock the conscience of the Guyanese nation.*

In Civil Appeal No 55 (1997), a matter of the Fundamental Rights and Freedoms of Individuals under the Constitution of Guyana (*Persaud and Rampersaud v Attorney General of Guyana and the Director of Public Prosecutions*), Kennard C added to this another element: 'I would add "the sensitivities of the world at large".' He considered that the lapse of a period of six and a half years between the date of the convictions and the reading of the warrant was not so unconscionable that to execute the appellants after this lapse of time was likely to shock the conscience of the Guyanese nation and the sensitivities of the world because 'things were always happening'. Positive actions were being taken at all stages. It was not a case where the relevant authorities were merely sitting idly and taking no action since the date of the convictions.

## FUNDAMENTAL PRINCIPLES

In *Omar Persaud v Jaitoon*, Criminal Appeal No 70 (1974), Haynes JA declared the following:

> It is the duty of the prosecutor to tender all material and relevant evidence available to him and necessary to establish a *prima facie* case, before he closes his case. But if for one reason or another he fails to do so, that is not the end of the matter. He would have no right to reopen his case to lead further evidence. But the magistrate has both a statutory and a common law inherent discretion to allow the prosecution to reopen for further evidence. This discretion is to be exercised judicially, not arbitrarily or capriciously or as a matter of course. The prosecutor must disclose to the court a judicially acceptable reason or excuse for the omission, and satisfy it that the ends of justice require that the discretion be exercised in his favour. But the court will bear in mind that, as the interests of justice include the interests of the defence as well as those of the prosecution, it would be wrong to allow the prosecution then to repair their omission, if this would or might cause injustice or improper prejudice to the defendant or be otherwise unfair to him.

> The court may properly allow a reopening before the defence opens or during its course or even after its close, and then let in evidence without which the complaint might be dismissed. Such evidence might be proof of a purely procedural matter or might form a vital part of the proof of guilt itself. But a prosecutor should make his application at the earliest possible opportunity, because the later the stage at which he acts the heavier is the onus of justifying the claim to the exercise of the discretion in his favour. And although this discretion is the magistrates and his alone to exercise as he thinks fit once he acts judicially, yet the circumstances of a case might be such that it becomes his duty to exercise it in one particular way.

## SELF-DEFENCE

In *Donald Gunputh v State*, Criminal Appeal No 17 (1991), Persaud JA dealt at length with the issues of self-defence and provocation, and the duty of the trial judge in presenting the evidence on these issues to the jury. The jury, he held, should have been told that if they were of the view that the attack on the appellant was such that defence was reasonably necessary, it would be recognized that a person defending himself cannot weigh to a nicety the exact measure of his defensive action. If the jury thought that in a moment of unexpected anguish the appellant had done only what he honestly and instinctively thought necessary, that would be the most potent evidence that only reasonably defensive action had been taken. The trial judge should have left for the jury's determination the issue of self-defence which was raised by the defence. Once there is material sufficient to raise the issue, it becomes a matter for the jury, and not for the judge to decide whether or not the material is adequate to determine the issue in favour of the accused. He cited with approval the following *dictum* from Luckhoo JA in *R v Wilbourne and Walters* (1971) 17 WIR 100:

> Even though it might well be said that it was not probable that they would have so concluded, so long as it is possible that they might have done so, the question ought not to be left for their determination.

## PROVOCATION

In the same case, Persaud JA dealt with the issue of provocation in the following terms:

> Provocation has long been held to be 'some act or series of acts done or words spoken by the deceased to the accused which would cause in any reasonable person and actually causes in the accused a sudden and temporary loss of self-control, rendering the accused subject to passion, as to make him for the moment not master of his mind'. Provocation included provocation emanating from sources other than the victim. Provocation consists of three elements: '... the act of provocation; the loss of self-control; both actual and reasonable, and the retaliation proportionate to the provocation.'

In that case, in his direction to the jury the trial Judge had omitted to point out to them that the plea of provocation might still have arisen if the appellant had formed an intention to kill or inflict grievous bodily harm which resulted in death, but his intention to do so arose from sudden passion induced by the provocation. That was a grave omission. The withdrawal of the issue of self-defence from the jury by the learned trial judge, and the grave misdirection on the question of provocation had deprived the appellant of a fair chance of acquittal. Consequently the verdict of murder must be set aside and a conviction for manslaughter substituted.

# IDENTIFICATION

## Identification at the police station

In *Wilfred Methews v State*, Criminal Appeal No 15 (1996), the Court of Appeal was faced with the issue of confrontation between accuser and accused at the police station. After an extensive review of the cases, Kennard C noted that they had clearly established that evidence of such a confrontation should be criticised by the trial judge and if that is done the weight to be attached to this type of identification would be a matter for the jury. (See also *Kirpaul Sookdeo et al v State* (1972) 19 WIR 402 on Dock Identification.) The evidence is certainly relevant so far as the issue of identification is concerned and is, therefore, admissible.

In the instant case the trial judge did not criticize the type of identification used by the police. She merely repeated what took place at the police station but did not in any way highlight the weakness in that type of identification. Kennard C cited the following passage of George Ch in *State v Ramesh Ramdat*, Criminal Appeal No 40 (1988):

> As I have said the whole body of judicial wisdom frowns on an identification that is made as a result of a confrontation between the witness and the alleged assailant especially where the latter was hitherto unknown to the former. The proper course in such a circumstance is to hold an identification parade with all the attendant safeguards which such a parade requires in order to give it authenticity by avoiding any premature meeting between the witness and the suspect prior to the parade. This was not done. Nor were the dangers endemic in the confrontation highlighted to the jury. It was not pointed out to them that the tendency in such a situation would be for the witness to assume that the person in police custody, or, if the identification is first made in court in the dock, he must be the person, who was involved in the offence, as it is unlikely that the police would deliberately arrest someone, other than the person whose description had been given to them ... In my opinion these were serious mistakes.

## The Turnbull Rules

The Court of Appeal has endorsed the English Turnbull Rules on identification evidence. In *State v Michael Greene and Walter Alleyne*, Criminal Appeal Nos 24 and 25 (1978), decided on 24 May 1979, Massiah JA summarized these rules as follows:

> First, there is the requirement that the judge should warn the jury of a special need for caution before convicting the accused in reliance on the identification evidence of one witness, and even where more than one witness identifies him; and he should go on to explain the reason why such caution is needed. He should also refer to the possibility that a witness might be positive and sure of his identification and still be honestly mistaken. This special need for caution must be directed in fit cases even when the identification was made after a long period of observation or in satisfactory conditions by a relative or a neighbour or a close friend or a workmate or the like. For mistakes in identification have been known to occur even in such cases. Secondly, the jury must be told to examine closely the conditions under which the witness or witnesses saw the person identified as the accused at the trial.
>
> Thirdly, he must discuss as such any specific weaknesses in the identification evidence, meaning any circumstances which might tend to weaken its value.
>
> Fourthly, even when a witness is purporting to recognize someone whom he knows, the jury should be reminded that in human experience mistakes in recognition of relatives and friends have been made.
>
> Fifthly, if the quality of the identifying evidence is poor, as for example, when it depends solely on a fleeting glance or even on a longer observation made under difficult conditions, the judge should withdraw the case from the jury and direct an acquittal, unless there is other evidence which goes to support the correctness of the identification. This other evidence may be corroboration in the sense lawyers use that word. But it need not be, if its effect can be to make the jury feel sure of the correctness of the identification evidence in spite of its weakness. For example, a witness gets only a fleeting look at a man's face as he snatched a purse and ran off. Later at a parade he identifies the accused as the thief. If this is all the proof, it would be poor quality identification. It might require the judge to withdraw the case from the jury. But if, in addition, there is evidence that the snatcher was seen to run into a house nearby and it turns out that the accused lived there, this could be sufficient to justify safely leaving all the evidence to the jury to assess its value.
>
> Sixthly, if there is any evidence in the case capable of supporting the identification, the judge should identify it to the jury for them to decide if it does make them feel sure no mistake was made. Similarly, if there is any evidence or circumstance which the jury might think was supporting, when it could not be, the judge should tell them so. For example, he should warn them, where the accused does not give evidence, that this by itself cannot support the identification, and also that if they felt that he told lies about where he was at the material time, this does not by itself prove that he was where the identifying witness says he was. If they believe his alibi, then clearly it would

be a positive case of mistaken identity. But if they disbelieve it, then their duty is to examine closely the prosecution's evidence of identification to see whether a mistake *might* (not *must*) have been made. If so, the jury should be told, the prosecution's case would not have been proved beyond reasonable doubt.

These directions are aimed at guiding the jury to a just verdict in these cases. What underlies it all is the judicial recognition of the possibilities of mistakes in identification, and of the tendency of juries to underestimate the dangers or brush them aside all together and to attribute too great probative value to the fact that the witness is positive and honest. Judges too often sum up in terms which contribute to this, or, at least, do not help to avert it. A direction that they may convict if they 'believe' an identifying witness or think him 'a truthful person', might be faultless if the accused is well known to him and the conditions for recognition are so good that a mistake is a mere remote possibility and the real issue becomes one of credibility. But if it is a case of the identification of a stranger, particularly upon a fleeting glance of his face only, such a direction could result in the conviction of an innocent man and a miscarriage of justice. For then what the jury have to decide would be whether the circumstances of the identification are such that the witness was in a position to make an identification on which it would be safe for them to rely, and not merely whether he is 'honest' or 'truthful' or 'sure'?

So a judge should take care to warn the jury strongly about these matters in such cases. What is required is not a bare or perfunctory and passing reference while reciting the evidence, or at the beginning or ending of the summing up like, for example, 'mistakes are sometimes made' or 'an honest witness might be mistaken', and nothing more. When viewed as a whole, the summing up must ensure that the minds of the jurors are alerted to the practical possibilities of mistake (if any) on the evidence of identification and to the aspects of it to be carefully considered in this respect.

## Identification parade

In *State v Ken Barrow*, Criminal Appeal No 94 (1975), one Richard Beharry had been robbed of a quantity of jewellery by several men, one of whom was alleged to have been the appellant. Beharry told the police that he could identify only one of the men whom he described as a short, dark Negro man with a scar on the left side of his face. An identification parade was held, the appellant being the suspect on it, and, while he bears a scar on the left side of his face, he was the only person on the parade with that distinguishing mark. Beharry identified him without difficulty as the man who held on to him during a brief struggle in front of his door beneath a light while another wounded him and two or three others entered his house. The appellant was convicted for felonious wounding and robbery under arms and was sentenced to a term of imprisonment of five years on each count.

Counsel for the appellant submitted, *inter alia*, that the identification parade was unfair. The court drew counsel's attention to *R v Gerard Frederick Jones* reported in *The Times* of 22 July 1969, where, on an identification parade, the appellant, the suspect on the parade, was dressed in his working clothes covered in oil while the others were well dressed in lounge suits. The police had tried to offset this disadvantage by placing benches in front of the men and draping blankets over them, but the appellant's dirty trousers were visible under the benches and an outsize coat which the police gave him to wear made him more conspicuous. He was readily identified. The English Court of Appeal considered the identification parade to be 'a complete farce' and quashed the appellant's conviction. On the other hand, counsel for the State referred to *R v John* [1975] Crim LR 456, where John had been convicted on the evidence of three witnesses who said he wore a leather jacket when he committee the offence. An identification parade was held and John alone wore a leather jacket on that parade. He appealed against his conviction and his appeal was dismissed, the court holding that the witnesses had based their identification on what they recalled of the man's features, and dress played no part in it. Further, all the witnesses had excellent opportunity to see him.

In the *Ken Barrow* case, Haynes Ch was of the opinion that the *John* case was distinguishable in that there was no evidence that the identification was based on the features rather than the scar, and Beharry never said that he had a good look at his assailant face to face. As already stated the appellant was *the only person* on the parade with a scar on his face. It was this compositional defect about the parade that caused the court much disquiet and led the Chancellor to think that the whole exercise was a farce (p 7). Crane JA reached the same conclusion; to have staged the parade with only one man with a scar on his face was, in his opinion, a 'glaring impropriety' (p 7). Luckhoo JA described it as a 'disadvantage' (p 6) and 'a factor which was likely to militate against him (the appellant)' (p 7).

Having reached the conclusion that the identification parade was unfairly conducted it became important for the court to consider what effect, if any, the identification of the appellant at the parade had on the proof of identification on oath at his trial. The Chancellor stated the general proposition that the two things were interrelated and that the probative strength and reliability of identification at the trial depended on what happened at the parade, a matter which many persons were apt to overlook. In connection with this specific aspect he referred to *United States v Wade* (1967) 388 US 218, pp 235–36, noted in [1974] Crim LR (December) p 682, and to an article on identification parades by Professor Glanville Williams appearing in [1963] Crim LR 479 (pp 479–80, 482). At pp 12–13 the learned Chancellor summarized his views thus:

> The identification at the parade is to my mind the crucial test and not the identification in court. What the witness does in court is just to identify under oath the person he identified not under oath, at the parade. He does not then scan the features of the accused in the dock to decide then if he is the guilty man. He did this at the parade ...

> So that the reliability of the identification in courts truly rests on the reliability of the identification at the parade; and this, in turn, depends in substantial measure on the fairness of the parade itself ...
>
> If the test (the parade) is not completely fair then as a result the identification at the trial might not be as completely reliable, as it should be, for a conviction.

It was the Chancellor's view that since the identification parade was unfair it became important for the trial judge to discuss this aspect with the jury in his summation. But the trial judge failed to do this. It was against this aspect of his summation that much of the court's criticism was directed. At pp 17–18 the Chancellor said:

> In the circumstances of this case, he (the trial judge) should have directed the jury specifically on the need for a parade to be a fair test and on the relevance of any proved unfairness to the reliability of the trial identification. He should have pointed out to them that there was an element of unfairness disclosed in the evidence, and that it was for them to consider and decide how far – if at all – it affected the weight of the trial identification. But nowhere in his summation did the trial judge deal even briefly with this matter. All he did was to read out from his notes the relevant evidence about the parade and the scar ...
>
> A jury is entitled to more assistance than this, where the proof of identification rests wholly on a brief visual observation at night by the victim of a crime of violence during a brief encounter, and an identification parade held 17 days later was manifestly unfair.

These defects in the summing up were considered to be sufficient ground to quash the conviction.

Crane JA agreed. At p 4 he said:

> All he (the trial judge) did was to draw the jury's attention to what Beharry told them in relation to the scar, compared it with what he said in the magistrate's court about the scar, and told them that any inconsistency was a matter for their attention. In other respects he gave them no assistance, for he positively made no mention that there was anything wrong or could be wrong with a parade comprising only one person with a scar; nor did he indicate what effect he thought that fact would have on its value or reliability in proving the identity of the accused.

Crane JA was of the further opinion that at the identification parade Beharry should have been given an adequate caution in the nature of a 'savings clause' to ensure that he understood that he was under no compulsion to identify someone on the parade and that he should only do so if he were positive that his assailant was on the parade. What Beharry was actually told by the police was that 'he should look at the parade and should he recognize any of the persons who visited his house on Monday he must touch the person'. Crane JA considered this to be inadequate in the sense just explained.

Luckhoo JA shared the opinion of his learned brethren that the trial judge's directions in relation to the issue of identification were inadequate. He referred to the circumstances of the parade and then said at p 7:

> It was incumbent on the learned trial judge to draw to the attention of the jury these factors, and to instruct them that such factors must affect the reliability of the parade that was held and diminish the cogency of an identification made in those circumstances. No such warning was given. The dangers inherent in an identification which had taken place in those circumstances were not pointed out to the jury.

In the result, because of the inadequacy of the summation insofar as it related to the circumstances of the identification parade which was patently unfair and its effect on the probative value of the identification of the appellant at the trial, the court was unanimously of the opinion that the appeal should be allowed and the conviction quashed.

## CONFESSION STATEMENTS

In the cases of *Gobin* and *Griffith,* the Court of Appeal considered the law for Guyana on the admissibility of confession statements. In the case of *Gobin,* he had made a statement confessing his misdeed and, at his trial, objected to its admissibility on the ground that it was not made by him nor on his instructions. He alleged that the signature was elicited from him by threats of violence, and by actual violence he was forced to sign and write on the statement. The trial judge admitted the statement without holding a *voir dire* telling the jury that as the accused was saying it was not his own statement, its admissibility was a matter of fact for them to decide.

In the *Griffith* case, the accused objected to the admissibility of a confession statement on the ground that force and violence were used in order to obtain it from him. He alleged he had been pushed about, cuffed in the abdomen and as a result was induced to sign the confession. At the *voir dire,* it turned out that he was complaining that the statement had been prepared beforehand by the investigating officer and he was ill-treated in the manner described to sign it. At this point, the trial judge halted the trial within a trial and ruled that as the accused was not saying he was beaten to sign a statement of which he was the author but a statement concerning which another person in fact was the author, it became a question of fact for the jury whether or not the statement was that of the accused. He thereupon refrained from ruling on voluntariness, although he admitted the statement and caused it to be read to the jury.

The Court of Appeal held in each case that the trial judge had erred in ruling that the objection did not raise the issue of voluntariness; and in not ruling on all the evidence upon the *voir dire,* including the defence evidence of inducement, whether the statement was voluntary or not, the court found, in each case, the objection raised challenged the voluntariness of the written statement and a ruling after a trial within a trial was essential upon all the evidence including the evidence of the accused (if any) of any compulsion exercised by any police officer to induce him to sign it. In each case, the omission to rule was a fatal irregularity. In each case, as a result, the confession was received in evidence although not duly shown to be voluntary. In the *Gobin* case it was legally impermissible to leave it to the jury to determine whether or not it was voluntary.

The Court of Appeal added that, the lower court had deprived itself of the opportunity to learn facts relevant to determining whether or not to exclude the evidence on discretion, even if voluntary. In the *Gobin* case, the Court of Appeal further held that the trial judge was wrong in ruling that the admissibility of a confession statement was a matter of fact for the jury to decide, because admissibility of evidence is always a question of law for the trial judge and not for the jury to decide on. In most cases, if not in all cases, a trial within a trial should be held to decide and rule on the admissibility, eg, the voluntariness of confession statements. It is not the law that the accused must raise by way of challenge objection to voluntariness by alleging there was an inducement to him to confess, so as to entitle him to a *voir dire* and ruling thereon, because no matter what the ground of challenge, the accused is entitled to a ruling on voluntariness *vel non*. Voluntariness of a confession statement automatically arises whenever admissibility is in issue.[1]

# EVIDENCE

## Unsworn evidence of a child

In *Queen v Boodram Lall*, the Court of Appeal held: (1) the unsworn evidence of a child could not be used to corroborate the sworn testimony of another person; (2) the directions of the judge were of such a nature that it was impossible to say whether the jury relied for their verdict of Guilty on the uncorroborated evidence of the mother alone coupled with the warning that they were so entitled to do, or, on the evidence of the child as corroborative of the mother's testimony.

# SENTENCING POLICY

In *Ryan Spencer and Rodewell Fraser v State*, Criminal Appeal Nos 10–11 (1996), Kennard Ch had the following to say on sentencing:

> I intend no disrespect to anyone when I say that I find some sentences to be startling in their leniency. Too often are killers put on bonds to be of good

1 Law Reports of Guyana (1975), p 113.

> behaviour for a period of time, as if guilty of some minor summary offence, or sentenced to a very short term of imprisonment seemingly inappropriate to the gravity of the offence. Serious questions of public safety are involved, and so to trivialize homicide is to treat human life with a casualness that is both frightening and dangerous. I believe that we must solve our own problems according as our own circumstances dictate and require, and in the present state of criminal activity I cannot bring myself to think that it is prudent to err on the side of undue leniency.
>
> My own opinion is that some offenders, for the protection of society as a whole and as a deterrent to others and to themselves as well, ought to be kept in custody and so away from society for some time. I do not wish it to be understood that I look askance at rehabilitative notions, or that I set no store by the fact that each case must be dealt with on its own facts, or that I am an advocate of cruel and inhuman punishment, but I believe that deterrence is still one of the objects of punishment, and that punishment should be condign.[2]
>
> Counsel had submitted that the period of delay of three years coupled with the conditions on 'death-row', that is to say, the exacting conditions of confinement including lack of fresh air and some basic amenities, constituted a state of affairs amounting to inhuman or degrading punishment. There can be no doubt that the conditions under which prisoners are held on 'death-row' are extreme and exacting. I have already referred to the balance which must be maintained between the public interest and the fundamental rights of the condemned man. The Guyanese nation, struggling as it is to maintain the most basic amenities for the public weal, would expect improvement of prison conditions at a pace and level that was fair and just according to the financial resources of the nation. And I reject any criticism which suggests that a nation that cannot afford special amenities for its prisoners cannot afford the death penalty; a nation that chooses to retain the death penalty must ensure a fair distribution of its resources to achieve a fair balance between the public interest and individual rights. And whether or not the conditions under which condemned prisoners are kept, amount to inhuman or degrading treatment is a question directly relevant 'to our standards of decency and the level of our maturity', using the expression in the widest possible sense so as to reflect our culture, our humanity, and our morality.[3]

## RETRIAL

In *Hardat Ketwaru v State*, Criminal Appeal No 32 (1998), decided on 21 June 1999, Kennard Ch dealt with the issue of retrial as follows:

> An order for a retrial in accordance with s 13(2) of the Court of Appeal Act, Cap 301 is not to be made as a matter of course. Such an order should be made only if the interests of justice so dictate and the interests of justice comprise the

2 Original judgment, pp 1, 13–14.

3 Churaman JA.

> interest of the appellant, the interests of those responsible for instituting criminal proceedings and the interests of public welfare ...

He recalled that in *Sattaur and Mohamed v State* (1976) 24 WIR 157, Haynes Ch, p 170 had set out the various factors which a Court of Appeal should take into consideration in determining whether or not to order a retrial. These included the length of time the appellant had been in custody, the length of time he might have to remain in custody awaiting the retrial, the strength of the State's case and the prevalence and the seriousness of the offence:

> The interests of the public must be considered by seeing to it (generally speaking) that those who are guilty of serious crimes should be brought to justice and should not escape it merely because of a technical blunder by the trial judge in the conduct of the trial or in his summing up to the jury. (See Lord Diplock in *Reid v R* [1979] 2 All ER 904 and *R v Turner* [1975] 61 CAR 7, p 69.)

In the instant case the offence had been committed on 5 October 1996, the trial took place in 1998, the appellant was on bail prior to his trial and he had been in custody for less than one year. The Chancellor recognized that the appellant would be saddled with additional legal expenses for representation for the retrial if one was ordered:

> However, this must be weighed against the prevalence and the seriousness of the offence and the strength of the State's case. It is a known fact that offences involving the use of violence in the society are on the increase, and the offence with which the appellant is charged is indeed a very serious one as the legislature has prescribed a maximum period of imprisonment for life on conviction for such an offence. Apart from the evidence of Samantha Ketwaru and Seeram Jagbir, there is strong circumstantial evidence against the appellant. When all the relevant factors are taken into account, this is a case where justice demands that the appellant be retried and I so order.[4]

## CONCLUSION

It is in this chapter that one feels in places a sense of pride in the Guyana Court of Appeal. One cannot help the thought: had the judges been pre-eminent, rather than the party, how different the fate of Guyana would have been.

One sees the same striving for legality in other areas of the law, such as the law of torts which we touch upon briefly in the next chapter.

4 Kennard Ch Had earlier taken the same position substantially in *Shazam Ibrahim, Surendranauth Chattergoon v State*, Criminal Appeal Nos 28 and 29 (1998), decided on 8 February 1998.

# CHAPTER 7

# LAW OF TORTS

## INTRODUCTION

This work is an introductory essay on the Guyana Court of Appeal. It can therefore only provide an introduction to the flavour being given to the law of torts in the context of Guyana.

## PLEADINGS

In *1 Peter Mangroo, 2 Bissessar called Baata v Dhanmatie Singh*, Civil Appeal No 22 (1974), decided on 14 July 1977, the point of major concern was the respondent's challenge of the effectiveness of the following pleading: 'Save as is hereinbefore expressly admitted, the defendants deny each and every allegation contained in the Statement of Claim, as if the same were set out *verbatim* and traversed *seriatim*,' which was employed by THE solicitor for the appellants. The Court of Appeal considered the meaning of this encapsulated form of pleading; its range and limitations.

The facts were that an accident occurred on 28 November 1966 on the public road at the village of Land of Canaan on the East Bank, Demerara. A motor car and a lorry were involved in the accident. The respondent was a passenger in the motor car. The second appellant was the driver of the lorry. As a result of the accident the car caught fire and the respondent sustained severe burns about her body. Some of these were on her face. She spent three months in hospital.

She sued the appellants, alleging that the first appellant was the owner of the lorry driven by the second appellant, his servant or agent, whose negligence, she claimed, caused the accident. Her Statement of Claim consisted of three paragraphs and ran as follows:

(1) The first-named defendant was at all material times the registered owner of motor lorry No GT 934. The second-named defendant was at all material times the servant and/or agent of the first-named defendant.

(2) On the 28th day of November, 1966, at about 4.20 am the plaintiff was a passenger in motor car No PE 196 which was being driven by one James Baldeo in a northerly direction along the Land of Canaan public road on the East Bank of the Demerara River in the county of Demerara when the second defendant drove the first-named defendant's said motor lorry No GT 934 so negligently that he collided with the said motor car.

(3) As a result of the said collision the plaintiff was seriously injured and had to be hospitalized and has been put to loss and expense and has suffered damage.

There followed particulars of negligence, injuries and special damage.

For the appellants it was pleaded in defence as follows:

(1) Save as is hereinbefore expressly admitted, the defendants deny each and every allegation contained in the Statement of Claim, as if the same were set out *verbatim* and traversed *seriatim*.

(2) The defendants admit that on the date and at the place mentioned in the Statement of Claim a collision occurred between motor car PE 196 driven by James Baldeo and a motor lorry No GT 934 driven by the second-named defendant. Save as aforesaid para 2 of the Statement of Claim is denied.

(3) The second-named defendant denies that he was guilty of the alleged or any negligence or that the said collision was caused as alleged in the Statement of Claim.

(4) The second-named defendant says that he was driving motor lorry No GT 934 north along the public road at Land of Canaan, East Bank, Demerara, when motor car No PE 196 driven by the said James Baldeo and which was travelling at the rear of him in the same direction passed the said lorry and without any warning or signal, the said motor car pulled up almost instantly in front of the said lorry, thus causing the collision.

(5) Further or alternatively, the matters complained of were caused wholly or in part by the negligence of the said James Baldeo, the driver of the said motor car No PE 196.

(6) No admission is made as to the alleged or any injuries, loss or damage.

There was no further pleading and the trial proceeded. When the respective cases were closed counsel for the appellants submitted that the case against the first appellant failed since there was no evidence that he was the owner of the lorry or that the second appellant was his servant or agent as alleged. Indeed, no such evidence was adduced, counsel for the respondent contending that there was no need to do so, for the allegations not having been specifically denied by the appellants were to be treated as having been admitted.

In Guyana the 'Rules of Pleading' are contained in Order 17 of the Rules of the High Court, Cap 3:02. The trial judge considered them. In his conception the danger from the concise form of pleading employed in para 1 of the Defence was that since it was not a specific denial of the allegations as envisaged by Order 17, Rule 13, it was to be considered as an admission of them. He stated his conclusions on this aspect of the matter as follows:

> In the pleadings to which reference has already been made the plaintiff made the allegation of fact that the first-named defendant was at all material times the registered owner of motor lorry No GT 934. The allegation of fact was not specifically denied or denied by necessary implication, nor was it stated to be not admitted by the defendant. It would seem, therefore, that that allegation should be taken to be admitted in terms of Order 17, Rule 13.

And later he said:

> When I apply those expressions of opinion, which I adopt, to the statement of defence in this case, it is my opinion that the general traverse in the defence falls short of what would be required to put in specific issue the fact that the first-named defendant was the registered owner of motor lorry No GT 934 and the fact that the second-named defendant was at all material times the servant and/or agent of the first-named defendant.

The trial judge thus took the view that the allegations in relation to ownership and agency were admitted. He went on to consider the question of negligence and found that the second appellant was wholly responsible for the accident. He therefore gave judgment for the respondent against both appellants in the sum of $7,000, costs $600. The appeal was brought against that decision.

In the Court of Appeal counsel for the appellants contended that the trial judge had misconceived the relevant rules of court. Order 17, Rule 13, by which the judge set great store reads as follows:

> Every allegation of fact in any pleading, not being a petition or summons, if not denied specifically or by necessary implication, or stated to be not admitted in the pleading of the opposite party, shall be taken to be admitted except as against an infant, lunatic or person of unsound mind not so found by inquisition.

Massiah JA, delivering the judgment of the Court of Appeal, invoked Order 17, Rule 19, as the rule that bore directly on this issue. That rule provides:

> It shall not be sufficient for a defendant in his defence to deny generally the grounds alleged by the Statement of Claim, or for a plaintiff in his reply to deny generally the grounds alleged in a defence by way of counter-claim, but each party must deal specifically with each allegation of fact of which he does not admit the truth, except damages.

It was the submission of counsel for the appellants that the general denial pleaded in para 1 of the defence was in compliance with the provisions of Order 17, Rule 19, and that the effect of such pleading was to put the plaintiff to the proof of the allegations in respect of ownership and agency since the other allegations had been dealt with specifically. Since there was no proof of those matters, the argument ran, then the case against the first appellant failed. He cited several authorities to support his contention. Counsel for the respondent disagreed. He asserted that the form of pleading under discussion was in clear violation of Order 17, Rule 19. He took the view that there were important allegations in para 1 of the Statement of Claim which required to be dealt with specifically; since they were not specifically denied, he contended, they were to be regarded as having been admitted. There was therefore no need to prove them.

After considering the English case law on the issues, Massiah JA concluded that the effect of a general denial is to put the plaintiff to proof, no more and no less:

> Since it puts the plaintiff to proof it is inconceivable that it could at the same time be considered as an implied admission (under Order 17, Rule 13, or otherwise) which is the position contended for by counsel for the respondent in this matter. The position is axiomatic; an admission is an acceptance of certain facts. If, therefore, you accept the truth of certain allegations, how then can you at the same time require proof of them? The two concepts are mutually exclusive. You cannot say 'I admit it, but you must prove it, nevertheless', or put another way 'I desire you to prove it, although I admit it'.

On this reasoning, he concluded that para 1 of the defence was not evasive and admitted nothing; it had the effect of putting the respondent to the proof of the allegations in respect of ownership of the lorry, and the relationship existing between the appellants. Since there had been no adduction of evidence in relation to those matters, it followed that they had not been proved, and since the respondent could have succeeded against the first appellant only if she could have satisfied the court in relation thereto, it followed that the first appellant's appeal must be allowed.

He added:

> Although I express no view on it the position may well have been different if the defence consisted only of a bare, general denial, but all the allegations in the Statement of Claim, save those contained in para 1 thereof, were specifically dealt with in various paragraphs of the defence; and the allegation of negligence, the most important and material allegation of all, was specifically denied, the appellants giving in a separate paragraph their own version as to how the accident occurred.

He considered it important to bear in mind that the main purpose of the rules under discussion in the case was to bring the parties by their pleadings to an issue and so diminish expense and delay. This was secured by requiring each party to fully admit or clearly deny the material allegations made against him so that the issues would be clearly designated.

In the end result, the Court of Appeal allowed the appeal of the first appellant and dismissed the appeal of the second appellant against whom the judgment stood.

## Could the Transport and Harbours Department be sued for negligence?

In *Deonarine Singh v Transport and Harbours Department*, Civil Appeal No 47 (1975), the question to be decided upon appeal to the Court of Appeal was whether a person who had purchased a ticket on the railway could sue the Transport and Harbours Department for damages for personal injuries while travelling as a passenger thereon. Crane JA held:

> Bitter pill as it might be at the present day to many constitutionalists, the fact remains that government departments are still not under the law generally;

> they are immune from suit and cannot be sued in our courts of justice unless permission is granted by statute to the citizen to do so. Meanwhile, a lead on this vital matter is awaited, particularly in view of the new social order that has come about since independence. Until then, it means that a citizen who is seriously injured by the fault of a government department, can recover as of right no compensation, save by way of *ex gratia* award.

In the same case, R Luckhoo JA sought to give a steer towards a new jurisprudence in the following declaration:

> I would like to add that we are swiftly moving away from the days when litigants approach the judgment-seat in uneven combat, some being in an advantageous and privileged position. With the modern trend in social legislation within a welfare state, there is reason to hope that soon all litigants will stand on equal terms before the law for a determination of their rights and obligations, and that everyone who has suffered loss or damage or injury through a breach by a defendant of his duty of care will not be turned away without compensation.

## Meaning of a 'public official'

In Civil Appeal No 12 (1973), involving an application for a Writ of Certiorari by Gordon Yaw and VJ Correia, the appellant was dismissed by the Permanent Secretary of the Ministry of Housing and Reconstruction whilst in the service of the Government of Guyana. If, in law, his status was that of a 'public officer', only the Public Service Commission or its delegated agent, and no one else, could have legally secured his dismissal, as the competent authority vested with this power under the Constitution of Guyana. The Court of Appeal, EV Luckhoo C presiding, came to the conclusion that the appellant, a night watchman, came within the direction and control of the Permanent Secretary by virtue of Art 45 of the Guyana Constitution since his services were paid for by the ministry from the block vote under the Head – Wages, Ministry of Housing and Reconstruction.

## Damages awarded in foreign currency

In Civil Appeal Nos 51–56 (1983) and Nos 69 and 73 (1989), decided on 26 May 1993, multiple claims were considered following an accident that resulted in the loss of several lives and injuries to others. One of the deceased had been living in the United States and was visiting Guyana at the time of the accident. At the time of the deceased's death her minor children were aged 10 years and 16 and a half years, both living with her in the United States of America.

George Ch held that their dependency under the Accidental Death and Workmen's Injuries (Compensation) Act should be calculated at about 30 per centum of the deceased's net income, or US$3,200.00 per annum. Having regard to the fact that judgment was not delivered until some seven years after the accident it would be the total amount assumed to have been lost each year during that period. Therefore, in the case of one child, Nadira, this would be one and a half years amounting to US $4,800.00 and in the case of the other child, Chandra, she would be entitled to seven and a half years' dependency, or US$24,000.00.

As to the deceased's estate, George Ch fixed the damages for the lost years at US$17,280.00 out of which each of her nine children would be entitled to US$1,920.00.

## CONCLUSION

A question that arises for reflection is: how will Guyanese conditions impact upon the future development of the law of torts in the country. This, we hope, will be the subject of future research and scholarship – as indeed of the law of contracts, to which we now turn briefly.

# CHAPTER 8

# LAW OF CONTRACTS

## INTRODUCTION

We have here the same question as in the preceding chapter: how are local circumstances influencing the development of the law?

## REPUDIATION OF CONTRACT

In *Ramasingh v Janakdai Bacchus*, Civil Appeal No 4 (1995), Kennard C dealt with the law on the repudiation of contracts in the following terms:

> The law as to repudiation as I understand it is this: if before the time arrives at which a party is bound to perform a contract, he expresses an intention to break it or acts in such a way as to lead a reasonable person to the conclusion that he does not intend to fulfill his part, this constitutes an anticipatory breach of the contract and entitles the other party to take one of two courses: (1) He may accept the renunciation, treat it as discharging him from further performance and sue for damages forthwith ... or he may wait till the time for performance arrives and then sue. If the breach is accepted the innocent party is relieved from further performance of his obligation under the contract.
>
> If the breach is not accepted, the contract subsists at the risk of both parties and the anticipatory renunciation is ineffective ...
>
> Where there is an anticipatory breach or the breach of an executory contract, and the innocent party wishes to treat himself as discharged he must normally make his decision known to the party in default ('accept the repudiation') ... Unless and until this is done, the contract continues in existence for ('an unaccepted repudiation is a thing writ in water') ...
>
> Acceptance of a repudiation must be clear and unequivocal.

In the instant case, the court held that the appellant, having expressed an intention to repudiate the contract by a letter dated 24 April 1990, one would have expected the respondent, if she were going to accept that repudiation, to have indicated her acceptance of that repudiation within a reasonable time. The learned Chancellor did not consider that a period of eight months was a reasonable time, having regard to the nature of the subject matter of the agreement (sale of property). There being no acceptance of the repudiation by the respondent, the appellant was entitled to treat the contract as still subsisting in which case it continued in force for the benefit of both parties.

# VARIATION OF CONTRACT

In *Toolsie Persaud Ltd v Durga Persaud*, Civil Appeal No 9 (1974), the plaintiff, Durga Persaud, had been employed by the defendants over a period of time in the unloading of sand, stone and quarry-sifting from boats and pontoons moored alongside the defendant's wharf at Canje. Up to October 1968, the plaintiff had been in receipt of a wage calculated on the basis of 15 cents per tonne of sand unloaded. He was paid at the end of every week. In October 1968, without any prior discussion or agreement having been made between the parties, he found his wages had been reduced to such an extent that it worked out at eight cents per tonne. The defendants contended that as from October 1968 it was agreed that a new rate would be payable in respect of sand. The trial judge found against this contention and held that the act of the defendants in reducing the rate of pay amounted to unilateral variation of the contract of service and awarded a sum of money which represented the difference of the wages between the old and the new rates.

Upon appeal, Civil Appeal No 9 (1974), Persaud JA held that the trial judge was right when he came to the conclusion that the defendants could not unilaterally have altered the terms of the contract of employment. Handing the plaintiff his pay envelope with a reduced wage could not amount to a termination of the old contract, and a new offer at the new rate when the workman protested the new rate. Nor could the continuation of work by the workman at the new rate be regarded as his acceptance of the new rate under these particular circumstances. To vary a contract, or to enter into a new contract, there must be agreement on both sides, or as it has been described, *consensus ad idem*.

# SPECIFIC PERFORMANCE: HARDSHIPS SHOULD BE JUDGED AT THE TIME OF CONTRACT

In *Dropratte Singh v Raymond Bayse*, Civil Appeal No 61 (1991), the respondent/plaintiff made an application for specific performance of a contract of sale of the appellant's rights, title, and interest in and to a long lease in respect of a property. The purchase price was $115,000.00. In the particular facts of the case, the application was made some years after the original contract of sale and the matter reached the Court of Appeal some seven years after the original contract of sale. In the meantime the property had increased considerably in value.

George Ch called in aid *Fry on Specific Performance*, 6th edn, p 214:

> The question of the inadequacy of the consideration must of course be decided at the time of the contracts and not by the light of subsequent events ... It is now ... well established that the time of the contract is the time for judging of its consideration.

The learned Chancellor continued:

> A vendor can easily insure against creeping inflation by the simple device of including a clause in the agreement making time of the essence of the contract, and even if the agreement contains no such provision there is nothing in law to prevent such a term from being engrafted, giving reasonable time, after there is default in completing within the originally stated time. In my opinion, the view expressed by Megarry VC in *Lazard Bros and Co Ltd v Fairfield Properties Co (Mayfair) Ltd* (1977) SJ 793 would seem to accord with present-day thinking. He is reported to have said:
>
>> If specific performance was to be regarded as a prize to be awarded by equity to the zealous and denied to the indolent then the plaintiffs should fail. But whatever might have been the position over a century ago, that was the wrong approach today. If between the plaintiff and the defendant it was just that the plaintiff should obtain the remedy, the court ought not to withhold it merely because the plaintiff had been guilty of delay. There was no ground here on which delay could properly be said to be a bar to a decree of specific performance.
>
> In other words, in the absence of a special provision as to time the emphasis should be on the justice of the case as between the parties. And in considering this issue, the circumstances of persistent or chronic devaluation of currency can hardly be of very great significance. Indeed, it has been said that for changed circumstances to be relevant they must be so fundamental as to strike at the root of the agreement and render its performance in the manner contemplated by the parties impossible. (See *Hangkam Kwingtong Woo v Liu Lan Fong (Alias Liu Ah Lan)* [1951] 2 All ER 567, p 573.)

Later in his judgment, George Ch did entertain the possibility that subsequent hardship might influence a decision on an application for specific performance. He stated:

> ... the hardship that motivates a court to exercise its discretion to refuse an order for specific performance is that which existed at the date of the agreement or which is due in some way to the fault of the plaintiff who seeks the order. A passage at p 199 of the 6th edn of *Fry on Specific Performance* accurately sets out the position. There the author says:
>
>> The question of the hardship of a contract is generally to be judged of at the time at which it is entered into; if it be then fair and just and not productive of hardship, it will be immaterial that it may, by the force of subsequent circumstances or change of events, have become less beneficial to one party, except where these subsequent events have been in some way due to the party who seeks the performance of the contract. For whatever contingencies may attach to a contract, or be involved in the performance of either part, have been taken upon themselves by the parties to it. It has been determined that the reasonableness of a contract is to be judged at the time it is entered into, and not by the light of subsequent events ...

George Ch continued:

> But although the general principle is that the issue of hardship should be judged at the time that the contract is entered into, as the passage acknowledges, it is not an inexorable rule, and, intervening circumstances can in exceptional cases impel the court to refuse an order for specific performance. A recent example of this is *Patel v Ali* [1984] 1 All ER 978 where a vendor who, subsequent to the contract of sale of her home, became an amputee, and who thereby and for other reasons had become grossly handicapped as regards everyday living, successfully invoked these facts to resist a claim for specific performance of the contract.

## TRAVEL TAX ON AN UNUSED AIRLINE TICKET SHOULD BE REFUNDED

In *J Goel v Attorney General*, Civil Appeal No 33 (1989), decided on 11 November 1991, the appellant had paid the fare for two return tickets to India; travel tax amounting to 100 percent of the cost of the ticket; a miscellaneous charge order for excess baggage; and travel tax levied at 100 per cent of the cost of the excess baggage voucher. The tickets were never used and replacement tickets and MCOs were reissued before the expiry date of the ticket. In 1986, after the expiry of these replacements, the appellant sought a further renewal which was refused. The cost of the tickets and MCOs was refunded but not the tax paid. The appellant was subsequently informed by the Ministry of Finance that he was not entitled to a refund of the tax whereupon he instituted proceedings for the recovery of the sum outstanding.

The contention of the Commissioner of Inland Revenue was that while the taxes had been remitted to him by the airline, since the validity of the MCOs had expired, the refund claimed was statute-barred by s 12(3) of the Travel Voucher Tax Act, Chapter 80:09. On appeal, George Ch held that under s 10 of the Act the carriers/charterers were made the statutory agent of the commissioner and under s 12 of the Act, two or three circumstances were contemplated where a refund of the tax could be obtained. These were:

- Where a claim was made by the purchaser of the ticket from the Commissioner of Inland Revenue for a refund of excess tax paid.
- Where the purchaser claimed from the carrier or charterer for tax paid on any unused portion of the ticket.
- Where the carrier claimed from the commissioner a diminution of liability because of his repayment of travel tax to a traveller.

Only in these three circumstances did the three-month limitation period prescribed by sub-s 3 apply.

The use of the word 'proportion' in s 12(b), George Ch continued, was merely intended to indicate the measure by which the refund of the tax was to be calculated. If the whole of the ticket was unused and the traveller was entitled to a refund of the whole of its cost, the proportion of the tax to be refunded was the whole.

Churaman JA held that the appellant's claim for a refund was being made under the general law. Nothing in the Act expressly or by necessary implication suggested that tax, once paid, could never be reclaimed. If a person were entitled to a rebate under sub-s 2 for unused portions of a ticket *a fortiori* a person who had never left the country would be entitled in accordance with accepted commercial practice, to a refund of ticket money as well as tax.

## CONCLUSION

When the Law Reports of Guyana are finally published for the years 1976–2000 (25 years), it will be easier to trace further how local circumstances are impacting on the law. Here also ,there is an invitation to future scholarship.

The law of real property in Guyana is a combination of Roman-Dutch Law, Common Law, and local legislation, and presents special challenges. We shall now finally turn to this important area in the development of a Guyanese jurisprudence.

# CHAPTER 9

# PROPERTY LAW

## INTRODUCTION

It is interesting that it is in relation to property that we see the Court of Appeal more recently grappling with the rights of the subject as against the rights of the State.

## RIGHT TO PROPERTY

As we saw in an earlier chapter, in Civil Appeal No 43 (1994), decided in January 2000, the Court of Appeal had to deal four square with the right to property in the 1980 Constitution of Guyana. Kennard Ch and Prem Persaud JA held that: '... the power of Eminent Domain is an essential attribute of sovereignty and it connotes the legal capacity of the State to acquire private property for public purposes ... and there is no need to confer this authority expressly by the Constitution as it exists without any declaration to that effect.' Churaman JA entered a powerful and magisterially-reasoned dissent which is certain to command attention in the future. He stated:

> The consequence according to this majority view is that the State has the power and the constitutional capacity to deprive citizens of choices in action – the right to sue for money – so long as it is in the public interest so to do, and the State is prepared to give bonds redeemable twelve or so years after. In other words, the citizen's right to the immediate enjoyment of the fruits of their judgment can be taken away by the issuance of paper bonds. This seems to me a serious violation of the citizen's rights to property, and one specifically proscribed by the combined effects of Art 40(c) and Art 142 of the Constitution of the Co-operative Republic of Guyana ... The majority decision has the effect also, without either of my brethren saying so, of overruling the much respected decision of *Inland Revenue Commissioner v Lilleyman and Others* (1964) LRBG 221, a landmark decision of the British Caribbean Court of Appeal ...

The facts of the case, taken from the judgment of Churaman JA were as follows: In 1992, Caterpillar Americas Company was owed some US$950,000 by Guyana Mining Enterprise (Guymine), a public corporation in Guyana. The Government of Guyana held all the shares in Guymine through its nominee, The Bauxite Industry Development Co Ltd. Guymine was unable to pay its debts to Caterpillar, so the government decided to restructure Guymine. It made an order under the Public Corporations Act, 1988, the effect of which was, *inter alia,* to transfer liability of the debt from Guymine to the Government of Guyana who, in turn, would discharge the indebtedness to

Caterpillar by the issuance of bonds to mature some 12 years later. Caterpillar wanted their money forthwith. Caterpillar moved the High Court by motion, alleging that the order made by the minister under the Public Corporations Act contravened the provisions of the Constitution and was therefore *ultra vires*, invalid and void. The trial judge agreed with the contentions of Caterpillar and struck down the provisions relating to the issuance of bonds to be redeemed after 12 years as being violative of the Constitution. The Government of Guyana appealed to the Court of Appeal.

Counsel for the appellant based his arguments on two grounds: First, that on the doctrine of Eminent Domain, the government had both the power and the duty, in the national interest, to make the order it did in 1992 to preserve the bauxite industry; and, secondly, that there was no 'taking of possession' by the government of Caterpillar's property in contravention of the Constitution. Counsel for the respondent contended that Eminent Domain had no applicability in the jurisprudence of Guyana and that by the combined effect of Arts 40 and 142 of the Constitution, Caterpillar was deprived of its property in blatant contravention of the Constitution.

Art 40 of the Constitution reads in its relevant portions:

> Every person in Guyana is entitled to the basic right to a happy, creative, and productive life ...
>
> (c) protection for the privacy of his home and other property and from deprivation of property without compensation.

Art 142(1) reads thus:

> No property of any description shall be compulsorily taken possession of, and no interest in or right over property of any description shall be compulsorily acquired except by or under the authority of a written law
>
> (a) providing for compensation for the property or any interest in or right over property so possessed or acquired and specifying the principles on which the compensation is to be determined and given; and
>
> (b) giving to any person claiming such compensation a right of access either directly or by way of appeal, for the determination of his interest in or right over the property and the amount of compensation, to the High Court.

In his dissenting judgment Churaman JA made the point that is worth keeping in mind at the very outset:

> One must keep in the forefront of one's mind that our Constitution does not, neither in Art 40 nor 142, speak of compulsory acquisition or deprivation of property *for public purposes*. It is important to bear this in mind for this reason pivotal to the reasoning of my brethren in the instant appeal is the argumentation in each judgment that 'public purpose' is an essential prerequisite for the right of the State to acquire property, that is to say, the property must have been taken for some public purpose. With all due respect, our Constitution simply does not say so, and it seems to me, with deep respect, to be something of a confusion of thought to engraft upon our Constitution the essential prerequisite of the American concept of Eminent Domain in justification of the conduct of the Government of Guyana in this matter. Our

> Constitution is the supreme law of the country. It does not exempt the government from the constraints imposed by the Constitution, by taking property for public purposes. However public the purpose, however noble the purpose, the government – the executive – simply cannot take private property under the guise that it is being taken for public purposes ...

Churaman JA ended his dissent on the following stirring note:

> I entertain no doubt, from the review that I have attempted to undertake, that the question of Eminent Domain simply has no place on our jurisprudence. We cannot and must not rewrite the Constitution of Guyana by superimposing on Art 142, or on the combined effect of Arts 40(c) and 142, some such concept that whenever the State is of the view that a public purpose is involved, that the State may, by the applicability of some alien concept, deprive people of property and then use noble intentions to justify that deprivation. If that is so, one wonders whether, for example, a bank or any financial institution taking in depositors' money which happens to be a public corporation may, under appropriate conditions, leading up to restructuring, with relevant legislation in place, issue depositors with bonds, in lieu of cash, redeemable after 12 or so years! Citizens of Guyana, alike with others, would no doubt see this as the extreme mockery of our Constitution.

On the side of the two majority judges, Prem Persaud JA considered that the power of Eminent Domain seemed to be an essential attribute of sovereignty and connoted the legal capacity of the State to take private property from individuals for *public purposes*.

> Since it is an inseparable incidence of sovereignty there is no need to confer this authority expressly by the Constitution, and it exists without any declaration to that effect. But because it is used for *public purposes* there must be constraint within certain limits and there must be safeguards subject to which the right may be exercised.

In his judgment, Arts 40(c) and 142 could be said to deal with the topic of Eminent Domain:

> ... the property of the respondent was not acquired by the State by the order. it merely guaranteed the payment of the debt owing. The debt was not disputed. The respondent could not have recovered the sums owing from Guymine, and the government has acted clearly with the intention of salvaging the industry with the assistance of overseas financial assistance, and to protect and preserve the debts owing to the respondent, in order to ensure that they be paid in due course. The economy of the country depended upon the viable performance of the bauxite industry, and a substantial section of the population depended upon it for their livelihood and well-being. There is nothing in the record or otherwise to question the intention of the government.

Later in his judgment he added:

> The respondent is a creditor and is not deprived of the entirety of his rights to which he is entitled by being the owner of the promissory notes. The test is whether it has been dispossessed substantially from the rights held by it. There is no evidence that the bonds are not convertible in the commercial market; no evidence was led to show that the respondent was prejudiced by the deferment

of payment or that the bonds are worthless. It can and is free to sell or dispose of its rights and interests in the bonds to anyone. No one has taken away the notes from him. Its legal and beneficial interest is left intact. I rely on the Indian cases cited and come to the conclusion that even if the deferment of the payment can be said to be depriving the respondent of its property, in my judgment, that deprivation is not substantial enough to merit a finding that the constitutional rights of the respondent have been violated. Deferring payment ensures that the rights of the respondent will be honoured by the State itself.

# TITLE TO, PRESCRIPTION, LIMITATION AND POSSESSION OF LAND

The case of *Samuel Glen*, Civil Appeal No 9 (1971) involved, in the words of Crane JA, 'an enlightening exercise ion the law relating to title to, prescription, limitation and possession of land'. In that case, both the appellant and the respondent claimed to be in possession of the same field at the same time. The respondent, who was the plaintiff in the High Court, was the owner of lots six, seven and eight of Plantation Millmount, West Bank, Demerara. His case was that he got possession of lot nine in 1964 by virtue of an agreement of a lease from its owner, one Donald Walker, although he produced in evidence neither lease nor Walker to prove the origin of his possession and to support his assertion that the appellant was never at any time in possession of the land. It was his complaint that the appellant had trespassed upon lot nine on two occasions – first in the year 1965, when he uprooted coconut trees, and again in April and May 1968, when he uprooted cane tops valued at $1,000, without even speaking to him about his occupation of the lot in dispute. There was conflicting evidence concerning Walker's existence. Two of the witnesses who testified on the respondent's behalf were in conflict on the matter. However the Court of Appeal accepted that Walker was indeed in being at one time, particularly as one of the appellant's witnesses who had been residing on the plantation continuously from the year 1910 reputedly referred to lot nine as Walker's land.

The appellant had testified that he was born in the year 1917 in a house on lot nine occupied by his father, Charles Glen, and mother, Ada Steward, until 1938, when the house broke down from disrepair. Thereafter, before his death in the same year, Charles Glen had gone to live in a rented house one mile away at a place called *Vive la Force*. After his father's death, the appellant said he had taken possession of and continued to cultivate lot nine until 1960, after which he had moved elsewhere to earn his livelihood cutting cane. The trial judge accepted these facts but did not accept the following: firstly that there was a sub-division of lot nine into three strips, one of which (ie, the southern strip adjoining lot eight) was the subject of the dispute between the parties; secondly, that although the appellant personally ceased cultivation in 1960, it was not his intention to abandon lot nine, he having let it out to small farmers, including one Burleigh Forde, in 1964, when peasant cane farming was first introduced into the district of West Demerara.

In analyzing and assessing the evidence led on behalf of the appellant, the learned trial judge said it was of such a contradictory and conflicting nature that he found himself unable to rely on most of what was told him, and on this aspect expressed himself as follows:

> In the context of the very contradictory and conflicting nature of the evidence given by the defendant and his witnesses I can set very little store by the greater part of what they have said. I believe the defendant was born at Free and Easy and lived there with his father until the year 1938 when they left for *Vive La Force* because of the very bad state of disrepair into which the house had fallen. I further believe that after his father's death he continued to cultivate the land at Free and Easy until 1960 when he *abandoned* it, and that thereafter he never cultivated the land or rented any portion of it or permitted anyone to occupy any portion. He returned to the land in 1964, soon after, according to him, peasant 'cane farming was introduced to West Bank Demerara' only to find the plaintiff in occupation of certain portions of it. I accept the plaintiff's evidence that his cultivation spanned the width of the land and was not as the defendant would have me believe only one rod in width. I also believe that the total length bulldozed and cultivated by the plaintiff was 100 rods east of the public road and 312 rods west of it.

In his judgment, Crane JA remarked that the above finding of an abandonment of lot nine was in the teeth of evidence that the appellant had assumed full and uncontrolled dominion and exclusive occupation of it for a period of 22 years prior to the year 1960. He proceeded:

> But I cannot doubt that it is not permissible to add to this period that of his father's occupation which the evidence affords, eg that from at least 1917 until 1938, because of the appellant's illegitimacy. (See *Re Pouderoyen* (1914) LRBG 73). This is why I must agree the relevant period to consider for prescription is not as claimed in the amended statement of defence, eg, the period of upwards of 33 and one-third years, but only that for which the appellant had, in his own right, been in exclusive possession, eg from 1938 onwards.

Crane JA held that where the trial judge had initially erred was in his finding that the appellant had 'abandoned or relinquished' lot nine when he, personally, ceased to cultivate it as from 1960. He noted that nowhere in his judgment did the learned trial judge refer to the matter of intention to abandon nor on whom lay the burden of proof of it, although, in his view, it was clear from the joint operation of ss 3, 5 and 6, Cap 184 of the Laws of Guyana that the onus of proof of dispossession or discontinuance lay on the adverse possessor.

In reaching his conclusion the judge had made a thorough examination of both the 30 year and 12 year periods of prescription in the enacting part and in the proviso to s 3 of the Title to Land (Prescription and Limitation) Ordinance, Cap 184 Crane JA commended the trial judge for the way in which he had explained the operation of those two periods and had reached the conclusion that the 12 year period was not retrospective. The trial judge had concluded that as the proviso to s 3, dealing with the shorter period of 12 years' adverse possession for prescriptive title, was not retrospective in operation, the plea of prescription could not avail the respondent, he having in his own right neither the 30 year period nor the shorter 12 year period (which must be counted only as from 1952) because he had abandoned possession of lot nine in 1960. (This issue had earlier been dealt with by Crane JA in *Kadar Lall Gobind v HS Cameron et al* (Civil Appeal No 35 (1969), dated 30 December 1970).)

On the facts in the instant case, there had been altogether 14 years' adverse possession *immediately* prior to 1952. Was the appellant entitled, on this account, to have considered the claim in his plea to have acquired a prescriptive title within the proviso to s 3 of the Ordinance? Crane JA considered that the learned judge had rightly considered that it did not avail the appellant and continued:

> I think it is immaterial whether the whole of the 12 year period be *immediately* prior to 1952, or partly *prior* to and partly *after* that year, for so long as the vested rights of an owner will be impaired, the rule is that the ordinance must not be given a retroactive operation. It seems to me, however one looks at the matter for one to add a period after 1952 to another period *before* that year so as to make up the shorter 12 year period of prescription, would be depriving a landowner of his property to which he is entitled until 30 years of adverse possession and would have deprived him of his title to it, because that was the law before 1952. To express the same thing in terms of an analysis of the right: Before 1952 there would have been no right in an adverse possessor to prescribe for less than the statutory period of 30 years. At the same time, there was the corresponding right in the true owner not to be deprived of his *title* by adverse possession within the same period. The true owner would therefore have the right to expect that his title would not be destroyed by adverse possession short of 30 years, and in all probability he may well have been relying on that right so as to regain possession by peaceable re-entry at a future time within that period. This, to my mind, was the nature of the right vested in him by law even though he was debarred from bringing an action to recover possession after the lapse of 12 years.
>
> In *Gobind's* case (above), the argument was rejected that a period of 12 years' adverse possession acquired sometime before, though not, as in the instant case, immediately before 1952, was operative to defeat the rights of co-owners who had re-entered possession under title in 1948. I held the view that as the rights of the defendant co-owners were vested both in title and in possession, it would have done them an injustice to hold that immediately on the coming into force of the 1952 legislation, they were automatically deprived of their title.
>
> Applying the principle of what has been said above to the present appeal, I find the position to be as follows: Prior to 1952 the true owner of lot nine, whoever he was, was out of possession. That lot was then in the adverse possession of the appellant for a period of 14 years immediately preceding 27

> December 1952. The right of the true owner to recover possession by action under the law as it then stood, will have been barred (see s 4(2) of the now repealed Civil Law Ordinance, 1916), though his *title* will have remained intact along with his *right to re-enter possession peaceably* and to restore his *status quo ante* at any time within the prescriptive period of 30 years. (Section 15(a) of the Limitation Ordinance No 1 of 1856 (repealed).) Before 1952 both of these were rights vested in the true owner. So that if retroactivity of the 1952 Ordinance is favoured, the joint effect of ss 5 and 13, above, would, contrary to principle, certainly operate to extinguish them both notwithstanding they were acquired under an existing law. This is what the rule we have just been considering says is an injustice and ought to be avoided. Retroactive interpretation in such a case is not only absurd, but is inconsistent with the very basis on which the legislature usually sanctions the retrospective operation of statutes, viz, that Parliament does not intend what is unjust.

After examining the cases and deciding not to follow the British Caribbean Court of Appeal, Crane JA continued:

> If I am right in saying that these rights continued in their respective owners after 1952, then it seems to me s 13 cannot operate so as to extinguish the true owner's title until 12 years after 1952. It is because of the continuity of these rights after 1952 that an adverse possessor is permitted to prescribe thereafter, both in respect of the 30 year period and the 12 year period with a view to bringing his petition for a declaration of title in respect of either, whichever affords him the shorter time within which to do so. There is, however, this difference in respect of the 30 year period: It is quite permissible for him to add a period of adverse possession *after* 1952 to one *before* that year so as to make up 30 years because of his accrued rights in that period, but he may not do so with respect to the shorter period of 12 years because *title* before 1952 was a vested interest in the true owner which carried with it the right to enter possession at any time before the expiration of 30 years. Therefore I think it must be clear that after 1952 an adverse possessor could not, in view of the owner's vested interest, justly take any period of time before that year and add it to another thereafter, so as to help assist in extinguishing the owner's title before the 30 year period.

Later in his judgment Crane JA elaborated further as follows:

> Depending upon how long a period he has to his credit, a petitioning adverse possessor may use either one or the other of the two periods so as to enable him to bring his petition within the earliest possible time after 1952, but, with this limitation: it would not be within the spirit and intendment of the ordinance, until at least 1964, in the light of the principle stated above, for him to rely merely on a 12 year period of adverse possession acquired before that year to enable him to acquire the title of the true owner ...

Having regard to the facts and the law, Crane JA felt that the trial judge had erred on some issue(s) mentioned below and that he had misdirected himself in the following passage from his judgment:

> Having come to the conclusion that the defendant was not in possession for the required statutory period, it is not necessary for me to examine the effect which his relinquishment of possession in 1960 would have, if he could have taken advantage of periods before and after the ordinance came into operation, in order to take advantage of the shorter 12 year period.

Crane JA dealt with this misdirection as follows:

> I am clearly of opinion that the learned judge was in error here. It was not, I think, vitally necessary to the success of the appellant's case for him to prove to the hilt a prescriptive title to the extent of either of the two periods mentioned in s 3 of the ordinance. If he succeeded in so proving, then, *cadit quaestio*; but if he did not, the matter ought not necessarily to have ended unfavourably for him, as the trial judge appeared to think. There still remained to be considered the legal implication of the appellant's contention which was found as a fact to have existed, viz, that he was in sole and exclusive possession of lot nine for a period of 22 years prior to 1960, and that he had returned to its physical re-occupation in 1964, the very same year the respondent went into possession of it. In my view, the appellant was also entitled to have considered not only his plea to have been in possession for the full statutory period, but also any other lesser period of time which, on the evidence, was sufficient to confer on him possessory rights since these give such a title as would enable him to maintain possession against anyone other than the true owner of the lot. This, I think, was really the implication in his plea for prescriptive title to lot nine.

Counsel for the respondent had asked the Court of Appeal to consider both parties as being in the position of trespassers to the disputed lot, and had formulated the following proposition:

> A trespasser's possession is only protected so long as he remains in actual possession. If he removes from, or gives up actual possession before the expiration of the statutory period and a third person enters into possession, then that third party can maintain an action in trespass against the original trespasser.

After disagreeing with this presentation of the facts, Crane JA continued:

> The true situation would, however, appear to be that if, though not in actual physical possession for the full statutory period, a prior possessor with possessory rights re-enters with the intention of asserting his possession *immediately* upon being dispossessed, his dispossessor does not in the eye of the law have such a possession as would enable him to sue trespass. The cases, however, show re-entry must be *immediate* in the sense that there must have been no appreciable space of time between the dispossessor's entry and the re-entry so that it can be found as a fact that the dispossessor has acquired possession. But it will always remain a question of fact for the court to decide whether there has been a sufficient lapse of time between entry in the one case and re-entry in the other to confer possession. That will depend on all the circumstances of the case.

In the instant case, Crane JA, with the concurrence of the other two judges of appeal, held as follows:

> I entertain no doubt at all that the respondent is a naked trespasser. The evidence has truly exposed him to be a land grabber who, in his quest for expansion, unscrupulously seeks to do so at the expense of a weaker neighbour. I am firmly of opinion, having been convinced from both principle and the decided cases, that he is a mere trespasser without a sufficient possession to enable him to maintain this action for trespass. In my judgment, the truth is inescapable – he has never been in possession of lot nine.
>
> For these reasons, we allowed this appeal and set aside the judgment of the learned trial judge with costs here and below.

The judgment of Crane JA, 31 pages, is a masterful piece of judicial artistry. It is all the more surprising that one would find him later, as Chancellor, seeking to please the government of the day with a lecture on socialist legality, the main parts of which are reproduced later in this volume.

## LEGAL EFFECT OF A MORTGAGE DEED IN GUYANA

In *Leon Vansluytman; Philomena Vansluytman v New Building Society Ltd, CJ Thrift Shop Ltd,* Civil Appeal No 68 (1992), Bernard JA clarified the legal effect of a mortgage deed in Guyana as follows:

> In a Treatise on the Law of Immovable Property in British Guiana by Edgar Mortimer Duke, the view is expressed that a mortgage deed in Guyana is in reality a judgment under which the mortgagor admits that he is justly and truly indebted to the mortgagee in the sum named in the deed, and consents to being condemned in the payment of the said sum and interest. Sir Charles Major, CJ in the case of *Re Demerara Turf Club* (1915) LRBG 193, explained the position in this way: 'In this colony, the remedy under an instrument of mortgage is sale, and not the mortgagee's acquisition by means of a decree for foreclosure of the mortgagee's interest in the mortgaged property without sale.'
>
> Therefore the only remedy which the mortgagees, NBS, had against Khan under the mortgage executed in January 1979 was sale of the mortgaged properties ...

## CONCLUSION

In reading the decisions in some of the cases discussed above, one's respect for the judges and the lawyers involved grows immensely. The quality of research, arguments and decisions is striking. There is no doubt that Guyana has had and continues to have gifted lawyers and judges. Its travail has been the paramounting of the party in power rather than the paramounting of the law. It is to the paramounting of the law and the Courts that Guyana's Court of Appeal must now return the country. That is its historic challenge.

# CONCLUSION

At the outset of this work, we sought to show that the rule of law is vital for the achievement of development in developing countries. The breakdown of the rule of law has, unfortunately, led to the impoverishment of so many developing countries.

In this study we have set out a peoples' historic quest for freedom during the times of slavery and of indentured labour. We showed how the vindication of human rights was a battle cry of the struggle for independence.

In the preceding chapters we have seen the stresses and strains to which constitutional government and the maintenance of democracy were submitted during three of the four decades in the history of the country considered. Against this background, we set out the place of the Court of Appeal, the highest court in the land, under the Constitution of 1980.

From the evidence presented and the cases examined, we have seen problems that surfaced shortly after independence in maintaining integrity in the constitution and membership of the court. Alas, these problems of integrity and propriety in the constitution of the court would recur even at the end of the fourth decade when, in 2000, the Bar Association would agitate over the fact that the president had not followed the recommendations of the Judicial Service Commission as mandated by the Constitution. In this sense, the travails of the rule of law are, alas, still not over.

This study has shown that after 1980 the courts were called upon to function under a Constitution that was brought in through a fraudulent referendum. The Court of Appeal was thus required to uphold the rule of law in a situation of fundamental illegality. The court has never addressed this issue, which presents a conundrum for the rule of law: if the constitutional groundnorm is legally invalid, can, or should, the courts challenge the very illegal groundnorm from which they derive their existence? This is an issue that lawyers interested in the rule of law would need to reflect upon deeply.

The state of the legal profession during this period was examined generally and through the cases. The picture presented is not an edifying one. The Court of Appeal, in one case, effectively held, in respect of a senior lawyer who was also Speaker of the Parliament, that his story in court – in a case in which he was plaintiff – strained credulity. Nevertheless, the legal profession continued oblivious to this holding and the person proceeded to receive the highest honour in the land. The Bar Association still has only a draft code of conduct and it is not clear what the regulatory authority of the legal profession is.

It would be fair to say that with regard to the criminal law one saw the brilliance of local judges and the majesty of the law in operation. One could also see the brilliance of the legal profession through the cases dealing with the criminal law, the law of contracts, the law of torts, and property law. When it came, however, to the protection of fundamental rights, one cannot avoid the impression that the individual was left to the whims of the court.

The application of international human rights law by the Court of Appeal has hardly even begun. While one has seen cases where the court based itself on international law generally, as regards prison conditions and standards of fair trial, voices on the Court of Appeal have argued for the standard of what the country could afford. There is no evidence of the courts insisting on the application of international standards in defence of fundamental human rights. This is a cause for serious concern.

One has seen bewildering behaviour on the part of highest judges in the land, chancellors of the judiciary. One would argue for 'socialist legality'; another would leave his position on the bench to become the Attorney General of the government; and a third would contend that women had no place in active practice at the Bar. All of this is cause for dismay.

In the midst of all of this, the Law Reports of Guyana were last published in 1975 and so, for the past 25 years, the decisions of the courts, including the Court of Appeal, are largely inaccessible. It was partly to remedy this deficiency that we set out at the beginning of this work a list of the notable cases of the Court of Appeal containing those decisions that were selected by its staff for binding and eventual publication. This is a distressing situation for a country that aspires to the rule of law.

Notwithstanding all of this, it is important, in our submission, to identify and build upon those strands in the jurisprudence of the Court of Appeal that can be built upon, in the future, to provide the foundations for the rule of law and respect for human rights. That has been a principal aim of this introductory study.

# APPENDIX A

## THE GEORGETOWN CONCLUSIONS ON THE EFFECTIVE PROTECTION OF HUMAN RIGHTS THROUGH LAW

During the past eight years an important series of judicial colloquia has taken place concerned with the application within national legal systems of international human rights norms. The meetings have been held under the auspices of the Commonwealth Secretariat and Interights (the International Centre for the Legal Protection of Human Rights). The participants have included judges from various countries of the Commonwealth, together with participants from common law countries outside the Commonwealth, from countries of the civil law tradition, and from international courts and other fora concerned with the legal protection of human rights.

The seventh meeting in the series took place in Georgetown, Guyana, between 3 and 5 September 1996. It was convened by the Chancellor and Head of the Judiciary of Guyana, the Hon Mr Justice AFR Bishop. The gathering was organised by Interights and the Caribbean Community Secretariat (CARICOM), with generous assistance from the Commonwealth Secretariat, the Overseas Development Administration of the United Kingdom, Cable and Wireless, and the World Council of Churches.

The colloquium was honoured by the opportunity to discuss with His Excellency the Hon Dr Cheddi Jagan, President of Guyana, the protection of human rights and the rule of law in a democratic society in their wider economic, social, and political context.

The participants at the colloquium were:

**Antigua and Barbuda**

The Hon Mr Justice Albert Redhead, High Court of Justice

**Barbados**

The Rt Hon Mr Justice Telford Georges, PC, Member, Judicial Committee of the Privy Council and former Chief Justice of the Bahamas, Tanzania and Zimbabwe

Ms Sandra Mason, Chief Magistrate

**Belize**

The Hon Madame Justice Cynthia Pitts, Family Court

**British Virgin Islands**

The Hon Mr Justice Ephraim Georges

The Hon Mr Justice Stanley Moore

**Dominica**

The Hon Mr Justice Odel Adams

**Grenada**

The Hon Mr Justice Brian Alleyne, SC, Justice, Supreme Court of Grenada and the Eastern Caribbean States

**Guyana**

The Hon Mr Justice Aubrey Bishop, Chancellor and Head of the Judiciary

The Hon Madame Justice Desiree Bernard, Justice of Appeal

Dr Bertrand Ramcharan, Director in the United Nations Secretariat, United Nations, New York

**India**

The Hon Justice PN Bhagwati, Former Chief Justice of India and Vice-Chairman of United Nations Human Rights Committee

Mr Soli J Sorabjee, SC, Senior Advocate, Supreme Court, former Attorney General of India

**Inter-American Commission on Human Rights/Organization of American States**

Ms Elizabeth Abi-Mershed, Staff Attorney

**Jamaica**

Dr Lloyd Barnett, attorney-at-law

Mr Laurel B Francis, Member, United Nations Human Rights Committee

The Hon Madame Justice Hazel Harris, Judge, Supreme Court

The Hon Mr Justice Carl Rattray, President, Court of Appeal

The Rt Hon Mr Justice Edward Zacca, Chief Justice (Retired)

**New Zealand**

The Hon Justice Keith, Court of Appeal of New Zealand

**Saint Lucia**

The Hon Mr Justice Dennis Byron, Chief Justice (acting), Eastern Caribbean Supreme Court

The Hon Madame Justice Susie D'Auvergne, Puisne Judge, OECS Supreme Court

**Trinidad and Tobago**

The Hon Mr Justice Anthony Lucky, Judge, Supreme Court of Trinidad

The Hon Madame Justice Jean Permanand, Judge of Court of Appeal

**United Kingdom**

The Hon Mr Justice Laws, Royal Courts of Justice, London

**United States of America**

The Hon Judge Betty Fletcher, United States Court of Appeals (Ninth Circuit)

**United Nations Human Rights Committee**

Mr Andreas Mavrommatis

**Zimbabwe**

The Hon Mr Justice Anthony Gubbay, Chief Justice

**Observing Judiciary from Guyana**

The Hon Mr Justice MA Churaman, Justice of Appeal

The Hon Mr Justice Prem Persaud, Justice of Appeal

The Hon Mr Justice Oslen Small, Puisne Judge

The Hon Mr Justice Carl Singh, Puisne Judge

The Hon Mr Justice Deonaraine Biscessar, Puisne Judge

The Hon Mr Justice Rudolph H Harper, Retired Chief Justice

**Commonwealth Secretariat Representative**

Mr Reginald Austin, Director of Legal and Constitutional Affairs

**INTERIGHTS Representatives**

The Rt Hon The Lord Lester of Herne Hill, QC, President

Ms Emma Playfair, Executive Director

Ms Natalia Schiffrin, Legal Officer

Ms Helen Cooper, Barrister

**Caribbean Community (CARICOM) Secretariat**

Mr Duke Pollard, Legal Consultant

Ms Thelma Rodney-Edwards, Assistant General Counsel

Dr Gloria Richards-Johnson, Assistant General Counsel

1 The participants reaffirmed the general principles stated at the conclusion of the Commonwealth Judicial Colloquium in Bangalore, India, in 1988, and developed by subsequent Colloquia in Harare, Zimbabwe, in 1989; in Banjul, The Gambia, in 1990; in Abuja, Nigeria, in 1991; in Balliol College, Oxford, in 1992; and in Bloemfontein, South Africa, in 1993.

2 Fundamental human rights and freedoms are universal and are inherent in all human kind. They find expression in constitutions and legal systems throughout the world; they are anchored in the international human rights instruments by which all genuinely democratic States are bound; their meaning is illuminated by a rich body of case law of international and national courts.

3 The universality of human rights and freedoms derives from the moral principle of each individual's personal and equal autonomy and human dignity. That principle transcends national political systems and is in the keeping of the independent judiciary.

4 The international human rights instruments and their developing jurisprudence enshrine values and principles of equality, freedom, rationality and fairness now recognized by the common law. They should be seen as complementary to domestic law in national courts. These instruments have inspired many of the constitutional guarantees of fundamental human rights and freedoms within and beyond the Commonwealth; they should be given constitutional status in all dependent territories.

5 Commonwealth Caribbean judges in the discharge of their functions should give increasing effect to relevant international human rights norms (including those of the Inter-American international human rights instruments) when interpreting and applying their national constitutions and laws. The constitutional guarantees should be interpreted with the generosity appropriate to charters of freedom, avoiding the austerity of tabulated legalism.

6 It is the vital duty of an independent, impartial, well-qualified judiciary, assisted by an independent well-trained legal profession, to interpret and apply national constitutions and ordinary legislation, and to develop the common law in the light of these values and principles. As Commonwealth Law Ministers recognized, at their meeting in Kuala Lumpur, Malaysia in April 1996, the independent and impartial judiciary plays a crucial role in a healthy democracy. 'The protections enjoyed by judges, including financial independence and security of tenure, are an important defence against improper interference and free the judiciary to discharge the particular responsibilities given to it within national constitutional frameworks.'

7 Both civil and political rights and economic, social and cultural rights are integral, indivisible and complementary parts of one coherent system of global human rights. The implementation of economic, social and cultural rights is a primary duty for the legislative and executive branches of government. However, even those economic, social and cultural rights which are not justiciable can serve as vital points of reference for judges as they interpret their constitutions and develop the common law, making choices which it is their responsibility to make in a free, equal and democratic society. Respect for human rights under the rule of law provides the best environment for the economic, social and cultural development of everyone in all parts of the world.

8 Fundamental human rights and freedoms are more than mere pious aspirations. They form part of the public law of every nation, protecting individuals and minorities against the misuse of power by public authorities of all kinds. It is the special province of judges to see to it that the law's undertakings are realised in the daily life of the people. In a society ruled by law, all public institutions and authorities – legislative, executive and judicial – must act in accordance with the Constitution and the law.

9 The legislative and executive branches of government have a duty to provide the necessary means to secure the equal protection of the law, speedy and effective access to justice, and effective legal remedies. To achieve this, there is a need for adequate funds for the proper functioning of the courts, and adequate legal aid, advice and assistance for people who cannot otherwise obtain legal services. It is also essential for each branch of government to introduce and maintain appropriate rules and procedures to promote compliance, in discharging their functions, with the international human rights instruments by which they are bound.

10 The provision of equal justice requires a competent and independent judiciary and legal profession trained in the discipline of the law and sensitive to the needs and aspirations of all the people. It is fundamental for a country's judiciary and legal profession to enjoy the broad confidence of the people they serve.

11 Judicial review and effective access to the courts are indispensable, not only in normal times, but also during periods of public emergency. It is at such times that basic human rights are most at risk and when courts must be especially vigilant in their protection.

12 Freedom of expression must be jealously protected as essential to the safeguarding of democracy and human rights. The courts must be zealous to protect free speech and expression in their widest sense and at all times.

13 In relation to the death penalty, the participants recommended:

(i) that it should not be extended to any new offences to which it is not now applied in the particular State;

(ii) that States whose independence constitutions preclude the determination by the courts as to whether the sentence is inhuman and degrading, if the punishment was lawful prior to the achievement of national status, should amend their constitutions to remove this fetter on judicial determination;

(iii) that the death penalty should not be carried out until the exhaustion of all domestic and international legal remedies available to the applicant.

14 There is a need for courses in law schools and other institutions of learning to educate the next generation of judges, legislators, administrators and lawyers in human rights jurisprudence. The urgent necessity remains to bring the principles of human rights into the daily activities of government and public officials alike and of ordinary men and women. In this way a global culture of respect for human rights can be fostered.

15 The participants recognised the need to adopt a generous approach to the matter of legal standing in public law cases, while ensuring that the courts are not overwhelmed with frivolous cases. The courts should allow themselves to be assisted by well focused *amicus curiae* submissions from independent NGOs, such as Interights, in novel and important cases where international and comparative law and practice may be relevant. National laws should enable NGOs and expert advocates (whether local or otherwise) to provide specialist legal advice, assistance and representation in important cases of public interest. Bar associations and law societies should ensure that public interest cases can be effectively presented *pro bono publico*.

16 The participants expressed concern that the legislatures of some countries pass amendments to their constitutions or laws designed to erode or diminish fundamental rights and freedoms as interpreted and applied by national courts and by international human rights fora. They recommended that this practice of diluting the internationally and nationally guaranteed human rights of the individual should not be resorted to, and that no amendment should be made which would destroy or impair the essential features of democratic societies governed by the rule of law.

17 The participants urged closer links and co-operation across national frontiers by the judiciary of the Commonwealth Caribbean and beyond on the interpretation and application of human rights law. They attached the highest importance to disseminating to the judiciary and other lawyers, knowledge about the human rights norms of international law, the jurisprudence of international and regional human rights bodies, and the decisions of courts throughout the Commonwealth. They greatly welcomed the publication by Interights of the Commonwealth Human Rights Law Digest as an important means of improving access by judges, lawyers, NGOs and the public. They expressed the hope that the

Commonwealth Secretariat will provide within its human rights programmes the resources necessary to service the Commonwealth Judicial Human Rights Association, in collaboration with Interights, as recommended by previous colloquia.

18 In these ways a global culture of knowledge and respect for human rights can be fostered, and the noble words of international human rights instruments will be translated into practical reality for the benefit of the people we serve, but also ultimately for the benefit of people in every land, with the Commonwealth properly at the forefront, as befits its high ideals.

# APPENDIX B

# CODE OF CONDUCT APPROVED BY GUYANA BAR ASSOCIATION (1985)

## PREAMBLE

This Code of Conduct is intended to lay down minimum standards to which attorneys-at-law are required to adhere. Its promulgation is not intended to deny the existence of such other duties and rules of conduct at the Bar as were extant immediately before our attainment of independence on 26 May 1966, and which, unless specifically varied by legislation, are deemed to be continuing and are to be equally observed with this Code.

Where an attorney-at-law is in doubt on any matter touching professional conduct or where he requires ethical guidance he should immediately get in touch with the Secretary of the Bar Association. The underlying aim is that an attorney-at-law should at all times conduct himself in a manner that promotes public confidence in the integrity and efficiency of the legal system and the legal profession.

Integrity and judicial independence are the twin pillars of justice.

The Appendix includes recommendations which the Bar Council offers to all attorneys-at-law as useful guides that they should follow.

All references to the masculine include the feminine and all references to the singular include the plural and vice versa.

## RULE I – CONFIDENTIALITY

1 An attorney-at-law shall so arrange his business and office to ensure that his clients' affairs are treated with the utmost confidence.

2 Every attorney-at-law has a duty to hold in strict confidence all information received in the course of the professional relationship from or concerning his client or his clients' affairs and this information should not be divulged by an attorney-at-law unless he is expressly or impliedly authorized by his client to do so.

3 The duty of confidentiality survives the professional relationship and continues indefinitely after the attorney-at-law has ceased to act for the client whether differences may have arisen between them or not.

4 The duty of confidentiality enjoins an attorney-at-law to avoid indiscreet conversations, even with his spouse or family about a client or his affairs and he should shun gossiping about such things even though the client is not named or otherwise identified.

5 The relationship of client and attorney-at-law compels the latter to eschew personal intimate relations with clients of the opposite sex.

6 An attorney-at-law shall not use undue influence on a client to obtain a gift under his client's will or testamentary instruments, nor shall the attorney-at-Law in any way exploit the aforesaid confidential relationship for making personal profits or investments by himself or those acting through him.

## RULE II – RULE OF LAW

1 All attorneys-at-law shall be deemed to subscribe to the rule of law, which they shall use as an unalterable and fundamental guide in the conduct of their professional affairs.

2 Every attorney-at-law shall encourage public respect for, and strive to improve, the administration of justice.

3 Any criticism by an attorney-at-law of the system of justice or its functionaries must be reasoned and soundly based. Attorneys-at-law shall avoid criticisms that are petty or intemperate.

4 Attorneys-at-law shall not subvert the law by counselling or assisting in activities which are in defiance of it, nor do anything to diminish the respect and confidence of the public in the legal system of which they are a part.

5 Attorneys-at-law shall refrain from making irresponsible allegations of corruption or partiality that may tend to weaken or destroy public confidence in legal institutions.

6 Attorneys-at-law shall obey the law and show respect for the law.

## RULE III – INTEGRITY

1 Attorneys-at-law shall discharge their duties to courts of law, their clients, members of the public and their professional colleagues with integrity.

2 Neither in his private nor in his professional activities shall there be dishonest or dishonourable conduct on the part of an attorney-at-law.

3 A legal opinion should be given frankly based on an objective consideration of actual facts and fair judgment, and should not be influenced by the interests of the client.

4 Honesty, honour and reliability are the fountainheads of integrity.

## RULE IV – CONFLICT OF INTEREST

1 An attorney-at-law shall not advise or represent more than one interest in a matter nor shall he act or continue to act in a matter when there is or is likely to be a conflicting interest; which includes but is not limited to the financial interest of the attorney-at-law or his associate, and the duties and loyalties of the attorney-at-law to any other client or prospective client including the obligation to communicate information.

2 An attorney-at-law shall make adequate disclosure to the client so that he may make an informed decision as to whether he wishes the attorney-at-law to act for him despite the presence or possibility of conflicting interest.

3 When acting for more than one side, the attorney-at-law shall inform the parties that no information received in connection with the matter for or from any one side can or will be treated as confidential as far as any of the others may be concerned and that if a conflict develops he cannot continue to act for any of them, and he will have to withdraw completely.

4 It shall not be improper for any attorney-at-law to act against a former client in a fresh and independent matter wholly unrelated to any work he has previously done for that person.

5 The burden of establishing the disclosure of conflict of interest shall be on the attorney-at-law.

6 An attorney-at-law engaged wholly or partly at the criminal bar shall not accept membership on the Police Service Commission.

7 An attorney-at-law who is an official of a company or corporation or any other organization shall not accept a brief against such company or corporation or organization, or in favour of a member thereof against another member in respect of a dispute arising out of their common membership.

8 An attorney-at-law who engages in another profession, business or occupation concurrently with the practice of law shall not allow such outside interests to jeopardize his professional integrity, independence or competence.

## RULE V – COMPETENCE

1 An attorney-at-law shall not accept a brief in a matter or field in which he does not have the requisite expertise, knowledge, skill or ability to effectively and properly represent the interest of his client.

2 An attorney-at-law must be alert to recognise his lack of competence for a particular task and the disservice he will do his client if he undertook such a task. Should the client insist on his retention, the attorney-at-law shall consult and collaborate with an attorney-at-law who is competent in that field.

3 An attorney-at-law shall perform all the work and services which he undertakes on behalf of his client in a competent manner, providing a quality of service at least equal to that which attorneys-at-law generally would expect of a competent legal practitioner in a like situation.

4 An attorney-at-law who displays incompetence does his client a disservice, brings discredit on his profession and may bring the administration of justice into disrepute.

5 Without derogating from the generality of the foregoing rules, an attorney-at-law shall (a) keep his client reasonably informed; (b) do work for which he is retained promptly and not belatedly so that its true value to his client is diminished; (c) avoid slipshod work, such as mistakes or omissions in statements or documents prepared on behalf of his clients; (d) inform his client properly of proposals for a settlement or determination of a matter; (e) avoid misleading a client as to the position of a matter in order to cover up his neglect or mistakes, and (f) ...

## RULE VI – ADVERTISEMENTS

1 Advertising professional legal services in or through any medium is strictly forbidden. Advertising is incompatible with the honour of the profession and can be detrimental to the public interest. Brief announcements of a change in address or telephone numbers are permitted.

2 An attorney-at-law shall not compensate a reporter or otherwise pay to have his name included in the report of a case.

3 The foregoing prohibitions extend also to law firms, and all the attorneys-at-law connected with the erring firm shall be deemed to have transgressed those rules, unless he can establish that the matter occurred without his knowledge or consent.

4 An attorney-at-law may use the following – letter heads, cards, office signs or legal and directory listings, and no others, in a restrained and dignified form:

(i) A letter head and professional card identifying the attorney-at-law by name and as an attorney-at-law giving his decorations and degrees (legal or otherwise), his addresses, telephone numbers and the name of his law firm or professional associates, provided that such cards are not published in the news media and are only handed out on request.

(ii) A sign on or near the door of the office, and in the building directory identifying the law office, provided that it is of a size and design compatible with the existing practice of the profession.

(iii) A listing in a telephone directory, a reputable law list, legal directory or biographical reference giving brief relevant information and not calculated to attract clients to himself or his firm.

5 An attorney-at-law may permit limited and dignified identification of himself as an attorney-at-law:

(i) in public notices where the announcement of his professional status is required or authorized by law;

(ii) in or on legal textbooks, articles or publications and in advertisements thereof;

(iii)in announcements of any public address or lecture by him on legal topics, provided that such announcements do not emphasize his own professional competence and are not likely to be regarded as being concerned with the giving of individual advice by him.

6 An attorney-at-law shall not solicit appearance on radio or television or any other public forum in his professional capacity as an attorney-at-law or attempt to use any appearance as a means of professional advertisement.

7 An attorney-at-law shall not offer generally to provide legal services at reduced rates for the purpose of attracting clients.

8 The provisions of this Rule shall not prevent such reasonable advertising as may be necessary to bring to the attention of underprivileged persons the existence of Legal Aid facilities or organizations engaged in the provision of such facilities as may be approved by the Bar Council.

## RULE VII – ADVOCACY

1 Attorneys-at-law shall respectfully bow to all courts in session on entering and leaving them, and on the occasions of the presiding judge or magistrate entering or leaving the court and bowing to same.

2 When an attorney-at-law is appointed a judge or a magistrate, he shall comport himself with dignity on the Bench displaying good manners, humility, patience, detachment, and a respectful attitude towards other participants in the trial, avoiding arrogance and pomposity.

3 An attorney-at-law shall treat the court with courtesy and respect, while representing his client resolutely, honourably and within the limits of the law.

4 Attorneys-at-law have a duty to their clients to fearlessly raise every issue, advance every argument and ask every question, however distasteful, which they think will help their client's case; and to endeavour to obtain for their client's benefit any and every remedy and set up any defence which is authorized by law and in a manner consistent with their duty to treat the court with candour, fairness, courtesy and respect.

5 Attorneys-at-law shall not indulge in angry verbal exchange in court, even if made *sotto voce*. All objections shall be addressed to the court and not to fellow attorneys-at-law.

6 Attorneys-at-law shall not conceal documents that their opponents are entitled to see.

7 It is prohibited for attorneys-at-law to engage in abusive or threatening language and physical attacks in court (or out of court).

8 An attorney-at-law shall always stand when addressing the court. Where an attorney-at-law is being addressed by a judge or magistrate he shall

stand at the Bar Table. It is not permissible for either to use language that is not courtly or Parliamentary; nor to shout.

9 It is forbidden for an attorney-at-law to appear in any court in a state of intoxication.

10 An attorney-at-law shall not abuse, intimidate, inconvenience or harass a witness. Intemperate cross-examination or the abuse of the privilege of advocacy to insult, annoy or degrade a witness is impermissible.

## RULE VIII – STANDARDS OF CONDUCT

1 An attorney-at-law has a special duty not to advise or assist in the violation of the Law. Likewise, he shall not knowingly assist or permit his client to say anything which the attorney-at-law knows to be dishonest or dishonourable.

2 When advising his client an attorney-at-law shall not knowingly assist or encourage any dishonesty, fraud, crime or illegal conduct or instruct his client to violate the law or how to avoid punishment. He shall be on his guard against becoming the tool or dupe of an unscrupulous client or those who are associated with that client.

3 An attorney-at-law who appears in a matter in which another attorney-at-law was previously acting, is obliged to inform the latter of his appearance in the matter.

4 An attorney-at-law shall not attempt to intervene in a case for which another attorney-at-law has been retained. An attorney-at-law should not unreasonably interfere with the desire of his client to have another attorney-at-law participate in the case.

5 By his oath an attorney-at-law is required to appear for clients for whom he has been retained, regardless of their political affiliations and notwithstanding the connection of the cause or matter with politics. When an attorney-at-law so appears he is entitled as of right to be treated with the same courtesy as in cases which do not have political overtones.

6 An attorney-at-law shall not without good reason decline matters which have been referred to him by government authorities. A court-appointed defence counsel shall not attempt to be retained by the defendant as private counsel in connection with the same case.

7 An attorney-at-law whether for the prosecution or defence shall not endeavour or suffer anyone else to endeavour, directly or indirectly, to influence the decision or action of a court or any of its officials in any case or matter, whether by bribery, personal approach or any means other than open persuasion as an advocate.

8 An attorney-at-law shall not coach witnesses.

9 An attorney-at-law shall not attempt to deceive a court or influence the course of justice by offering false evidence, knowingly misstating facts or

law, presenting or relying upon a false or deceptive affidavit, suppressing what ought to be disclosed or assisting in fraud, crime or illegal conduct.

10 An attorney-at-law shall not knowingly misstate the contents of a document, the testimony of a witness, the substance of an argument or the provisions of a statute or like authority.

11 It is the duty of every attorney-at-law to draw authorities to the court's attention and not to conceal any authority that is or may be against his proposition.

12 An attorney-at-law shall not dissuade a material witness from giving evidence or advise such a witness to absent himself, nor shall he knowingly assist a witness to misrepresent himself or impersonate another.

13 An attorney-at-law shall not express his personal opinions or beliefs in the conduct of a case. He shall not in effect make himself an unsworn witness. If he becomes a necessary witness in a case conduced by him, he should testify and the conduct of the case shall be entrusted to another attorney-at-law. An attorney-at-law who was a witness in proceedings shall not appear as an advocate in any appeal from the decision in those proceedings.

14 Attorneys-at-law who are elevated to judicial or magisterial office shall discharge their duties by giving prompt decisions, in the case of the latter within the time prescribed by any statute; and in the case of the former within a reasonable time.

15 Any attorney-at-law who has served as a magistrate shall not upon embarking or resuming private practice accept a brief or appear for any party in a matter which had been previously called before him while he served as a magistrate.

## RULE IX – CLIENTS' INTERESTS

1 An attorney-at-law owes a duty to his clients to keep in safe keeping any of his clients' property that is entrusted to him; and he shall take the same care of such property as a careful and prudent man would take of his own property of a like kind.

2 An attorney-at-law shall keep adequate records of client's property in his possession, and upon request he shall promptly account for or deliver it to or to the order of his client.

3 Documents such as wills and minute books shall be treated by attorneys-at-law with the same reserve as confidential information.

4 An attorney-at-law shall only withdraw his services from his client for good cause and upon appropriate notice to his client.

5 An attorney-at-law who is deceived by his client shall have justifiable cause for withdrawal.

6 Upon withdrawal and due discharge of such reasonable fees as an attorney-at-law may have charged, he shall deliver to or to the order of his client all papers and property to which his client is entitled; give to his client all information that he may require in connection with the case or matter; and co-operate with the attorney-at-law who succeeds him to facilitate the orderly transfer of the case or matter to him.

7 Unless warranted by special circumstances, an attorney-at-law shall not contact or negotiate directly with the opposite party who is represented by an attorney-at-law, without the consent of such attorney-at-law.

## RULE X – RELATIONS WITH FELLOW LAWYERS

1 The conduct of an attorney-at-law towards other attorneys-at-law shall be characterized by respect, courtesy and good faith.

2 Any ill feeling which may exist or be engendered between clients, particularly during litigation, shall not influence attorneys-at-law in their conduct and demeanour toward each other or the parties.

3 Attorneys-at-law shall answer with reasonable promptness all professional letters and communications from other attorneys-at-law which require an answer, and they shall be punctual in fulfilling all commitments.

4 Attorneys-at-law shall avoid ill-considered or uninformed criticism of the competence, conduct, advice and charges of other attorneys-at-law.

5 Assistance and advice in matters of law and procedure from one attorney-at-law to another attorney-at-law shall be readily available on request by an attorney-at-law, subject to any interest the requesting attorneys-at-law may have in the cause or matter.

6 Before accepting a retainer to act as a substitute or successor attorney-at-law, an attorney-at-law shall properly satisfy himself that the predecessor attorney-at-law has withdrawn or has been duly discharged by the client, and the successor attorney-at-law shall not embark on the retainer unless outstanding fees for work done have been settled with or secured to the attorney-at-law from whom he is taking over.

7 Only when the trial or hearing is in progress and the client would be otherwise prejudiced, is an attorney-at-law allowed to substitute for another where fees to the latter have not been settled or satisfied.

8 Unless otherwise directed by the Bar Council, an attorney-at-law in court shall hold the brief of an absent attorney-at-law on request and do all that is reasonable to assist his absent colleague. He shall report or cause a report of his intervention in court to be promptly reported to his colleague.

9 An attorney-at-law shall not attempt to influence the attorney-at-law for the opposite side by offering a benefit in connection with the case.

## RULE XI – PUBLIC LAW OFFICERS

1 An attorney-at-law regardless of which public office he holds shall bring to the discharge of his duties the same high standards of conduct which he is required to observe as an attorney-at-law in private practice.

2 Unless an attorney-at-law has given cause for treatment to the contrary his word shall be accepted as his honour.

3 The acceptance of public office shall in no way militate against an attorney-at-law treating with those in private practice with respect, courtesy and good faith; and vice versa.

4 An attorney-at-law who holds public office *qua* attorney-at-law shall not allow his personal or other interests to conflict with the proper discharge of his official duties.

5 An attorney-at-law holding public office *qua* attorney-at-law shall not engage in private practice as a legal practitioner.

6 Justices of the Court of Appeal and judges of the High Court shall not appear at the Bar itself following their retirement or their ceasing to hold such offices.

7 Confidential information acquired by an attorney-at-law by virtue of his holding public office shall be kept confidential and shall not be divulged or used by him merely because he has ceased to hold such office.

8 Attorneys-at-law performing judicial or magisterial functions shall not adjudicate in cases in which they have an interest or are personally connected with one of the leading parties involved in the case.

## RULE XII – APPEARANCE

1 In the Supreme Court, attorneys-at-law shall always be attired in sober colours. The standard accepted colours shall be black, dark blue and grey – trousers shall always be of full length and jackets and shirt jackets shall always be of long sleeves. The material chosen shall be of good quality.

2 Attorneys-at-law shall always appear in court neatly attired, tidy and clean.

3 Attorneys-at-law shall always wear close fitting shoes (with socks or stockings) in court. Except for medical reasons, sandals of any kind and yachting or track shoes shall not be worn in court. Footwear shall also be of a sober colour.

4 If a sari or shalwar is worn, it shall be of sober colour.

5 Courts shall have the right to refuse to hear attorneys-at-law who are not properly attired.

6 Attorneys-at-law shall conform with the practice directions given from time to time by the Chancellor as to attire in court.

## RULE XIII – TOUTING

1 'Tout' shall bear the same meaning set out in the Legal Practitioners Act, Chapter 4:01.

2 An attorney-at-law who is connected with touting or who associates with touts shall be deemed unfit to practise as an attorney-at-law.

3 Attorneys-at-law shall not permit known touts on their premises or in their offices.

4 An attorney-at-law who becomes aware, or reasonably suspects that a person who, not being entitled to practise as an attorney-at-law or not being a public officer acting in execution of his duty, for or in expectation of a fee, gain or reward, draws or prepares or offers to draw or prepare any legal document other than a will, shall be obliged to report the same promptly to the Bar Council.

5 An attorney-at-law shall not speak derogatorily of another attorney-at-law in good standing; nor shall he by disparaging remarks or otherwise of another attorney-at-law seek to attract clients to himself in preference to that other attorney-at-law.

6 An attorney-at-law shall not solicit retainers or briefs in any manner; nor shall be given any inducement to have his services retained.

7 Attorneys-at-law shall avoid giving confident assurances to clients or potential clients as to the results of a case or matter, more especially when his retainer depends on his advising his client or potential client in a particular way.

## RULE XIV – PROHIBITED BUSINESS

Practising attorneys-at-law shall not engage in or be associated with any illegal, disreputable or unsuitable business or transactions.

## RULE XV – BAR ASSOCIATION

1 All practising attorneys-at-law shall be required to be members or associate members of the Guyana Bar Association.

2 As a continuing condition of practice all attorneys-at-law shall be members or associate members in good standing in the Guyana Bar Association.

3 An attorney-at-law shall promptly respond to a request from the Guyana Bar Association or committee or agent thereof for comments or information on matters raised by the Association with him.

## RULE XVI – FUNDS

1 All monies received by attorneys-at-law for their clients shall be scrupulously accounted for.

2 An attorney-at-law shall promptly notify his client of the receipt of any property of or relating to his client unless he is satisfied that this client is aware that it has come into his custody.

3 Attorneys-at-law shall promptly discharge and pay out costs damages judgments or other disbursements on behalf of their clients from monies received by them from or on behalf of their clients.

4 Attorneys-at-law shall keep adequate records of their clients' monies that come into their custody and shall keep such money in a bank in a separate account from their own.

## RULE XVII – DISCIPLINE

1 An attorney-at-law who suffers a conviction involving moral turpitude shall be disqualified from practising at the Bar.

2 An attorney-at-law who is declared an insolvent shall be disqualified from practising at the Bar, but may apply to the High Court to restore his right to practise if he is discharged.

3 An attorney-at-law shall promptly answer reports from the Legal Practitioners' Committee established under the Legal Practitioners Act, Chapter 4:01 and ensure his punctual attendance before same when he is requested to attend.

4 Except where otherwise stated, a breach of any of the foregoing rules of conduct shall render an attorney-at-law liable to a reprimand, a fine not exceeding $2,000.00, suspension from practice for a period not exceeding six months and disbarment from practice.

5 Before being found in breach of any rule of the Code of Conduct for Legal Practitioners, an attorney-at-law shall be afforded an opportunity to exculpate himself from any charge thereto before a Disciplinary Code Committee established by the Bar Council.

6 An attorney-at-law duly found in breach of the Code of Conduct for Legal Practitioners shall have a right to appeal to the Bar Council within 14 days of the decision.

## ANNEX

1 Read and Digest:

(ii) Advocacy in Court and Preparation of Cases by Justice JC Gonsalves-Sabola.

(ii) A Practitioner's Perspective on Advocacy and Decorum in Court and the Preparation of Cases by Adams, BO, SC, BA, LLB, BCL.

2 Out of court conduct particularly at places of public entertainment should be that expected of a gentleman or lady.

3 Before filing a writ or summons against a fellow attorney-at-law, or at all events at the time of so doing, a note or memo to this effect should be sent by the attorney-at-law who is filing same to the attorney-at-law who is being sued.

4 In the normal course of things, an attorney-at-law on visiting the offices of another attorney-at-law on legal business shall on request be promptly accorded an audience with his professional colleague.

5 Attorneys-at-law practising in the same firm or partnership shall not conduct or hold a case against an attorney-at-law of the same firm or partnership. In joining or establishing the firm or partnership, incompleted contentious matters between attorneys-at-law in the same firm or partnership shall be transferred to attorneys-at-law outside of the said firm or partnership.

6 Attorneys-at-law shall be properly groomed in court.

7 Brothels, spirit shops, strip shops, and betting shops are considered unsuitable business as referred to Rule XIV.

8 Newly admitted attorneys-at-law should normally take advantage of the courtesy of being introduced to the judge or magistrate preferably in Chambers before appearing before such judge or magistrate for the first time. This is a courtesy which ought to be appropriately followed up by direct personal introductions to senior members of the Bar (and attorneys-at-law within the same circuit).

# APPENDIX C

# EXCERPTS OF ADDRESS ON THE FUNCTIONS OF THE COURTS IN CONTEMPORARY GUYANA

*By*

*The Honourable VE Crane (Chancellor of the Judiciary) to the Guyana Bar Association on 28 October 1981*

Having made preliminary observations in which he established that the aim was to achieve greater social justice for all, the Chancellor proceeded to examine this from three standpoints: (1) maintenance of the rule of law; (2) the administration of justice and (3) the development of the law. He continued:

## 1 MAINTENANCE OF THE RULE OF LAW

**The rule of law remains a principle of our Constitution notwithstanding its recent transformation and socialist orientation. In its clearest connotation the rule signifies the absence of arbitrary power in the State** and has come to be regarded as the hallmark of a free society. In all democratic constitutions, the rule of law is identified with the liberty of the individual in a free society. In the Universal Declaration of Human Rights, 1948, it is laid down that **the end of the rule of law is the attainment of justice and consequently of order and freedom.** A breakdown of it necessarily leads to tyranny, oppression, rebellion and anarchy.

In Guyana, the rule of law is very necessary so as to provide the right environment for socialist orientation and nation building which are the dominant preoccupations of Parliament and the Government of the Co-operative Republic of Guyana. The judiciary is now a necessary and integral part of the political, economic and social system, and the judiciary must look upon itself as having a crucial role to play in this task by ensuring that in the all-important field of socialist development, basic values like the rule of the law and, consequently, justice, are to be maintained. This is, without any doubt, one of the most important of the judiciary's functions in contemporary Guyana.

Article 32 makes it obligatory that the rule of law shall prevail by insisting that 'it is the joint duty on the State, the society and every citizen **to combat and prevent crime and other violations of the law,** and to take care of and to protect public property'. This clearly means that since the Constitution imposes a duty of the aforesaid entities in Art 32, then there must be a corresponding legal right to seek redress in the courts available to those persons with violated rights. A conjoint reading of Arts 32 and 39 makes this quite clear. And though the expression 'rule of law' is not expressly mentioned in the present as it was in the preamble to the previous Constitution the object is very much the same – to secure the citizen's rights and freedoms 'in a democratic society founded upon the **rule of law**.'

## THWARTING POLICY

But specific reference to the expression, 'the rule of law', in the preamble of the last Constitution and its absence from the present has caused the uninformed and certain agents of destabilisation to say that means an end to the rule of law; that the universality of the rule of law has been abolished in Guyana. Nevertheless, as I have shown, the object is the same in the old as well as in our new socialist Constitutions. The rule of law in Guyana is quite alive and continues unabated and guaranteed to the subject just as it always used to be. Article 40 dealing with fundamental rights and freedom of the individual, and Arts 138–51, inclusive, providing for the protection of these rights, are all indications of the existence of the rule of the supremacy of the law, notwithstanding that expression is not repeated in the present Constitution. Integrally connected with the rule of law are the judicial officers of the State.

Judicial courage is closely associated with judicial independence. A judge must always have the courage of his convictions, irrespective of whether he is right or wrong in what he decides. It sometimes requires a great deal of courage to give judgment in some criminal cases involving the public interest, and in civil cases between the State and the subject involving the liability to the State in regard to the rights and interests of the citizen; also in cases involving the invocation by the court of its control and jurisdiction over the executive in the exercise of ministerial or statutory powers or functions ...

This, of course, does not mean that the judiciary should be pressurised by the executive, only that the judiciary ought not to set itself up in opposition to that organ of government ...

But while the approach of the judiciary in Guyana should be to march in step with the aspirations of the people and the government, it must not hesitate, if the occasion ever warrants it, courageously to demonstrate the principle of its independence. Sometimes this principle is performed in the interpretation of the Constitution and may involve the very life of the government. I shall have more to say about it later on.

## 2 THE ADMINISTRATION OF JUSTICE

'Hereby it is manifest that during the time men live without a common power to keep them all in awe, they are in that condition which is called war; and such a war as is of every man against every man ... Whatsoever therefore in consequent to a time of war, where every man is enemy to every man, the same is consequent to the time wherein man live without other security than what their own strength and their own invention shall furnish them withal ... In such condition there is no place for industry ... no arts, no letters, no society, and, which is worst of all, poor, nasty, brutish, and short.' (Hobbes, Leviathan, Chapter 13.)

## ADMINISTRATION

Hobbes, however, was not altogether right. Philosophers have disputed the correctness of the above statement and the point whether it has even been really the true nature of man to live continuously at war with his fellow man. However, while on this aspect, I need not delve too deeply into the necessity for institutionalized law enforcement. The need for it must be self-evident to us all. But suffice it to say, lying beneath the veneer of civilisation is the ever-present danger that man is wont to resort to force or violent extrajudicial self-help to settle grievances with his rivals. This tendency is not new, and to arrest it, in medieval times the Statute of Marlborough in the days of King Henry III decreed that: 'All persons as well of high as of low estate, shall receive justice in the King's Court, and none from henceforth shall take revenge or distress of his own authority without award of Court.' (52 Hen III C 1.) But this is not unusual for all early codes demonstrate the gradual method in which the voice and force of the State become the exclusive instrument of declaration and enforcement of justice.

The chief function of the judiciary, however, is the administration of justice. It is essentially concerned with adjudication, eg, the resolution of conflicting rights and interests. It is intended to highlight a few major problems of administration of justice that Guyana has in common with some new Commonwealth countries of which I have been speaking and which I have considered necessary to compare with Guyana in illustration of our topic.

## DELAY

No matter where trials take place, it seems there will always be complaint of delays in hearing.

It has been rightly said of the law's delays that they have become proverbial. It is neither new nor peculiar to any period in history nor to any country. It has been the characteristic of all countries and is, perhaps, as old as the law itself. One can read of it in Herodotus. It confronted the Greeks (Athenians) who appointed six men to overhaul their legal system. It stared the Romans in the face, and they appointed 10 men, the Decemvirs, to tackle the problem. It has been the theme of tragedy and comedy. Hamlet included the law's delays among the seven burdens of man. It made Goethe change from law to letters. Chekhov and Moliere wrote tragedies based on it; Dickens memorialized it in *Bleak House*; and Gilbert and Sullivan it in song.

Quite recently too, following on strictures and accusations of laziness from the Lord Chief Justice of England, judges at the Old Bailey in London devised a scheme to defeat the law's delays by beginning daily sitting half an hour earlier. Instead of starting work at the traditional hour of 10.30 am they began at 10.00 am. The results were startling. It was calculated that the extra 30 minutes per day worked by 23 courts effectively provided the Old Bailey with the equivalent of an additional two working judges each week, and a backlog of 1,200 cases had been reduced to under 800 within the space of three weeks. But whatever the contributory causes of the delay in dispensing justice, it cannot be denied that 'justice delayed is justice denied'.

After pointing to the independence of judges and magistrates under our Constitution and to the English principle that judges should be absolutely independent of the government, he continued:

## VIEWPOINTS

But, it appears to me, the difference between English and socialist viewpoints springs from historical antecedents. The English judiciary was not always in the same pre-eminent position in which it finds itself today. As one eminent writer expressed it, far from being as they are today, 'lions *beside* the throne', in the days of the Stuart Kings, they were merely 'lions *beneath* the throne'. And it was only after the Act of Settlement 1701, that the English judiciary can be said 'to stand between the Executive and the subject', and that an end was put to the claim of the monarchy that judges held office during the King's good pleasure. Henceforth, they could no longer be removed at will. In former days, right up to the close of the 17th century, the executive in England was suppressive of the rights of the subject. It was the work of the Glorious Revolution of 1688 that achieved their independence. This was how the judiciary in England became a referee, so to speak.

On the contrary, a judge under a co-operative socialist-type constitution, whilst maintaining his independence, must needs work in conjunction with, and not inseparably from the executive. There is no rigid sphere of constitutionally assigned jurisdiction with regard to the judiciary. There is no longer any theory, as there is in England, about a judge in a co-operative socialist State 'standing between the State and the citizen' because, under socialism, it cannot be envisaged that the State and the citizen can even be in conflict: they ought never to be if they are pursuing the same goals towards socialist democracy and co-operation. The courts are in duty bound, just like Parliament and the government, to be guided in the discharge of their functions by the principals and based on the political and socio-economic system (Art 39) and so it is the duty of the socialist judge to work in unison and co-operatively with the Administration in furthering these principles.

## CO-OPERATION

The high point of the present-day arrangement is that while he maintains his judicial independence and conscience, the Guyanese judge works in co-operation with the Administration for the advancement of socialism; but the courts are not mere mouthpieces of government policy, because the courts are quite competent to try issues because the State, the society and the citizenry under their joint duty under Art 32 and adjudge either the State or other entity to be in default of duty. Judicial independence, however, does not mean that a judge in contemporary Guyana should stay aloof from the realities of life and the *modus vivendi* of Guyanese citizenry as he used to do. Rather, he must further their interests whenever possible, in accordance with the principles as set out in Chapter 2 wherein are set out a number of national goals or objectives, and directive principles for achieving them.

In Guyana there was never a problem of administration concerning an indigenous legal system such as exists in places like Africa and Asia when the English common law was received as part of our legal system in the year 1917. Speaking about this topic Dr Shahabuddeen in his work *The Legal System of Guyana*, p 190, tells this story: 'In British Guiana the conditions were very different. Since its colonization in the 17th, century and, more particularly, since its surrender to the British in 1803, it possessed a highly organised flexible system of common law which, but for the special conditions of the colony, would have proved as suitable for all commercial and social requirements as a similar form of jurisprudence and done for the larger and more important British and Dutch settlements in South Africa and Southern Rhodesia.'

## 3 THE DEVELOPMENT OF THE LAW

On the development of the law, he stated:

> Now that Guyana has a Constitution into which is entrenched the principles and concepts of socialism the courts are now faced with the challenge, even more than before in the evolving constitutional experiment, to develop it by judicial exposition and analysis and to apply those principles to such factual situations as are brought before them. From the legal standpoint, this is how the principles and bases of the political socio-economic system will develop. In the exercise of their constitutional interpretative functions, courts will make positive declarations on rights and duties. However, the courts cannot declare on rights and duties unless they are specifically asked to do so and, in some cases, unless enabling legislation is enacted as an aid to enforceability. That this is the intention of the Administration is to be seen from what it has in prospect–the establishment of two committees headed by two eminent experts in their own field – former Minister of Agriculture Gavin Kennard and Justice Desiree Bernard.

## COMMITMENT

And this is where I think the Bar as protectors of the rights of the citizens can render an invaluable service to the community in helping to build the system under which we now live. It behoves every lawyer to exercise a greater sense of commitment to the country's socialist ideology and to spare no pains to have the principles of socialism tested and expounded by the courts. But just how are they to condition their minds to the tasks? I would respectfully suggest to practitioners they should abandon all previous common law notions and approaches to continuously fix their eyes on the Constitution and to begin to think individually, collectively, imaginatively and consistently about socialist democracy that is now an inseparable and organic part of our national ethos. I have already referred to the need for co-operation between Bench and Bar as a *sine quo non* for furthering, developing, aiding and co-ordinating the work of the courts. And though it is very necessary for both Bench and Bar to continue to inform themselves from Commonwealth and other law reports in particular, and other legal periodicals in general, on the progress and development of the law, we must learn to think for ourselves, to be self-reliant and to look for solutions to problems locally and within the ambit of our Constitution.

When deciding cases our judges, in point of principle, ought first to pay regard to local law reports on what has already been decided in Guyana and in West Indian jurisdictions. Our own reports date from about 1865, eg, during the days when the old Roman-Dutch law was the common law of Guyana. And it will be of interest to note that Dr Shahabuddeen has raised practically the same point I now seek to make about the duty of our courts to pay regard to local decisions in the preface to his work *The Legal System of Guyana*, p ix.

## FOREIGN AND LOCAL

In *Singh v McLoggan* (1961) LRBG 38, the Federal Supreme Court has brushed aside counsel's reference to Roman-Dutch law when it was informed of the rule that execution could not levy on immovable property when movables were still available. Admittedly, Roman-Dutch law did not apply to the case, but the fact that there was a similar rule applicable in Guyana some two hundred years old, apparently meant nothing to the court. The judges in *Singh v McLoggan* (Rennie, Archer and Wylie JJ), all expatriates, evidently had no incentive to record that fact, and that was why the learned author hoped a wholly national judiciary would be more watchful of the lines along which the future will tend to rise out of the past.

So only if there is no help forthcoming from within, will a local judge be justified in referring to and considering foreign cases and judicial pronouncements on what has been decided on facts and circumstances non-Guyanese.

Practitioners, too should always cite local cases in preference to foreign ones, if they can. Quite recently in *Persaud v Barran* (1981) GCA Criminal Appeal No 36 (1980), dated 22 June 1981, I had occasion to speak out against this tendency of our judges to review copious citations and dicta in foreign authorities in support of legal principles when those principles are already amply illustrated by locally-decided cases. I referred to the habit as a backward tendency and suggested that if our Supreme Court in 1955 had only though it fitting to consider our local decision of *Williams v Sancho* (1917) LRBG 137, which laid down the principle of justice for conducting a view of the *locus in quo*, an appeal for the advice of Her Majesty in Council on that matter would hardly have been necessary in our local cases of *Karamat* and *Tameshwar*. I say without fear of contradiction that this nostalgic reverence for, and attachment to English and other foreign precedents by our national court of final instance in the fact of Act No 14 of 1970, abovementioned, has been one of the chief obstacles to the development of the law in Guyana.

A good example of what I mean is the attitude until recently, adopted by our own final Court of Appeal to the admissibility of confession statements. Until the recent decision of the Privy Counsel in *State v Adjoda and Chandree et al* our Court of Appeal and those of the several jurisdictions of the West Indies consistently persisted in refusing to accept the self-evident truth that 'in all cases where an accused denies authorship of the contents of a written statement, but complains that the signature or signatures on the document which he admits to be his own were improperly obtained from him by threat or inducement, he is challenging the prosecution's evidence on *both* grounds and there is nothing in the least illogical or inconsistent in his doing so'. See *State v Adjoda and Chandree et al*. It had to take a decision of the Privy Council to convince the Trinidad and Tobago and the Guyana Courts of Appeal that this was the right view to take, and that it was wrong to have changed the view it previously held on the matter in *Lindon Harper v State* (1970) 16 WIR 353. Had our Court of Appeal held firmly to what it decided in the *Lindon Harper* case and not reneged on it by faulty distinctions in *State v Fowler* (1970) 16 WIR 453, neither the appeal in *Dhannie Ramsingh* nor *State v Gobin and Griffith* would have been necessary, and I venture to say even that of the Privy Council in *Adjoda and Chandree* (above); but this is all history now.

In conclusion, he said:

> In summing up I will be very brief. The central theme of my address has focussed on the effort of the alternation of the 'Westminster Model' of constitutional government in so far as it affected the work of the courts. What has been achieved by that alternation ... should leave you in no doubt about the sort of role the courts are called upon to play in contemporary Guyana. It is, however, not true to say that since the changeover to socialism the courts have become mouthpieces of government policy. But it is not possible for the courts, if they are to be faithful to the Constitution, to ignore the political bases of the economic and social system of the State, they must guide themselves thereby in the evolving constitutional experiment, it is evident courts must work co-operatively with the government and other public agencies in the pursuit of the principles of socialist democracy as set out in Chapter II of the Constitution and in so far as the role the courts are expected to play in contemporary, eg, socialist Guyana, Art 39 gives the clue to it.

## RELENTLESS

I have also acquainted you with the relentless struggle for economic and social development that existed before independence and which continues to exist in our society also with the aims and aspirations of our peoples for better standards of living and a more prosperous way of life and gave you some idea of the role the judiciary could meaningfully play in maintaining the rule of law, in the administration of justice and in the development of the law in our present situation. I have also apprised you of how development of the law can take place by our unswerving devotion to our Constitution for ideas and inspiration, and have explained the need for both Bench and Bar to think locally for solutions that may be obtained from locally-decided cases, and gave you some specific examples of how best we, by concerted action, can achieve that end.

Members of our noble and learned profession, I have come to the end of my discourse. I will have been deeply honoured if you should have derived at least some benefit from it. You may, however, rest assured that it has been a pleasure to address you this evening. Before I take my leave of you, however, I will offer this bit of advice: that it is only by dint of diligent application and research that your contribution to the constitutional interpretative role of the judiciary will be of value to the progress and development of the law. See to it that you are equal to the task.

# APPENDIX D

# ADDRESS OF THE PRESIDENT OF THE GUYANA BAR ASSOCIATION, 2 MAY 1984

## 'Courts have long way to go' – Bar Association Head

The task of the courts in Guyana is 'to establish a jurisprudence that responds to the needs of our people and our times and in so doing to recognise the ascendency of none but the law'. So declared the new President of the Guyana Bar Association Miles Fitzpatrick as he welcomed the new Chancellor Keith Massiah and bade farewell to the retiring Chancellor Victor Crane in a packed courtroom on 2 May 1984. 'The courts have a long way to go in carrying out this task', Mr Fitzpatrick added.

The Bar Head warned the assembled judges, lawyers, diplomats and guests of the need for continuity of the law. 'However revolutionary and progressive' the changes may be, if we lose sight of the basic verities of the common law, we would 'cast ourselves adrift on the rocks of dictatorship and intolerance'.

'You take office, sir', he told Chancellor Massiah, 'at a time when the development of the law is at a watershed. Change in a post-independence Guyana is inevitable, but how that change occurs is not'.

'We can either go forward to a new flowering of the law, where the courts cast their protective cloak over the ordinary citizen, upholding his fundamental rights against ever-increasing encroachment by an ever-more powerful authority; or we can go backwards, to an authoritarian system, in which the power and interests of the establishment take precedence over the freedom, integrity and welfare of the underprivileged citizen.'

Two decisions handed down by the Appeal Court of Guyana, Mr Fitzpatrick said, had helped to define the task of the courts – *Peter Persaud v Plantation Versailles* in 1970 and *Guysuco v Teemal* a few months ago.

In the *Peter Persaud* case, even though the judges affirmed the independence of the new jurisprudence of Guyana from the external restraints of the British courts, they based their pronouncements firmly on the statements of the greatest English jurist of the 18th century, Lord Mansfield. It was this judge who in 1772 struck a mortal judicial blow to the institution of slavery.

# APPENDIX E

# EXCHANGE OF STATEMENTS BY THE GUYANA BAR ASSOCIATION AND FOUR SENIOR JUDGES ON THE LATTERS' RETURN TO PRIVATE PRACTICE AFTER LEAVING THE BENCH

## 1 RETURN TO PRACTICE BY RETIRED JUDGES UNDIGNIFIED, INDECENT*

The Guyana Bar Association (GBA) yesterday reiterated its opposition to retired judges returning to practise in the courts of this country. 'It is undignified, indecent, inappropriate and totally unacceptable', said a strongly worded statement released yesterday by the Secretary, attorney-at-law Mr Vidyanand Persaud.

He explained that it was delayed after a Bar Council (Executive) meeting in December. However, it did not name any of the former judicial functionaries in the criticized category.

'What started as an exception or isolated trickle over our objections has now turned into a deluge and appears set on becoming a norm', the professional body of lawyers noted.

'It is a most unfortunate development and strikes a crucial blow against our legal system and the independence of the judiciary, which is one of the main pillars of justice in the Republic. It signals a further decline in the standards of the judiciary in this country and is going to bring the law into ridicule and disrespect', said the GBA, whose President is another practising attorney-at-law, Mrs Pearlene Roach.

The declaration went on:

> Originally, appointees were elevated to their high and distinguished office on the known and accepted convention that judges, on retirement, do not return to practise at the Bar. The convention is so hallowed and of such veneration that it was accepted and regarded as tantamount to a rule of law.
>
> Recognizing that in ceasing to have the Privy Council as our final court of appeal and, through our republican status, the severing of certain linkages with English judicial practice, the Guyana Bar Association, in 1995, adopted a Code of Conduct by which all legal practitioners are bound.
>
> And that Code took into account the convention that retired judges should not return to the Bar to practise.
>
> At Rule XI, Clause 6 of the Code, it is specifically prescribed: 'Justices of the Court of Appeal and Judges of the High Court shall not appear at the Bar itself following their retirement or their ceasing to hold such offices.'

---

* Source: *Guyana Chronicle*, 16 March 1996.

'The rule, like the convention, is founded on sound principles, including the cardinal one that justice must not only be done but it must manifestly appear to be done,' the GBA said.

Arguing against the situation, the release said:

Critics of this rule that served the legal profession so well in the past should bear in mind that appearance of attorneys-at-law in court is with the leave of the court.

The courts have certain inherent jurisdictional powers in this regard.

It is necessary also to underscore that the rule does not prevent and the Guyana Bar Association is not opposed to retired judges earning through the skills of their professional qualification.

There are many other avenues through which that knowledge can be usefully employed, for example, in being a consultant in any area of law, legal drafting and the writing, for gain, of scholarly legal articles, chamber practice, lecturing and tutoring, research, authorship and directorships.

It is practice in the court itself, to which the prohibition attaches. It is undignified and indecent for a retired Chancellor, Chief Justice or a Judge of first instance or an Appellate Judge to return to practise in the courts before persons they may have helped to appoint as judges or who were subordinate to them and to be citing their own judgments as authority for any proposition they may put forward.

The Guyana Bar Association remains firmly opposed to a breach of the convention and its own Code of Conduct in retired judges returning to practise in the courts of this country.

## 2 MASSIAH, POMPEY AND GANPATSINGH RESPOND TO LAWYERS' BODY*

Three of four retired judges who returned to practise at the Bar have reacted to the recent stinging criticism by the lawyers' professional grouping.

Responding to a statement by the Guyana Bar Association (GBA), that what they are doing is 'undignified and indecent', they declared that they do not propose 'to match' the body's 'petulance and crude vituperation' which 'cannot provide the resolution of what is essentially a serious jurisprudential dispute'.

But, former Chancellor Keith Massiah and retired Justices George Pompey and Laurie Ganpatsingh pledged to debate the matter fully 'at the proper place and time'.

'Grave common law and constitutional issues require to be settled. This has to be done by authorities superior to the Bar Association – authorities constitutionally clothed with the power to address those issues. If and when

* Source: *Guyana Chronicle*, 23 March 1996.

that time arrives, we know that we would be afforded a fair hearing on the matter', they stated.

Noting that another in their category, Mr Rudolph Harper, who was Chief Justice, is out of the country, the three who put their signature to the response, said the GBA has 'once again ... arisen from its accustomed torpor to pontificate on the way retired judges should or should not practise their profession'.

'This time the tone is shriller, somewhat below the expected decorous level of that august institution', the trio observed.

According to them: 'The Bar Association should feel strange on the moral high ground that it has now sought to occupy, for it has not been making public pronouncements on the great moral and social issues of the day.'

Massiah, Pompey and Ganpatsingh asked: 'Where does it stand on the question of domestic violence, on the need for integrity legislation, on legal education? When has it shown concern on the question of the admission of Guyanese students to the West Indian Law Schools?'

'It is astonishing, to say the least' said the three former judicial functionaries, 'that the Bar Association distanced itself form the interesting debate on the important issue of abortion, uttering not even a mouse's squeak on the subject'.

Continuing, the reacting group wanted to know: 'Where is the doughty Bar Association when our judges are under attack, when it sees fit to sustain a stony silence when questions of the Rule of Law and the independence of the Judiciary arise directly, not tangentially?'

They went on: 'And perhaps the Bar Association can tell us what is its record on Legal Aid. Has it organized a group of lawyers who are prepared to grant legal aid to the unfortunate and indigent women in our society who have been battered and brutalised by violent men? Is the Bar Association's social conscience not pricked in the face of such destitution? Or is its concern only with retired judges?'

Massiah, Pompey and Ganpatsingh said: 'Since the Bar Association does not appear to be concerned with these and many other urgent moral questions, then one wonders what is its agenda in this matter? Why does it bestir itself so much over this matter?'

The three respondents said there is much important work the GBA can do. 'We cannot staunch the flow of millions into our colleagues' pockets. Nor are we so simple as to believe that the Association is driven by any high moral principles. Don't make us laugh.'

'We know one another only too well. So why does the Bar Association not disclose its true motives? Whom is it really pursuing and why? Is there more in the proverbial mortar than the pestle? Is this a witch-hunt tricked out in moralistic robes?' the response probed.

It continued: 'We totally disagree with the Bar Association's febrile and insubstantial reasoning. But here is not the place to expose its inadequacies and impractical suggestions.'

'Nor do we share the Association's antediluvian ideas', they said.

Massiah, Pompey and Ganpatsingh recalled that Lord Hailsham, then Lord Chancellor of Britain, was so stunned by the statutory divestment of some of the profession's high cherished ideals that he declared that Parliament was 'sitting on its head and thinking with its bottom'.

'He had to come to terms with the reality that we live in a world of constant change and new ideas', they commented.

Returning to Guyana the situation, the other three lawyers said: 'Parliament's recent statute on abortion exemplifies this notion. We also live in a real world where only those who live in a world of fantasy can ignore the market place.'

'So live and let live, Bar Association', was their plea.

They concluded: 'And of course we do not and will never accept that the Bar Association has the authority to erode our cherished human right to work, without even affording us an opportunity to be heard on the matter. We are not yielding our rights.'

## 3 JUDGES HAVE THE RIGHT TO WORK*

Dear Sir,

The Guyana Bar Association has made a scathing attack on those judges who have demitted office and sought to augment their pension by practicing the profession for which they were trained. That vilification was no surprise to me. 'The greater the divisor the smaller the quotient', we have all learnt since we were in standard one.

I was away from the country when the Bar Association pronounced its worthless 'edict'. I was also away when my three colleagues made a stately reply which has my full approbation. However, I am not wont to concur without expressing some thoughts of my own.

As far as I can recall only one Bar Association president, Mr Frederick Ramprashad SC, has ever evinced any concern with the conditions of judges after retirement. He genuinely endeavoured for judges to have a pension and conditions no less favourable than when they were employed, so that they can maintain their standard of living.

Sir Kenneth Stoby approached the Bar Association in the sixties with an idea of implementing an insurance scheme so that when legal practitioners

* Source: *The Stabroek News*, 29 March 1996.

fall on lean days they can have recourse to a fund. That idea was summarily dismissed by the Bar Association.

For this august Bar Association to say that judges' return to practice 'signals a further decline in the standard of the Judiciary in this country and is going to bring the law into ridicule and disrespect', is the most nonsensical statement in the whole diatribe. How will those practitioners' appearance in court lower the standard of judgment? On the contrary, their appearance can enhance the decision.

This erudite Bar Association must by now know of the far-reaching changes made in England during the last few years so that solicitors can now have audience in the High Court and further they can be appointed as judges. Coke perhaps had turned several times over in the grave on hearing of those practices. But so be it.

May I remind the Bar Association of Art 22(1) of our Constitution:

> Every citizen has the right to work and its free selection in accordance with social requirements and personal qualification. He has the right to be rewarded according to the nature quality and quantity of his work. Women and men have the right to equal pay for equal work.

Is the Bar Association endeavouring by its stated Code of Discipline – the less said of that code the better – to deprive us of that right to work which is enshrined in the Constitution?

It is better that the Bar Association try to discipline those many in its fold who with daring impunity rob their clients, whose recourse to the Legal Practitioners' Committee is almost a waste of time.

We shall always reserve the right to appear before any forum where our services are legitimately needed.

Yours faithfully,
Mr Rudolph H Harper CCH
Retired Chief Justice

# BIBLIOGRAPHY


**Official publications and legal journals**

Decisions of the Guyana Court of Appeal, 1975–2000 (unpublished)

*Guyana Law Journal*

Laws of Guyana

*Law Reports of British Guiana, 1865–65*

*Law Reports of Guyana, 1966–75*

Practice Directives of the Chancellor of the Judiciary, 1966–2000

*The Guyana Bar Association Review*

*The Official Gazette of Guyana*

*West Indian Law Journal*

*West Indian Law Reports*

**Books, articles and other materials**

Abraham, EAV, 'Marriage Law: British Guiana (1885–1886)' 1 West Indian Quarterly 188

Adams, BO, 'The argument for the establishment of the Commonwealth Caribbean Court of Appeal' (1972) 2 Leg Prac Rev 7

Alexis, F, *Changing Caribbean Constitutions*, 1983, Bridgetown, Barbados: Antilles

Arrot, D, *A Tabular Index* (alphabetically arranged) to the Laws and Ordinances of British Guiana as in Force (either wholly or in part) on 1 April 1864, Georgetown

Atkin LJ, 'Appeal in English law' (1927–29) 3 CLJ 1

Barnett, LG, *Constitutional Law of Jamaica, A Study in the Evolution and Adaptation of Responsible Cabinet Government and Constitutionalism in an Emergent Nation*, PhD thesis, 1966, University of London

Beaumont, J, *Speeches Delivered by Chief Justice Beaumont on 8th February, 1865, in the Court of Policy, Upon the Second Reading of the Gaol Delivery Bill*, 1865, Georgetown

Blue Books of British Guiana, miscellaneous years

British Guiana/Venezuela Arbitration, 1899

British Case, Appendix, Vols 1, 5, 6, 11

British Counter Case, Appendix

Oral Proceedings, Vol 1

Venezuelan Case, Vol 2

British Guiana Sessional Papers, miscellaneous years

Brumell, J, *The Handy Book of Village Law*, 1873, Georgetown

Carrington, JW (Sir), 'Modes of colonial legislation: British Guiana' (1896) 1 JSCL 140

Clementi, C (Sir), *A Constitutional History of British Guiana*, 1937, London: Macmillan

Dalton, LC, 'Review of WR Lee's introduction to Roman-Dutch law, 1915', *The Daily Argosy*, 25 December 1915

Davis, D, 'The beginnings of British Guiana' (1893) 7 Timehri 12

De Freitas, JE, 'Law reform in British Guiana' (1943) BG Law Society's Gazette 70

Duke, EM, 'Land registration in British Guiana' (1943) BG Law Society's Gazette 28

Fairn, RD, *A Review of Prison Administration in British Guiana*, BG Sessional Paper, No 15, 1956

Gouvelia, EV, *The West Indian Slave Laws of the 18th Century*, 1970, Carribean: Caribbean UP

Green, WA, 'The apprenticeship in British Guiana: 1834–38' (1969) 9 Caribbean Studies 44

*Human Rights in Latin America, 1964–1980*, a selective, annotated bibliography, 1983, Washington, DC: Hispanic Division, Library of Congress

Jayawardena, C, *Conflict and Solidarity in a Guianese Plantation*, 1963, London: Athlone

Kirke, H, 'Our criminal classes' (1888) 2 Timehri 1

Lee, RW, 'Roman-Dutch law in British Guiana' (1914) 30 Jo Soc, Comp Leg, NS, 11

Patchett, K and Jenkins, V, 'A bibliographical guide to law in the Commonwealth Caribbean', in *Law and Society in the Caribbean, No 2*, 1973, Mona, Jamaica: Institute of Social and Economic Research, University of the West Indies

Patchett, KW, 'English law in the West Indies' (1963) 12 ICLQ 922

Ramsahoye, FHW, *The Development of Land Law in British Guiana*, 1966, Dobbs Ferry, NY: Oceana

Shahabuddeen, M, *Constitutional Development in Guyana, 1621–1978*, 1978, Georgetown: Shahabuddeen

Shahabuddeen, M, *The Legal System of Guyana*, 1973, Georgetown: Guyana Printers

Singh, PG, *Local Democracy in the Commonwealth Caribbean: A Study of Adaptation and Growth, 1972*, Port of Spain, Trinidad, Kingston, Jamaica: Longman Caribbean

Some Aspects of Marriage and Divorce in the West Indies (1959) 8 ICLQ 632

Stafford, SL, van B, 'Roman-Dutch remnants in the civil law of British Guiana' (1943) BG Law Society's Gazette 8

'Statute law revision' (1890) 4 Timehri, NS, 225

Stevens, RB, 'The role of a final appeal court in a democracy' (1965) 28 MLR 509

'The abolition of the Roman-Dutch law in British Guiana' (1912) 2 Timehri 1

'The records of British Guiana' (1888) 2 Timehri 339

'The Chief Justices of British Guiana' (1894) 8 Timehri, NS, 378–81

Williamson, JA, *The English Colonies in Guiana and on the Amazon, 1604–68,* 1923, Oxford: Clarendon

Young, A, *The Approaches to Local Self-Government in British Guiana,* 1958, London: Longmans, Green

# INDEX

## D



## E



## F

## M



## N



## O



## P

## T



## U



## V



## W